The foreclosureS.com

Guide to Making
Huge Profits
Investing in
Pre-foreclosures
without Selling Your Soul

Guide to Making
Huge Profits
Investing in
Pre-foreclosures
without Selling Your Soul

Alexis McGee

BICENTENNIAL

1807

WILEY

2007

BICENTENNIAL

John Wiley & Sons, Inc.

Library of Congress Cataloging-in-Publication Data:
McGee, Alexis, 1960–
    The Foreclosures.com guide to making huge profits investing in
  pre-foreclosures without selling your soul / Alexis McGee ; with Susan J.
  Marks.
      p. cm.
  Includes bibliographical references and index.
  ISBN 978-0-470-17105-9 (pbk. : alk. paper)
   1. Real estate investment—United States.   2. Foreclosure—United States.
  I. Marks, Susan J. II. Title.
  HD255.M3725   2007
  332.63'24—dc22   2007028128

Printed in the United States of America.

10 9 8 7 6 5 4 3 2 1

To my husband and partner,
Tim,
who knew I had a book in me before I did.

And to my kids, Cooke and Kali, *who think it's cool.*

CONTENTS

This first *ForeclosureS.com Guide to Making Huge Profits Investing in Pre-Foreclosures Without Selling Your Soul* draws on what I've learned in more than 20 years in the real estate business. All those people who have touched my life have helped me understand the right way to do business, create happiness, and be successful in life. For that I thank each of you.

I owe special thanks to a number of others who influenced me and made this book a reality:

Tim, my husband and business partner, for his unwavering love of 25 years. Tim, you are the wizard behind the door at ForeclosureS.com, yet you rarely take credit for our successes. I am so glad we took the leap of faith together by leaving our corporate lives more than 15 years ago. We are far stronger together than as two separate parts. Most of all, thank you for believing in me and letting me be me.

Cooke and **Kaliope**, my children, who are the sunshine of my life. You are so authentic, creative, cool, and scary smart. I am thankful to have time to spend with you while you are still young. My life is full and blessed because of you, and I'm so proud of you both.

Carol Shea, my big sister, best friend, biggest cheerleader, and marketing research guru of the century from Olivetreeresearch.com. Your marketing and branding insight propelled our business into the stratosphere.

Chris and **Kally Zacharos**, my parents, for allowing me to ask questions, for not expecting me to be quiet, and for giving me very dangerous and very wise advice: "Say whatever you want as long as you say it with a smile and from the heart." And for helping me get to Arizona, where I met my honey.

James R. Hagerty, the *Wall Street Journal* reporter who interviewed me and wrote a front-page story that changed my life—"Slower Home Sales Open Up a Market for Some Investors. The Threat of Foreclosure Feeds a Real-Estate Niche That Thrives on Hard Luck. How to Be a 'White Knight.'" Thank you for sharing our story with the world in such a positive way.

Susan J. Marks, my get-it-done wonder woman. Without your expert research and writing skills, round-the-clock work ethic, and ability to make sense of an entirely new language, this book would have never happened. Susan, I can never thank you enough for helping me find my voice and sharing it with the world.

Cynthia Zigmund, my agent from Literary Services Inc., who cold-called me after reading that front-page *Wall Street Journal* article, and asked me to "tell the rest of the story." I never had planned to write a book, nor did I have the time to do so. Cynthia went above and beyond the call of duty to make this project happen. Thank you so much for putting together such a top-notch team and for bringing me Susan Marks and John Wiley & Sons.

Laurie Harting, senior editor at Wiley, who had the market insight and enthusiasm to take on a first-time author and help her reach the stars. Laurie, your patience, understanding, and on-the-mark editing were invaluable in this project. Thank you. I couldn't have done it without you.

Mary Kay, **Daryl White**, **Sarah Garlick**, and **Tim Rhode**, my clients, ForeclosureS.com coaches, and dear friends. I would not be where I am today without you. You truly represent the philosophy of what I teach: Give first. You have given everyone you touch more than we ever can repay. Thank you for staying true to your values and helping so many new investors achieve the successes they deserve.

Kobe Zimmerman and **Bob Pratt**, for taking the time to share your personal stories with the world and for doing the hard work that has rewarded you handsomely as true "white knight" foreclosure investors. I am so proud of you. And **Marsha Townsend** and **Michael Andrews** of ForeclosureLink.com for also sharing their stories and expertise on the business of foreclosure auctions and investing.

Kristy Boyd, my assistant whom I couldn't live without, and my entire loyal **team at ForeclosureS.com**.

Dante Perano, our dear friend who came back into our lives when "we didn't know what we didn't know." You brought it all together for us, Dante. And now we get to enjoy our successes together with our children. How blessed we are!

Bob Carr and **Dennis McGilvray**, from Grubb & Ellis Commercial, who gave me my first real job out of college as an investment broker. I can't thank them enough for taking a chance and hiring me (albeit initially as a research director). Special thanks to Bob, my first real sales manager, who took me under his wing and taught me the value of asking questions and listening for the real answers.

Dale Carnegie, **Stephen Covey**, **Napoleon Hill**, **Jim Rohn**, **Brian Tracy**, **Jerry Vass**, and **Ron Willingham**, who continually inspire me to be the best person I can be, to take the higher road, pay it forward, and never give up, no matter what.

And last, but definitely not least, **Barbara Corcoran**, **Diane Kennedy**, and again **Brian Tracy** and **Ron Willingham** for taking time out of their busy lives to read my manuscript and offer their glowing comments.

Property foreclosures are at record levels across the United States. In some areas, they're up 1,000 percent over last year. The owners of tens of thousands more properties face imminent default as they struggle to cope with overextended mortgages, flat appreciation rates, languishing sales, and other economic woes.

It's a market primed for would-be investors and entrepreneurs looking for big gains through foreclosure investing. Consider a few statistics:

- Nationwide, nearly 1 million foreclosure filings (983,290) were reported in 2006. That's up more than 53 percent from just over 641,500 filings in 2005, according to statistics from ForeclosureS.com, which tracks foreclosure filings in more than 1,500 counties and growing across the United States.

- In the first quarter of 2007, 2.01 percent of all U.S. residential real estate loans were delinquent. That includes loans secured by one- to four-family properties and home equity lines of credit, according to statistics from the Federal Reserve Board (see "Charge-Off and Delinquency Rates on Loans and Leases at Commercial Banks," at www.federalreserve.gov/releases/chargeoff/delallnsa.htm).

- Forty-nine out of 50 states plus the District of Columbia had an increase in overall mortgage delinquency rates in the fourth quarter of 2006; 44 states had an increase in foreclosure inventory, according to the National Delinquency Survey from the Mortgage Bankers Association, a Washington, D.C.–based national association representing the real estate finance industry.

- Early payment defaults on subprime loans (those made to people with no or bad credit) through mid-2006 more than tripled the rate of early 2005, according to Freddie Mac, the congressionally chartered private mortgage market investor (see Economic & Housing Outlook, March 8, 2007, "In Like a Lion . . . ," at www.freddiemac.com/news/finance/pdf/Mar_2007_FRECOM_Outlook.pdf).

The good news, however, is that the American dream of homeownership is alive. An estimated 69 percent of Americans owned their homes as of year-end

2006, with 75.6 million housing units occupied by their owners, according to the most recent data from the U.S. Census Bureau.

Housing supply/demand is stabilizing, too. As of January 31, 2007, 3.55 million existing homes were available for sale, according to the National Association of Realtors. That's unchanged from revised December 2006 levels and represents a 6.6-month supply at the current sales pace. The supply hit a high of 7.4 months in October 2006. A balanced market generally is considered one with a six-month supply. This puts in perspective the idea that we truly are in a normal supply/demand market even though foreclosure numbers remain high.

From record, unsustainable new home sales in 2005, builders also have slowed starts to catch up with supplies and stabilize markets. Looking at more economic statistics:

- Sales of new single-family homes in 2006 dropped 17.3 percent from 2005's all-time high, but they were up 4.8 percent in December from November numbers, according to U.S. government reports.

- In January 2007, however, sales of new single-family homes plummeted 16.6 percent below December's revised numbers, according to estimates released jointly by the U.S. Census Bureau and the Department of Housing and Urban Development.

- Sales of existing homes were down 10.1 percent in fourth quarter 2006 from fourth-quarter 2005 numbers, according to the National Association of Realtors. By the end of January 2007, however, sales were only 4.3 percent off January 2006 numbers.

- Inventories of new homes for sale hit a 10-month low in December 2006 with only a 5.9-month supply, according to the Commerce Department.

- Nationally, the unemployment rate continues to hover just over 4 percent (4.3 percent as of December 2006).

- Projections call for continued demand for new households. The latest Census Bureau numbers show 111.1 million households currently, with 114.8 million projected in 2010. Some projections peg the number of households even higher.

Whether you're only toying with the idea or seriously considering getting started in the foreclosure investing business, the first step is to learn what it takes to successfully find the right properties, negotiate with their owners, buy the properties with or without your own money, and then turn them around and sell them for big profits.

Unfortunately, the market is flooded with misinformation and self-proclaimed gurus who tout their systems to make a fast buck by beating down property owners in default. This book is *not* simply another of those glorified sales pitches and multilevel marketing schemes that take your money and give you little but commonsense advice and often shady dealings in return.

Get primed instead for a new and different approach. Forget typical high-pressure techniques. Buying a home out from under a homeowner who defaulted on his or her loan—or using fear and intimidation to force someone to sell at a huge loss so you can turn a fast buck—simply isn't the way to win ethically, win long term, or win big at the pre-foreclosure property buying game.

Consider the ForeclosureS.com white-knight foreclosure investing approach. It's ethical, it's honest, and it's an opportunity for hefty financial rewards along with the personal satisfaction of helping others. No prior experience required, either. Regardless of market ups and downs and even without cash in hand, you can make lots of money *and* make a positive difference in other people's lives. The nice guy does finish first. In these pages we show you how.

Instead of entering the business of buying foreclosures with the goal of making quick money at any cost, consider that true long-range financial success comes when you help others, too. Make a difference in others' lives, and your own financial gain will follow—so much gain, in fact, that you'll be amazed by your own success.

Rather than feeling as if you're stealing a property out from under a homeowner on the courthouse steps, we'll teach you how to locate and, when appropriate, approach and get to know the homeowner in default. You will help the owner understand all the options, and then be available if selling the property to you is what's right for that homeowner. If it isn't the best choice for that homeowner, that's okay, too. You'll feel good about yourself and you will have made a difference in the life of someone who truly needed you. That person will remember you when he needs your help again and will refer you to others in need as well.

Author Alexis McGee has helped steer many of those entrepreneurs onto the right track. She's *the* nationally recognized foreclosure industry expert and sets the gold standard for honesty and ethics in the business. She's the go-to person interviewed or quoted by media coast to coast, from the *Wall Street Journal*, *The New York Times*, *The Washington Post*, *The Boston Globe*, *Newsday*, *Los Angeles Times*, *San Jose Mercury News*, and *Chicago Tribune* to *Money* magazine, Manhattan Mortgage, Bloomberg.com, CNNMoney.com, MSN.money.com, CBSMarketWatch.com, DailyNews.com, InmanNews.com, CBS, NBC, ABC, FOX, and CNBC as well as National Public Radio.

A 20-year veteran of the foreclosure investing business, McGee knows first-hand what works and what doesn't. She's had her hand in more than $100 million in both residential and commercial foreclosure deals and has earned millions of dollars buying and selling foreclosure properties in good times and bad. She's helped thousands of others do the same by teaching them the skills and approach necessary to make big money with a clear conscience.

Californian McGee is the founder, architect, and mentor for one of the most popular and the longest-running foreclosure web sites in the country, ForeclosureS.com. Pioneered by McGee with her husband, Tim, in 1995, the site's goal is to share with others the proven ways to gain lasting success and satisfaction from buying properties in foreclosure. Hundreds of McGee's students, many of whom first went elsewhere for unsatisfactory and costly advice, sing her praises and that of her white-knight approach to the business. They have listened to her message, capitalized on her mentoring, and gone on to build their own fortunes.

"I did my first real estate deal at age 25," says McGee. "It involved $12 million in apartments, and I went into it with no money, no track record, and up against the 'Brooks Brothers' guys with a big portfolio of deals behind them. But I persuaded the property owners to list exclusively with me. I looked them in the eye and they believed that I would do as I promised. They knew I was the one who really cared about them and would give their project my heart and soul.

"That's when I first realized the power of connecting with people on a personal level and that it's not facts and figures and all business. In the end, people need to know they can trust you and have confidence that you will do what you say you will. Without that, nothing else matters."

On that first deal, McGee brought her brokerage $360,000 in commissions and put $180,000 in her pocket! After that she parlayed the same philosophy into a highly successful and profitable career in commercial real estate that eventually included working with banks and lenders, and building relationships with the people who managed their real estate–owned (REO) foreclosures. Then, as the investment climate began to change from a buyer's market (many homes and fewer buyers) to a seller's market (fewer properties and more buyers), McGee changed, too. "I started working with owners in default and discovered it was so much more gratifying to help owners directly," she says.

Still not convinced that the ForeclosureS.com approach works? Consider what a few industry notables and students have to say about it.

Attorney William Bronchick, author of the best-selling book, *Flipping Properties: Generate Instant Cash Profits in Real Estate* (New York: Kaplan, 2006), says:

> Alexis McGee reveals a refreshingly honest approach to the foreclosure-investing business in that she actually teaches her students how to help people in foreclosure instead of take advantage of them. Her personal success as well as that of her many students are rock-solid proof that her approach works.

Jerry Vass, sales trainer and author of *Soft Selling in a Hard World: Plain Talk on the Art of Persuasion* (Philadelphia: Running Press Book Publishers, 1998) and

Decoding the BS of Business, Selling to Executives (St. Augustine Beach, FL: Vass, Inc., 2006), has this to say:

> The best part about Alexis McGee's approach is that the investor in foreclosures can look in the mirror and be proud of who looks back. That is hard to do if the person in the mirror is dancing on the grave of a family buried in debt.
>
> Helping other people solve their problems is the surest way to make money and keep it. Helping people is the business; foreclosures is just the medium one works in. And you don't have look over your shoulder. In a dark world full of crooks and hustlers, Alexis' philosophy is a shining light of ethics.

John Burns, president of John Burns Real Estate Consulting and author of "U.S. Housing Markets," a highly respected and watched market research publication, comments:

> We use Alexis McGee's ForeclosureS.Com to keep updated on foreclosure statistics across the country and we like her investment approach to the market.

And from Deana Carter, award-winning recording artist and graduate of McGee's training program:

> I was intrigued by Alexis' philosophy of "Do unto others as you would have them do unto you," which is rare in any profession, especially one as sensitive as foreclosures. She (and her program) truly teaches you to look at life differently—not how to *get ahead*, but rather, *to get behind* your beliefs and that helping others is where you truly prosper. How refreshing!

This book is your kick-start introduction to what can be a very rewarding way to control your own future, a satisfying way to help others, and a lucrative way to generate sizable income as your own boss. All of this comes without having to worry about the ups and downs of the real estate market.

The book is divided into two parts. In Part I, "A Different Approach," we introduce you to this new and different approach to foreclosure buying and help you determine whether it's right for you. In Part II, "Getting Started," we detail the approach, processes, procedures, documentation, and deals necessary to get started in this financially and personally rewarding field.

Throughout the book, we explain state-by-state nuances, legal ramifications, communications concerns, money details, scams to avoid, and other issues for homeowners, entrepreneurs, and investors. You'll learn the importance of connecting effectively with people in distress and how to do so with compassion. The people side of the business often gets overlooked by other so-called experts, but it is crucial to long-term success. No matter how much you may pay an expert for his secret to success, if property owners aren't buying your message, there's a reason why they're not.

We recount dozens of success stories from entrepreneurs of all ages and backgrounds and from homeowners who have been able to put their lives back together, thanks to guidance from someone like you who understands the ins and outs of foreclosures. Throughout the book you'll also find "Tales from Foreclosure Experts," real thoughts from real people who are making the system work. And we talk about the failures, red flags, cautions, and questionable dealings that regularly destroy the lives of homeowners in default. In most cases, except for our experts, we've changed the names we use to protect individual privacy. In other cases the stories are compilations of real experiences, any similarities to real people are coincidental.

So, if you're ready to learn the basics, get an edge in the market, and launch a new chapter in your life, turn the page.

PART I

A DIFFERENT APPROACH

Being rich is having money; being wealthy is having time.

—Alexis McGee

CHAPTER 1

Pre-Foreclosure Investing: What It Is and Why It Works

If you commit to taking an honest, ethical approach to the needs of financially troubled homeowners first, your own tremendous financial gains are sure to follow.

—Alexis McGee

Forget what you've heard about the typical approach to buying foreclosure properties. We are not in business to take advantage of distraught people. Success in the foreclosure business is not about stealing homeowners' properties, turning financially down-and-out folks out on the street, or hiding your intentions behind convoluted contracts with property owners in trouble. Nor does success come from spending thousands of dollars on ineffective mailing or advertising campaigns, fancy web sites, billboards, or your own toll-free telephone number.

This book will teach you how to be financially free. You'll learn how to make a profit buying properties in foreclosure while helping those in financial distress at the same time.

The market is primed. Foreclosures have soared nationwide as hundreds of thousands of Americans find themselves financially short. For some homeowners, the culprit may be a recent layoff or the promised raise that never materialized, combined with escalating costs for everything from health care to food, energy, clothing, and more. For others, the issue could be the creative financing that allowed them to buy homes they couldn't afford in the first place. As monthly payments on those homes adjust upward, overextended homeowners are left with little recourse but default and foreclosure.

Consider a few numbers:

- Nationwide, 983,290 foreclosures were filed in 2006, up 53.3 percent from the 641,503 filings in 2005, according to statistics from ForeclosureS.com, which tracks foreclosure filings in more than 1,500 counties and growing across the country.

- In the first quarter of 2007, 2.01 percent of residential real estate loans in the United States were delinquent, down slightly from 2.11 percent in the fourth quarter of 2006, but up significantly from 1.57 percent for the first quarter of 2006. That includes loans secured by one- to four-family properties and home equity lines of credit, according to statistics from the Federal Reserve Board (see "Charge-Off and Delinquency Rates on Loans and Leases at Commercial Banks," at www.federalreserve.gov/releases/charge off/delallnsa.htm).

- Credit problems are the most pronounced in the subprime mortgage market (those loans issued to people with no or troubled credit), according to statistics from various government, industry, and private organizations.

- U.S. home mortgage debt totals $10 trillion. Subprime mortgages account for $1.3 trillion or about 13 percent of the aggregate outstanding mortgage debt, with hybrid adjustable rate mortgages (ARMs) as the primary product, John M. Reich, director of the U.S. Office of Thrift Supervision, reported to members of Congress in March 2007 (see his testimony before the U.S. House of Representatives, Subcommittee on Financial Institutions and Consumer Credit of the Committee on Financial Services, March 27, 2007).

- Approximately $567 billion of subprime ARMs are scheduled for rate (and payment) reset in 2007, Reich said at the time, adding that many of those borrowers are already facing financial hardship with their mortgages:
    - Of loans originating in 2005, 8.6 percent are seriously delinquent at the 11-month mark.
    - Of 2004 originations, 6.2 percent are seriously delinquent at the 11-month mark.
    - Of 2003 originations, 5.6 percent are seriously delinquent at the 11-month mark.

- The national median existing single-family home price was $219,300 in fourth-quarter 2006, down 2.7 percent from a year earlier. For all of 2006, the

Foreclosure Leaders

The following states led the nation in numbers of foreclosure filings at year-end, according to ForeclosureS.com:

State	2006	2005
1. California	157,417	81,012
2. Florida	120,989	95,384
3. Texas	106,845	79,001
4. Illinois	75,176	39,809
5. Colorado	68,310	43,951

Source: ForeclosureS.com

median price rose 1.4 percent to $222,000, according to the National Association of Realtors (NAR). By January 2007 that price had dropped to $210,600, down 3.1 percent from January 2006. (*Median* means half the homes sell for more, and half sell for less.)

- The Federal Reserve Bank has raised interest rates 17 times since 2004.

Laying a Foundation of Fairness and Values

The ForeclosureS.com approach to helping financially troubled homeowners is based on negotiating to create a win-win situation for you and for the homeowner. Armed with information, expertise, and the truth, you will learn how to become the white-knight investor who rescues homeowners in default from the many scam artists in disguise and from the sale of their home on the courthouse steps. This approach involves getting to know property owners, learning how to earn their trust, and then helping them understand their options—at no cost to them.

That's right: You share your knowledge and expertise free of charge! This approach *is* ethical, honest, and without the deception or trickery sometimes associated with many in this business. The goal here is to buy properties at a price that works for you, the investor, but also helps those who are in distress. This method is about helping people get through difficult financial times by walking away with some cash in their pockets, an improved credit record, and the ability to make a fresh start instead of losing it all at the foreclosure auction.

With the right kind of perseverance and tenacity, you will achieve great rewards both financially and emotionally.

*I define the word foreclosure as people in financial
trouble who cannot afford their homes.*

—Alexis McGee

Confused about how you can help distressed homeowners out of their financial troubles and not eliminate your own target market? The primary objective of this approach is to help homeowners keep their homes *if* they can afford to do so. For many that is simply not an option—they have borrowed too much money to cover their payments, and borrowing more would bury them financially and not be in their best interests. Doing nothing and hoping they get whatever extra money is left over after their home is auctioned is equally risky. At most foreclosure auctions, a home doesn't draw competitive bids and sells only for the amount owed the lender. Those homeowners get nothing except ruined credit and a visit from the sheriff to evict them.

Instead, consider the situation in which an honest person—yourself as the white-knight investor—helps homeowners in distress figure out the best way to resolve their financial troubles. If their options are limited and their lender won't agree to work with them on a plan to bring the mortgage current, the best solution may be to sell the property. You could be the person who gives that homeowner a fresh start.

If this ethic and approach appeals to you, read on.

*Embrace the potential you have to help make a
positive difference in the lives of others.
Your own financial gain will follow.*

—Alexis McGee

The Basics

Let's start with a quick look at some of the basics relative to foreclosures. We'll delve more deeply in later chapters.

First, the term *foreclosure* as it relates to real estate is the forced sale of a property to repay a debt (also known as a *lien*) that is in *default*. The default usually arises when a property owner fails to make loan installment repayments of interest or principal or both according to terms of the loan. That loan is known as a *mortgage* or *deed of trust*, which is a legal document that creates a lien on a property as security for repayment of a specified debt. A property can have multiple liens, but the *first mortgage* or deed of trust has priority and, in case of foreclosure, must be satisfied before other mortgages or liens are paid off.

State laws relating to foreclosure vary. Foreclosures can be *judicial*, in which case they must be executed by a court, or *nonjudicial*, meaning that a lawsuit need not be filed or a court order obtained in order to foreclose or sell the property. *Equity* is that amount of the property's fair market value that exceeds outstanding loans and liens.

In the foreclosure business, investors can agree to purchase a property or pay off its liens at a *discount* off the property's current appraised value. That discount represents the investors' cost of doing business and fixing up the house, as well as the profit in a deal.

Property owners facing foreclosure basically have seven options (we examine them in more detail in later chapters):

1. Putting together a workout plan with their present lender to cure the default.
2. Rewriting their existing loan with the same lender.
3. Working with a mortgage broker to get a new loan.
4. Working with a Realtor to find a homebuyer.
5. Filing bankruptcy to defer the foreclosure.
6. Selling their home to an investor before the foreclosure auction.
7. Doing nothing, losing their home—along with all their equity—at the foreclosure auction, and destroying their credit.

If you opt to get involved in this business, you can do so in several ways. Among the options: You can work directly with property owners in default in the *pre-foreclosure* stage, which is before a property is *auctioned* off to repay its defaulted debt. That's the approach we generally advocate because you truly can make a difference to others and provide a great living for yourself and your family. You can purchase a property from the homeowner using your money or someone else's. At the closing of the purchase, the seller gets his equity in cash, and you and/or your investor get your below-market-price purchase. You can then clean up and rehab the property, then turn around and resell it. (In some cases you may decide to keep the property and rent it out instead.) Or you can simply locate and structure deals using our proven formulas and then turn them over to another investor who puts up the money and pays you a *finder's fee* at the closing.

Another approach to the business, one that most gurus tout as the road to unimaginable (and unrealistic!) wealth, is to buy foreclosing houses at the auction at a discount, and then repair and sell them for big profits. These same gurus like the short-sale approach, too. That's when the loans on a property exceed its value, you buy it, and the bank forgives a portion of the debt so the house can be sold. (There's a lot more to it. We'll talk more about that later.) Still another option is to buy real estate owned (REO) property, or bank-owned real estate, from the lender after it has reclaimed the property from the homeowner in default, and then rehab and sell the property, again at a big profit. These foreclosure investing approaches are rigged with land mines ranging from possible damage caused by unhappy former owners to confusion over a property's title, liens, or ownership.

No Get-Rich-Quick Schemes

Whatever approach you decide to take—and no matter what you've read or what anyone else has told you or how much money the advice from self-proclaimed gurus has cost you—forget any idea of get-rich-quick, easy-money schemes in foreclosure investing. Without effort and without commitment, the big payoff just doesn't happen. If you think it does, put this book down and go out and buy a lottery ticket instead. The odds of winning are about the same.

There's no magic marketing scheme, either, and you won't achieve fabulous riches trying to shortcut the system. Instead, true success in this business comes from purchasing ordinary properties in pre-foreclosure from homeowners in default who have equity in their properties.

Property owners facing foreclosure find themselves at the mercy of investors, lenders, brokers, consultants, and plain old greedy people. Surrounded by sharks in a financial feeding frenzy, these homeowners often don't know where to turn. As a result, they are rightfully suspicious and distrustful of anyone who claims to want to "help" them. If you aren't honest and genuine, compassionate and caring toward them and their situation, you'll never earn the trust it takes to really help them. Neither will you develop the rapport or reputation that can inspire a property owner to sell his home to you, and in turn create the potential for your own financial gain.

Marie, 62, never finished high school, but she had worked hard all her life. A single mom of three, she was financially responsible for her oldest son's toddler, too. As a housekeeper, Marie earned $19 an hour working for an elderly bedridden woman but found it tough to make ends meet. She fell behind on her mortgage, and her lender was ready to foreclose. Uninformed of her rights and confused by the notices, documents, and bureaucracy, Marie was scared of what might happen. She was afraid to contact the lender and certainly had no idea that she could possibly negotiate with the company on a workout plan.

Before you throw up your hands at Marie's ignorance, keep in mind that she's not alone in her inaction. Very few homeowners in default talk to their mortgage holders until it's too late. More than 6 in 10, or 61 percent, of late-paying borrowers were unaware of workout options with their lender for short-term financial difficulties, according to a 2005 Freddie Mac/Roper Public Affairs and Media (part of GFK Customer Research NA) survey of delinquent borrowers. And 75 percent of those delinquent borrowers even recalled being contacted by their mortgage-servicing company.

Joaquin, 44, had defaulted on his mortgage and was scheduled to lose his house at auction. Several get-rich-quick folks had approached him to "help," but luckily he was wise enough to recognize they weren't interested in helping him at all. He grew concerned when one of the folks wanted cash from him up front. That's when foreclosure investor Anna K. entered the picture. As expected, Joaquin assumed she was like all the others and immediately distrusted her. He hung up on her phone calls several times and even slammed the door in her face at first.

But Anna persisted. She had done her homework and knew this was Joaquin's first time in default. Everyone she had talked to thought Joaquin was honest and aboveboard, too. Eventually she convinced Joaquin of her sincerity and worked with him to help him understand his financial options. With her guidance, he figured out that he could borrow money from his retirement account on the basis of hardship and negotiate with his lender to get his mortgage current.

The end result: Joaquin and his family of four kept a roof over their heads, and he's now debt-free except for the reworked home payment plan and his car loan. Anna walked away from the deal comfortable in the knowledge that she had helped someone who needed it, no strings attached. Although she had spent considerable time on the phone helping Joaquin, her payment was the knowledge that she had done the right thing. "I'm comfortable with the fact I didn't make any money," says Anna. "I saved the family's home instead, and that's plenty of gratification for me."

Several months after working with Joaquin, Anna closed two deals with other homeowners in distress who could not afford to keep their homes. "They both said they listened to me because I was persistent and kept saying the same things over and over. I didn't change my story like all the others who kept telling them only what they wanted to hear. My honesty and sincerity showed through. That's why I got those deals," Anna says, her satisfaction evident. And her paycheck for those deals more than paid for the time she spent helping Joaquin for free.

When Anna helped Joaquin, she put goodwill into her "karma bank," says longtime investor and ForeclosureS.com coach Tim Rhode. "When you work with any homeowner, you have the chance to deposit cash, karma, or both. Whatever happens, it boosts your bank account."

Dakota and his wife were thrilled when they purchased their first home. Although his wife stayed at home with their young son and didn't have a job, their lender was more than willing to work with them to give them a loan to buy the house. The only problem was that they paid too much for a house they couldn't really afford on Dakota's salary alone. At age 24, Dakota had a good, although entry-level, job as a computer engineer, and the lender convinced him that creative financing was ideal for his situation. Dakota would pay interest only on the loan for the first three years. By then he would certainly have the big raise he had been promised and would easily be able to afford the monthly payments that would begin adjusting dramatically upward.

Big mistake! As is so often the case, the raise never materialized but the higher mortgage payments sure did. The end result: The lender foreclosed on the couple's home, and the American dream was shattered for another young couple.

Property owners who end up in foreclosure cross all demographics. The auto industry executive who is downsized out of his job can fall behind on the mortgage for his $850,000 home in Grosse Pointe, Michigan, just as easily as Dakota did. So can the fry cook with the $75,000 home in Selma, Alabama; the struggling cell phone salesman with the $430,000 condo in San Diego, California; the single mom working two jobs to make ends meet in her $150,000 home in Lancaster, Pennsylvania, and the recent college grad with a $250,000 first home in Colorado Springs, Colorado.

The common denominator? They're all people in financial trouble who cannot afford their homes. That's how I define *foreclosure*.

How Much Money Can You Make?

Goodness and kindness aside, however, you're thinking about foreclosure investing to pay your own mortgage and support the lifestyle you deserve. So how much can the average foreclosure investor make in a year? *Zippo—zero, nada, nothing!* That's right. The average foreclosure investor won't make a dime in this business.

You have to be above average in your commitment to and enthusiasm for this business if you want to earn a fantastic living buying and selling pre-foreclosures for profit.

In my 20-plus years as an active real estate investor and trainer, I have found that clients who try something other than the white-knight approach to foreclosure investing come up far short of their own expectations and goals. Many drop out of the process before ever turning one deal. Others drop out after discovering how much work and commitment this business requires. Still other would-be investors are afraid to approach complete strangers or are unwilling to switch their focus from money to one that revolves around helping the homeowners in need first. This approach is the Golden Rule in action: Do unto others as you would have them do unto you.

There are no shortcuts in this business and, as I've said, it isn't easy. If you're serious about getting started, you must believe that you can make it work for you, your family, and your needs. This is a personal decision that no one can make for you. As with anything else you truly want, you must decide to give 100 percent of yourself.

The average net profit on a typical deal is about
$45,000 on a $300,000 home that you buy,
fix up, and sell for a quick profit.

—Alexis McGee

If you do make the commitment, though, the average income on a deal depends on market values in the area. But you can probably expect an average net profit of about 15 percent of the resale on a home that you buy, fix up, and sell for a quick profit. Or you can opt to turn over a deal to someone else. That other investor pays the bills and fixes up the house and you instead earn a finder's fee for putting together the deal—anywhere from $10,000 to $20,000 and up—depending on the profit in the deal. Not a bad paycheck.

But don't expect it to come quickly or easily. The typical deal may take a few months to find, depending on market conditions that include the supply of homes, conditions of those homes, how they're priced, and more. Chances are you'll end up with more than one deal at virtually the same time, so get ready for all hell to break loose! If you take the right approach, do your homework, make the commitment, and follow through, you could expect *at least* six profitable deals (netting a minimum of $30,000 each) during your first year! You'll learn how to create a winning investment formula in Part 2 of this book.

Consider two of the hundreds of stories of personal satisfaction and monetary gain from those pre-foreclosure investors who have decided to follow the path of helping others first and letting the monetary gains follow:

1. Art was single and using his home's equity like a credit card to finance his lifestyle. Faced with the fact that he couldn't run anymore to keep up with his growing house payments, he signed a deal to sell his home to Mary Kay, now a ForeclosureS.com coach. The deal netted Art enough money to pay his debts and thousands of dollars to start over, and Mary Kay walked away with a $40,000 finder's fee. "I stuck with this guy and he signed with me because, he said, 'You were the *only* person who tried to help me, not just buy my house. I trust you.' What kind words that man said and how good they made me feel. I know that helping another person out of a bad situation is what we are in the business for, but the benefits are wonderful. What a fantastic life I lead . . ."

2. Liz at first rebuffed Daryl White's efforts to help her out of her loan default woes. She insisted that she was working on getting another loan to solve the problem. Daryl, a successful pre-foreclosure investor and ForeclosureS.com coach, tried to follow up with her anyway, but she never returned his phone calls. Then out of the blue one day, Liz called in tears. Her home was scheduled for auction in two weeks and she was afraid she would end up homeless. Daryl researched Liz's options, put together the numbers, and made Liz an offer for her home that she accepted. Liz got about $60,000 to start over, and Daryl netted around $74,000 for himself. "This is exactly why I have a passion for what I do," says Daryl. "In one day I helped someone go from being scared to death of being homeless to being happy about her future."

Your Business Insurance

Referrals are your long-term insurance and insulation against the ups and downs of real estate markets. The deal that doesn't materialize will generally bring referrals to you down the road. Those people you help, whether you buy their properties in default or not, will come back to you when they're in financial trouble again, or they will refer their friends and acquaintances your way. It's those referrals, along with your sincerity, that separate you from the masses. With the right approach, timely information, and commitment, you'll find long-term success in the business regardless of whether markets are hot, cold, or in transition. When the others are out of business or scrambling to find their deals, you'll have more than you need.

While knowledge is necessary, sustained success comes to the person who's driven by strong values and ethics.

—Ron Willingham, author and founder
Integrity Systems, Inc.

No need to worry about the annual cyclical nature of real estate markets, either. Winter, spring, summer, and fall, the deals will be there for you. We live in the Sacramento Valley in California where, in winter, we often go weeks without seeing the sun. The gray skies can really get to you. In fact, scientific studies show that gray skies can cause depression in some people.

In this gray time, you would think that selling and moving out of a home

Take Our Quiz

Ask yourself the following questions to help you better recognize whether you should be interested in foreclosure-investing. If you answer yes to all of them, your heart and soul are right for this approach to doing business.

- Do you want to be a real estate entrepreneur and finally be able to quit your day job?

- Are you looking for a way to profit from foreclosure real estate investing honestly and ethically without any dishonest, illegal, or questionable schemes?

- Do you want to feel good about helping others, while also helping yourself and your family?

- Are you willing to do the work necessary to get the biggest return for your investment in time and energy?

- Do you want a way to reach not only your financial goals, but also your quality of life goals so you can be truly wealthy in every way?

would be the last thing on people's minds. But just the opposite is true among those with their financial backs against the wall. The peak buying season for fore-closures is November through March. My hottest time of the year is when the other guys who are looking for foreclosures go on winter vacation because they can't find deals. That's when homeowners in default find it easiest to just let go, move on, and start over. Gray days truly are pay days!

TAKEaway

Some key points to remember:

- Putting the welfare of a homeowner in default ahead of your own financial gain will net long-term success in this business. It's about negotiating win-win situations for a homeowner and for you, too.

- If you can't stomach—and many can't—the idea of giving away your expertise and knowledge free, then foreclosure investing is *not* for you.

- Don't expect to get rich quick, either. The business is filled with people who paid big money for so-called secrets to success, only to find they didn't work.

- Getting ahead in this business requires tremendous commitment and effort. But, combined with the right approach, your hard work will result in big fi-nancial gains and personal satisfaction for you.

CHAPTER 2

You Can Do It!

Nice guys finish first.

—Alexis McGee

Buying pre-foreclosure or foreclosure properties doesn't take a real estate degree or license. In fact, it doesn't take a college degree, work experience, or any cash on your part, either. What it does take is the right attitude, approach, information, and perseverance. Opening the doors to this business involves learning what works and what doesn't, doing your homework, and then applying your people skills.

Do tales of success like those of Anna and Mary Kay, whom we talked about in Chapter 1, strike a chord with you? Do you want to feel good about yourself and what you do for a living? Are you willing to invest the time it takes to learn the details? Are you willing to forgo the mind-set of "me and my money first" and replace it with "What you sow you will reap"? You must answer all these questions and more in the affirmative if you want long-term success in the foreclosure buying business.

Jeff K. did just that. A high school graduate with virtually no work experience or extra cash, he liked the idea of a solid financial future and enjoyed giving to others. So he decided to look into pre-foreclosure buying. He learned about foreclosure investing, did his homework, and after only three months in the business is on the brink of closing deals with a half-dozen homeowners in default. Jeff has helped several additional homeowners escape from the foreclosure and loan sharks and avoid losing their homes for now. "Next time they'll come to me, I'm sure," says Jeff.

Another novice foreclosure investor, Kobe Zimmerman, is connecting big-time with homeowners, too. Those people in distress welcome his genuineness and sincerity, which breaks down any resistance or distrust they may initially feel. "A weird side effect of all my dealings is that I feel like I need to take care of these people," says Kobe. "They actually need me. These people are like small fish in the ocean. They are being preyed upon, and I am educating, protecting, and helping them. Man, I love this!"

Successful people are always looking for opportunities to help others. Unsuccessful people are always asking, "What's in it for me?"

—Brian Tracy, world-renowned professional speaker, author, consultant

---

The threat of foreclosure hits even closer to home for Cliff W. Several years before he got into investing, Cliff was two weeks away from losing his own home at public auction. "I wasn't ignorant. I just made some poor financial decisions," he says. "I had been misled, taken advantage of, and overwhelmed by the investors who began to circle when I got into financial trouble. All they wanted was to give me a few bucks in exchange for the deed to my house. I thought the situation was hopeless."

Then, at the eleventh hour, a white knight in the form of a caring mortgage broker came forward and helped Cliff avoid foreclosure by using the equity in his home to refinance it. Although this may seem like a simple, obvious solution, Cliff was unaware he had the income to qualify to borrow the money. The less scrupulous investors were more interested in getting the deal for themselves than in explaining Cliff's options so he could keep his home. Since that time, Cliff has reworked his life and his finances and now helps others get back on financial track.

These are just a few examples of what you or anyone of any age and educational background can accomplish when you set your mind to it. With the right attitude and the right set of tools, you will be able to help yourself and your family, and countless others at the same time.

Overcoming Your Own Fears

Don't let your own fears prevent you from succeeding, either. Buying pre-foreclosure properties from homeowners in default is a people business. Once you're beyond the facts and details, it comes down to whether a seller trusts you and likes you enough to sell you his property. Arrogant investors rarely do well buying homes from owners in default. Instead, they're left to buy homes on the courthouse steps at the trustee sale auctions. They deal with the owner in foreclosures after the auction by evicting them. How would that make you feel? Just remember, nice guys can and do finish first.

It doesn't matter where you are coming from.
All that matters is where you are going.

—Brian Tracy

Consider the beginnings in the business for Mary Kay, the highly successful foreclosure investor and coach mentioned earlier. She wasn't always as confident and clear as she is now. She was literally petrified by the idea of picking up the phone and talking to strangers as a way to verify and sort through leads on potential homeowners in default. Instead, Mary Kay went door to door to talk to these homeowners and their neighbors. "I vividly remember the first home I stopped at because it took me over half an hour just to work up the nerve to go to the front door. I'm sure the homeowner heard my knees knocking before my knuckles hit the door! Actually, they were very receptive and we spoke for several minutes before I headed off to the next 15 or so houses for the day."

That was thousands of door knocks and phone calls—and scores of deals—ago. Today Mary Kay picks up the phone and knocks on doors without a second thought! You can, too.

Before you make any excuse why you simply *can't* get into the foreclosure investing business right now, keep in mind that we've heard all the excuses before. You can always dream up plenty of reasons why you can't do something. But if you truly are committed to changing your life and your family's future, there's no better means than through pre-foreclosure investing. None of the excuses counts. You *can* do it.

Since I started in this business in 1983, I've been told time after time, "You can't do that," or "That won't work." The doubters and deniers fail to recognize that honest profits can be made through foreclosure investing. On average, you will find that if you spend four hours a day making calls, working perhaps 100 foreclosure leads a week, you will net 8 to 10 deals in a year. (Of course, you can check out far fewer leads and make far fewer deals, too. After all, you are your own boss in this business!) Out of those numbers, though, you will make more money

Top Ten Excuses for Not Getting Started in the Business

1. Not enough cash.

2. Not enough time.

3. No deals in my market.

4. Too much competition.

5. Friends and family think I'm crazy.

6. Real estate bubble is going to burst.

7. Realtors ignore me.

8. Bad credit or no credit at all.

9. Don't want to lose money.

10. Don't know where to start.

than you ever could have imagined and you will probably have helped hundreds of homeowners keep their homes in that one year's time. Let's shed some reality on each of the top 10 excuses why you can't invest in foreclosures.

1. *I don't have enough cash.* The reality is that you don't need your own money to invest successfully in foreclosures. When you know where to find motivated sellers in your backyard—and learn how to buy their houses below market value—the money you need will find you. In this book, we guide you through how to put together the deals and find all the money you will ever need.

2. *I don't have enough time.* Many people end up working in a dead-end job for someone else's future. Why not channel your energies into your own future by working for yourself where the potential for reward is limitless? You say you don't have enough time—what about all that free time you already waste? A great many people spend much of it in front of the TV. Give up that junk time, and you'll be amazed at how much time you have.

Then spend that time learning. You can carve out time anywhere. You can read at home; you can pick up audio CDs and listen to them in your car; you can even try downloads on hand-held devices. Use your down time to build up your deal-making potential. That means reading or listening to what's going on in the real estate industry and the economy, and studying self-help books. A couple of my favorites are *Integrity Selling for the 21st Century*, by Ron Willingham (New York: Doubleday, 2003); and *The 7 Habits of Highly Effective People*, by Stephen R. Covey (New York: Free Press, 1989). For more books see the Resources section at the back of this book. You might also take a few detours on your way home to talk to neighbors and property owners. You'll see how close by those great deals can be and how easy it is to make new friends and get the ground-floor gossip on potential deals.

3. *There are no deals in my market.* I have yet to find a market that doesn't have motivated sellers. New investors often focus only on what they read in their local paper and then summarily decide sellers don't need them. These are the same would-be investors who think that if you want to sell a house right away, you simply put it on the market for top dollar. That's not quite how it's done. We explain why later, but for now, consider a few "what ifs":

   - What if one of those homeowners in your area got sick or lost his job and couldn't make his house payments?
   - What if his lender has started a foreclosure action?
   - What if he tried to qualify for a new loan but couldn't?
   - What if his house isn't in the best condition?
   - What if he couldn't find a qualified buyer quickly enough?
   - What if the buyer couldn't get financing quickly enough?
   - What if a couple is about to lose all their equity and credit in a foreclosure auction?

   Could any or all of these happen to someone in your neighborhood—whether the market is hot, cold, or lukewarm? Absolutely! Motivated sellers are everywhere, all the time. It's up to you to find them and create a win-win deal. But you must learn what to do and what not to do, or those deals will slip through your fingers as fast as they appear.

4. *There is too much competition.* In Chapter 1 we mentioned the hundreds of thousands of properties in foreclosure in 2006. That doesn't even include the hundreds of thousands more properties whose owners are in default, and more and more properties come into the pipeline every day. That translates to more than enough leads for everyone. Remember the tale of Krispy Kreme® Doughnuts? The company entered a totally saturated market and blew away its competition. The company hit a home run because it had a better plan and implemented it perfectly. So stop worrying

about the competition, and start working on making yourself a better, smarter investor.

5.   *My friends and family think I'm crazy.* So what! Real estate success takes *your* positive attitude, confidence, and courage. If you listen to the critics and pessimists, you'll convince yourself you can't do anything. Business philosopher, author, and motivational speaker Jim Rohn suggests that you must constantly ask yourself a series of questions and use the answers to improve your outlook:

- Who am I around?
- What are they doing to me?
- What do they have me reading?
- What do they have me saying?
- Where do they have me going?
- What do they have me thinking?
- And most important, what do they have me becoming?

Finally, ask yourself the big question: Is that okay? If it's not, do something about it! (For more information on Jim Rohn, visit www.jim rohn.com.)

6.   *The real estate bubble is going to burst.* Again? So what! The deals will always be there. Divorce, illness, death, job loss, and other life-changing events happen, and people lose their homes every day. Yes, real estate markets have cooled. But economics still remain solid, and home builders aren't flooding the markets with supply as they did the last time we faced similar economic trends. Today the right homes are selling at the right price. You just need to know what that right price is, and you're set. It's not too late to invest, but you have to quit talking about it, and just do it.

7.   *Realtors blow me off.* As an ex–real estate agent, I know how a Realtor can and cannot help you as a foreclosure investor. When markets are hot, agents are busy. That's not the time to ask them to hunt for unlisted, below-market deals, or to write a lowball, discount offer on a property. When those markets cool, Realtors want to earn the listings of bank-owned (REO) properties, so they price them high—in effect, buying the listings. No one wants to find you deals. If they have them, they want to keep them for themselves!

Your best approach in any market: Prospect for motivated sellers yourself, educate yourself in the laws of your state, and negotiate your own deals. It's not tough. Real estate isn't rocket science, and plenty of reputable sources are available to help you (check out the Resources section at the back of this book).

8. *I have bad (or no) credit.* If you want to buy, fix up, and then hold on to a property as a rental or until markets change, you'll need long-term financing options. And, yes, good credit is important in order to get that type of loan. But if, instead, you're planning to buy, rehab, and sell a property quickly for profit, you don't need credit and you don't need permanent financing. You do, however, need to know how to purchase a property using *subject-to* financing. That means you receive title to the property but actually take over the seller's existing loans and make payments on them until you turn around and resell the property. That's when both you and the former owner collect your paychecks.

   Creative financing approaches abound (we discuss a few in later chapters), so don't get hung up on money and credit issues. Once you find the deals, the money will fly at you. That's almost guaranteed.

9. *I don't want to lose money.* This is a prime time to consider some of the many Norman Vincent Peale books on *The Power of Positive Thinking* (Prentice-Hall, 1952, et al.). The more positive an approach you take, the harder you'll work, and the greater the chances of your success. Don't fill your head with negative thoughts, which lead to negative words, which lead to negative actions. Sure, plenty of books take the gloom-and-doom approach to the risks and pitfalls of real estate investing. But don't waste your time reading those books. Scores of ordinary people just like you and me have made more money in real estate than in any other investment arena. How about you? If you own your own home, how does it compare with your stocks as an investment? Based on your answer, I'll bet you wish you'd bought more real estate than securities.

   So instead of fretting about possible losses, take a leap of faith, educate yourself on the right way to invest in foreclosure houses for profit, and realize your dreams. The more you learn, the better you'll feel, and the safer your investments will be.

10. *I don't know where to start.* You've already started! You picked up this book and have begun to read about how pre-foreclosure investing honestly and ethically can work for you. Now it's time to make your dream of investing become a reality. Stop making excuses and keep reading. You don't need to know everything to get started. But you do need to continue to educate yourself with the help of reputable and ethical mentors and teachers.

Finding a Good Mentor

Many people tout their expertise in the field. It's up to you to identify who is truly an expert and who is simply a pseudo-expert more interested in multilevel marketing and collecting your money than in your success in the business of foreclosure investing.

Before you sign on the dotted line or plunk down cash for any hush-hush marketing techniques, check out those gurus thoroughly. Google their names. Check with local and national Better Business Bureaus (try BBBonline.com and click on "Consumers"). Check their names on your county recorder's "Grantee-Grantor Index" to see if any liens or lawsuits have been filed against them. Also check eBay (www.ebay.com) to see if a glut of the guru's programs is for sale secondhand. That's not a good sign. If the system works, why then are so many people dumping it?

Pay particular attention to what current and former students have to say about a foreclosure-investing teacher and program, outside of that teacher's web site. If the majority of comments you turn up about a specific person or program are negative, chances are something isn't right. Gut feelings are seldom wrong, especially in a people business where intuition counts. If it feels as if something is on the shady side, dishonest, illegal, or even convoluted, it probably is.

Always thoroughly check out any self-described foreclosure-investing guru before you pay a penny for any "words of wisdom." Otherwise, you might find those words are merely empty promises.

—Alexis McGee

Don't overlook checking out various blogs and chat sites on the web that discuss foreclosure-investing, mortgage fraud, real estate, and more. They can be invaluable reality checks as well.

Are Foreclosure Investments Risky?

Keep in mind that when you buy a pre-foreclosure, you're buying real estate. It's safe and it isn't going anywhere, plus it has great potential for capital gains. You can also buy real estate as an investment rental property to generate positive cash flow. Of course, you must buy right. That means the right property at the right price in the right location. That's where doing your homework, knowing your markets, and paying attention to price come in.

Why pay retail price for a property when you can buy it *wholesale*? Buying wholesale is what happens when you buy using our system. Typically the investor buys the property at a *discount*. As we've mentioned, sellers can be motivated to accept a lower price because of their financial need or other circumstances. In fact, people in your own neighborhood whose homes aren't listed for sale could be in pre-foreclosure or foreclosure right now and need your cash more than they need full price for their home. Some may have experienced job loss, a long illness, divorce, or the death of the main breadwinner.

Unfortunately, they're also often slow to realize they no longer can afford to keep their home. If they face that fact quickly, they could sell their home conventionally for full market value or close to it. By the time they realize the seriousness of their situation, however, the foreclosure auction could be only weeks away. A traditional sale can't happen in that time frame, so they end up at the point of losing everything—including what remains of their credit standing—in a trustee or sheriff's sale. Those same people would be delighted to sell their house at a discount, and your cash will bring them what they really seek: peace of mind; a fresh start; a safe place for their family, and a return to creditworthiness. Their other option is to wind up with nothing and nowhere to go as they watch a stranger buy their home on the courthouse steps and later evict them.

Should You Quit Your "Day Job"?

People often consider foreclosure investing as something they can dabble in part-time while they continue to work at their full-time job—sort of a weekend adventure to supplement your regular income.

It's possible to do foreclosure investing on a part-time basis, and some people have done so successfully while they get started in the business. But however you get started, recognize the degree of commitment required if you want to succeed. You must schedule the time for this business *first*, not last, on your list of things to do. You must be totally focused, organized, and systematic in your approach. Can you do that part-time or does it require your full-time commitment? That's a question you must answer for yourself. Before you come up with a quick answer, keep in mind what I've said about the income—or lack thereof—of an *average* (as opposed to exceptional) investor in this business.

Your success or failure is ultimately up to you.

—Alexis McGee

Roger and Louise T. were retired and enjoying life tremendously, especially the time they spent on the golf course. They had a moderately comfortable retirement income but decided that with escalating living costs, they needed to supplement it by working part-time. They considered their options. Louise was tired of secretarial work, and Roger was bored with hard work and routine. Roger had worked at a mortgage company and Louise at a title company, so the couple figured that with their background and a little training, foreclosure investing would be the perfect solution. They could have their free time and bring in the cash, too. All they had to do was read a book about their new hobby, hang up their shingle, advertise, and the deals would pour in. No sweat, and best of all, no worries. Boy, did that couple get a rude awakening—and quickly, too!

Take a chance! All life is a chance. The man who goes farthest is generally the one who is willing to do and dare.

—Dale Carnegie, motivational and self-improvement speaker and author of *How to Win Friends and Influence People*, Philadelphia, PA: Running Press Book Publishers, 2002

They lacked the commitment to details, the drive, and the focus to get ahead. Yes, you can work as little or as much as you like in this business, but generally that option works only *after* you're successful—after you have worked hard at it and established your business.

Ted Z., age 47, had been a successful Realtor—so successful, in fact, that he had a nice financial cushion. But the thought of retiring was out of the question. Ted loved working hard and with people. He looked to foreclosure investing as a new career that could fulfill those aspects of his personality as well as earn him a nice living. He attacked his new profession with the same vigor he had his old. Although he worked only 20 hours or so a week in the beginning, his commitment was such that he accomplished more than most people would have if they worked at it 40 or more hours a week.

"It's a tremendous challenge to help others solve their financial problems," says Ted. "And it's awesome to really be able to help someone and make money at it, too."

Spotting the Red Flags

Quitting your regular job is not an easy decision or one to be taken lightly. We all have responsibilities—financial, physical, and moral—that have to be satisfied. What you must realize, however, is that without truly making the commitment to succeed at this business, you seriously limit your chances of success.

This business is not for everyone, and no matter what anyone tells you, not everyone can be successful at it. Over the years I've noticed several red flags or demotivators that work against success in this business. If you can't deal with and overcome these red flags, the foreclosure buying business probably isn't your best career choice. The demotivators and ways to overcome them include the following.

Fear

This includes fears of rejection, fear of failure, and fear of what might happen. Fear has ended more property-buying careers than any other single factor. Pressure and paranoia cause fear, so remove both, and you're home free. Get rid of the pressure by recognizing that you can't and won't win over every homeowner or close every deal. Even Donald Trump doesn't do that, and you're just starting out. Don't even question why your deals aren't closing until you've established relationships with at least 25 homeowners. This approach concentrates your attention on meeting sellers and understanding them. After you've really listened to all 25, then work on finding the right solution and closing. Of course, if you happen to make a great deal in the mean time . . .

Failing to Put Together a Deal That Meets the *Seller's* Needs

You must be willing to take the time to talk with sellers and develop rapport with them, or they won't be truthful with you and will blow you off. If you don't put their interests first, they will recognize and see through your ploys. Plenty of potential deals are torpedoed by buyers who chatter on and on about all the cash they are going to give the seller. Worse still, the same potential buyer often tries to put together a deal that doesn't meet the seller's needs. How do you discover those needs? Start by asking questions and really listening instead of just making assumptions.

Failing to Ask Questions, Listen to the Answers, and Formulate Solutions

Again, it's about establishing rapport. You absolutely must be willing to ask questions and hear what a homeowner is saying in order to uncover the real truth behind their problems. Only then can you offer the right deal or helpful advice. When meeting with an owner, look for evidence of hobbies, memorabilia, and deferred maintenance as subjects to discuss. With the right questions, you'll build rapport and turn the focus onto the owner and his situation, what he would like to see happen, and what he will do if that doesn't work out. You may or may not even talk about buying his house.

Focus on the solutions to his needs. If that includes selling the house, discuss what he expects the money from the sale to do for him, and not just the amount of money itself. Once the seller can see the value of what you bring, the deal is yours if you want it.

Failing to Realize Your Responsibility for Your Own Success

In this business, you train yourself for success. If your buying career isn't going as you would like, take control and make a difference by attending teleconferences, buying CDs, reading books, and seeking hands-on training to learn how to identify and correct what ails you.

Don't join an easy crowd; you won't grow. Go where the expectations and the demands to perform are high.

—Jim Rohn, business philosopher,
motivator, and author

It's Your Choice

As we've said, the choice to pursue foreclosure investing is yours. Consider all the issues and concerns we've discussed. Ask yourself whether you're willing to accept them as part of doing business. Do you think you have what it takes to overcome any potential shortcomings as they relate to what we've covered? Are you willing to make the necessary commitment? Do you have the compassion to empathize with people in trouble rather than look down on them with disdain? Do you have the patience and persistence to prevail?

If Daryl White ever had any doubts about whether foreclosure investing was the right choice for him, they were vanquished after a deal about a year ago. Currently a ForeclosureS.com coach and pre-foreclosure investor, Daryl recounts the experience:

> It was a husband and wife in their mid-forties with two young children. The wife was a stay-at-home mom and the husband a general contractor. Their life was great until the husband was injured on the job, and his medical insurance ran out.
>
> With their savings depleted, it was just weeks until the foreclosure auction by the time I successfully contacted them. Initially, they were reluctant to talk with me because so many others had tried the hard-sell, shark approach. But I took the time to help them go over all their options, and they began to trust me. They decided selling the property to me was the best solution for their future. They would be able to walk away with well over $100,000 in their pockets, which they could use to buy a new home. The day of the closing the wife was in tears after seeing the check. She told me she now knew they would be okay because of me!

It doesn't matter which side of the fence you get off on sometimes. What matters most is getting off! You cannot make progress without making decisions.

—Jim Rohn

Think about your own life today and your vision for the future. Are you doing what you want to be doing, earning what you would like to be earning, making a difference in others' lives as well as your own? Are you satisfied with your life and your expected future? Do you work for someone else and find yourself frustrated or spinning your wheels? Would you like to be your own boss, choose your own hours, and control your own destiny? Do you dream of pursuing interests and activities that take more time and money than you have? Wouldn't it be great to spend more uninterrupted time with your family? And how about taking fabulous vacations that you also dream about?

That's a lot of questions, but they're all important to consider. There aren't any right or wrong answers, either. You may very well be content with your life already, and perhaps successful foreclosure investing isn't the best track for you.

Be honest with yourself. This isn't a quiz that anyone else ever will see. This is, instead, about you making the right choices for your future and the future of your loved ones. Great financial, personal, and emotional reward can be yours if you're willing to give of yourself for others and make the commitment to honest and ethical foreclosure-investing.

Will A. was a highly paid engineer in Silicon Valley. He had a sound income and didn't mind his job but was simply tired of giving away his time and knowledge to thankless people. He did the math on a typical foreclosure deal in his area and saw nothing but dollar signs. So he figured pre-foreclosure investing was a great way to get paid for his smarts. Perhaps, he thought, he should start with auctions so he wouldn't have to deal with people anymore. What's wrong with his approach?

Ellen S., on the other hand, also thought pre-foreclosure investing was a great new career. She loved working with and helping others, especially if she could earn a good living while doing it. It's pretty clear-cut: Ellen is cut out for this business. Will isn't.

One Last Hurdle

It may surprise you, but the biggest hurdle for new investors isn't related to any of the previous thought-provoking questions. Instead, it's building up the courage to talk to homeowners in default, to call or walk up to complete strangers and discuss the very personal issue of money problems. That's essential to identifying the best potential deals. For many wannabe investors, making the calls is as bad as going to the dentist or taking unpleasant medicine. The excuse for not doing so is the same, too: Can't we put it off another day?

The answer is, "Nope, not if you want to make it." You must get past the inertia and get moving along your road to success in foreclosure investing. In the following pages, we show you step-by-step how to start. Meanwhile, the rhetoric boils down to two things:

1. A true desire to help people in need from a selfless viewpoint.
2. The courage to strike up a conversation with a complete stranger who is in foreclosure.

The first requires integrity and empathy on your part. The second, which is about gaining courage, will come with practice, practice, practice.

Daryl's Tips

ForeclosureS.com Coach Daryl White offers a few tips for new foreclosure investors:

- Have the patience and willingness to learn what the business is all about. That includes understanding your state's foreclosure laws and how to deal with owners in default.

- Thoroughly research anyone from whom you're planning to learn the foreclosure investing business.

- Invest in continued learning and personal development by reading books and articles by successful people such as motivational speakers Dale Carnegie and Zig Ziglar, business philosopher Jim Rohn, and others.

- Surround yourself with successful, like-minded, positive thinkers.

- Do exactly as you promise to do in your dealings with homeowners and others.

- Understand that this is not easy. There is no shortcut to wealth in this business. It takes hard work.

TAKEaway

Some key points to remember:

- Buying properties in pre-foreclosure doesn't take past experience, a college degree, or even your own money. It does take commitment, hard work, and knowing how to structure deals.

- Don't get bogged down in all the excuses why you can't succeed at foreclosure investing. Think positive instead. You can do this if you take the right approach and make the honest commitment.

- Foreclosure investing is about buying real estate, which is safe and isn't going anywhere. The key is to buy the right property at the right price in the right location.

- Whether you choose to pursue this business is up to you. Be honest with yourself about your strengths and weakness, and then be willing to work to improve yourself. Pay attention to those skills that need to be honed, and you will boost your chances of success.

PART II

GETTING STARTED

We teach investors the fundamentals of successful pre-foreclosure property investing through ethical scenarios that are a win-win for the homeowner and the investor.

—Alexis McGee

CHAPTER 3

The Basics

Success is the natural consequence of consistently applying basic fundamentals.

—Alexis McGee

If you're looking for a stable real estate venture, look twice at pre-foreclosure investing. The white knight strategy is all about getting to homeowners in default *before* they lose their home, *before* the foreclosure, *before* they're left with nothing. That's when you truly can help them make the right financial decisions for their futures, and in many cases generate solid financial returns for yourself, too.

Opportunities abound regardless of inflation, deflation, market ups and downs, or seasonal cycles. A ready supply of sellers is always yours if you know how to find them, how to work with them, and how to help them.

The business doesn't have to be complicated, but you do need to enjoy talking with property owners and building relationships. Some distressed homeowners are more motivated to act than others, and some just need help finding the right solution to their foreclosure problem. Almost all of the homeowners, however, present opportunities for you to help them while helping yourself.

Basically, your job is to identify prospective properties for purchase, locate their owners, share your expertise by working with the homeowners to solve their financial problems, and then—if a purchase is their best option—structure a deal that makes sense for you, too. Even if you're simply finding the deals and flipping them to another investor, you do the legwork—except, of course, paying the bills. An aside, though: If you do your job properly, chances are the seller will want to work with you only, and you'll end up attending the closing or guiding the seller through the process.

Steps in the Process

- Identify the best deal in your area.

- Find the homeowners, develop a rapport with them, and uncover the real reasons for their situation.

- Develop a game plan similar to one you would provide for your brother or sister that includes how to best help the homeowners.

- Crunch the numbers (resale value, repairs, loans, and liens) to determine your purchase offer. Remember, every deal has a financial point at which it does or doesn't make sense.

- Determine your financing or find an investor to flip (hand off) the deal to.

- Negotiate and sign a legal contract with the seller.

- If you're the purchaser, develop a resale or hold plan for the property that includes a tax strategy to maximize your return.

Self-Assessment

Before we go into more detail, you need to assess your own skills. When you learn how to capitalize on your strengths and compensate for your weaknesses, you will find it easier to work with homeowners in default and be successful.

As with other aspects of this business, a self-assessment begins by asking yourself key questions. Writing down your answers will give you a clearer picture of your assets and liabilities. Some issues to consider:

- In what areas do you excel? How might you capitalize on those strengths to help others and to improve your likelihood of success? If you're personable and get along well with others, for example, you're one step closer to developing rapport with prospective sellers. If you're an organized, detail-oriented person, you will have an advantage in developing a system to generate leads. If you have the ability to visualize, you might spot the diamond-in-the-rough property that others dismiss.

- What are your weaknesses? If you're shy and leery of talking with strangers, that doesn't mean you can't be successful at foreclosure investing. Many shy people are caring and empathetic-valuable qualities in winning a homeowner's trust. Shyness or self-consciousness may simply indicate that you need to work on developing your self-confidence. For starters, you might try reading self-help books (check out the Resources section at the back of this book for ideas) and brushing up on your people skills. If your big weakness is that you're disorganized or forgetful, you'll have to develop a system of managing property leads that ensures you won't overlook those all-important follow-up calls with potential clients.

- Are you a good communicator? There's more to the art of communication than simply getting along with others. You must be able to convey your message clearly; ask the right questions without being abrasive, so that owners will tell you the full story; and truly listen to the answers to those questions. (We address the details of communication in Chapter 8.)

- Does the business of foreclosures bother you ethically? Despite the potential financial gains, some people just can't get beyond the shady image of foreclosure investing as it's presented in certain newspaper articles and supermarket tabloids. If you feel that making money in foreclosures is inherently unethical, immoral, or dishonest, you could have a problem in this business, where attitude plays a major role in determining the degree of one's success. The power of positive thinking can't be overstated. You must love what you do, and do it from your heart. If you're unsure about this, you will talk yourself out of making calls. You can persuade yourself to have a positive or negative self-image.

- Can you handle going into business for yourself without using any of your own cash? It's a bit unsettling to call homeowners without knowing where you'll get the cash. And even though this book will give you the tools to find all the money partners you'll ever need, until you close your first deal with someone else's money, you'll still worry about the "what ifs." This is when that positive mental outlook will carry you a long way!

These legitimate questions demand honest answers because this is, after all, a business based on honesty and frankness with others as well as yourself. We'll help you understand and deal with your answers, too. But remember, not everyone is cut out for this business.

Your attitude toward what you do can
determine its success or failure.

—Alexis McGee

Louisa N., a long-divorced and now-retired schoolteacher, always liked the idea of owning real estate. She had a little cash saved and plenty of time on her hands, so when she heard about foreclosure investing, she thought it seemed like just the thing for her future. After all, her many years spent dealing with students and their parents had taught her how to handle all kinds of people. She figured she'd be a natural in this business.

Louisa overlooked one thing, however. Although she was a good teacher and could stand up in front of a class with ease, she was uncomfortable talking with her students or their parents outside the classroom, and she never developed close relationships with any of them. Not only was she afraid of intimate, one-on-one re- lationships, but she also feared rejection and loss of control.

The thought of cold-calling homeowners as a foreclosure investor brought all Louisa's fears to the surface. She simply couldn't make those calls. Yet those calls are the lifeblood of the foreclosure investing business. Without the ability to com- fortably call strangers, including neighbors, friends, and family of potential pre- foreclosure property owners, it's impossible to develop your sales leads, let alone contact the homeowners themselves.

Unlike Mary Kay, who overcame her fear of the phone, Louisa never got off the ground in this business. Had she thoroughly understood the business at the outset and asked herself some of the key questions we've discussed, she wouldn't have had to spend a chunk of her savings before recognizing the fallacy of her dream.

You, too, must ask yourself questions and answer them realistically before committing your time and money to something that may not be right for you.

Not-So-Secret Principles for Success

I subscribe to the following not-so-secret principles for long-term success in this business.

- *Visualize your success before you make a move.* Picture achieving that dream, perhaps the Jaguar in the driveway, the summer home on the lake, financial security for the rest of your life, or even making a difference in the lives of others. You need a clear vision of your success before you can attain it.

- *Set goals that others consider crazy.* The ultimate reason for such goals is to entice you into becoming what it takes to achieve them. If you build on those goals, you'll grow with them.

- *Create your own road map to success.* To grow your property-buying business, you must have a destination in mind, and a map or a plan to get there. Where do you want your life to lead? What path will you take to get there? When do you plan to arrive at that destination? If you have a good road map, you'll most likely get where you want to go—on time!

- *Plan to win.* Organize your days, months, and years with your focus on the road ahead and reaching your destination. Don't be like most people who plan their vacations with more care than they plan their lives.

> *Most people spend more time planning their vacations than they do their lives. The reason: Escape is easier than change!*
>
> —Alexis McGee

- *Strategize what it will take to succeed.* Go over in your mind what's required for a specific deal to succeed. What is the property owner looking for? What's his or her motivation? When you find the person's hot button, you'll know better what direction to take.

- *Associate with people who have something of value to share.* Remember business philosopher Jim Rohn's pertinent questions from Chapter 2:

  - Who am I around?
  - What are they doing to me?
  - What do they have me reading?
  - What do they have me saying?
  - Where do they have me going?
  - What do they have me thinking?
  - What do they have me becoming?
  - Is that okay?

- *Commit to your plan.* Once you have your road map, leave little room to deviate. Many people are apprehensive about the future because they don't have their life well planned. Wouldn't it be nicer to anticipate tomorrow instead of being surprised by it?

- *Invest in yourself.* Evaluate and reevaluate what you could have done to better help a homeowner in default. If you keep coming back to the same issue or problem, address the problem by further educating yourself in that area. Never begrudge the money you spend on your own education.

- *Develop the habit of repetition.* Repeat what's worked for you in the past and make that a habit. Success isn't magical or mysterious. It's the natural consequence of consistently applying basic fundamentals.

- *Stay disciplined.* Keep committed to and focused on doing what needs to be done. Remember that success is a few simple disciplines practiced daily, while failure is a few errors in judgment practiced every day. The cumulative weight of our disciplines and judgments leads us to fortune or failure.

- *Think!* This is one of the most important things we all need to do to be successful. We must allow ourselves quiet time away from phones and meetings. Give yourself time to clear your mind and focus on what you're doing. If you learn to think and reflect, you'll be aware of the consequences of your actions.

Business philosopher Rohn shares the secret to his own success in a field where many others fail:

> I found it easy to set the goals that could change my life. They [those who failed] found it easy not to. I found it easy to read the books that could affect my thinking and my ideas. They found that easy not to do. I found it easy to attend the classes and the seminars, and to get around other successful people. They said it probably really wouldn't matter. If I had to sum it up, I would say what I found to be easy to do, they found it easy not to do. Years later, I'm a millionaire and they are all still blaming the economy, the government, and company policies, yet they neglected to do the basic, easy things.

It's that power of positive thinking again!

This Isn't Your Ordinary Home Sale

If, after your own soul-searching, you're still interested in the white-knight approach to foreclosure investing, let's take a closer look at what is and isn't involved in the process.

Purchasing a home in foreclosure or pre-foreclosure is quite different from an ordinary home sale. Sure, a property's title changes hands and a mortgage is involved. But everything happens in double time—in fast-forward. *Escrow* (the time between when a sale is agreed upon, with a deposit held by a third party, and the closing, when the full payment is due) is short, typically only one to two weeks. (See Chapter 12 for more on escrow.) A buyer doesn't have time to go through the loan approval process, appraisal review, or underwriting—all standard protocol for an ordinary home purchase and loan. Even if you tried to assume the homeowner's loan, that requires a time-consuming credit approval process.

Instead, foreclosure investing requires minimal financing. That might involve a party flush with cash or, as is preferable in many cases, the use of subject-to financing that we briefly mentioned earlier. Remember, subject-to financing is when you or another investor takes over the property owner's existing loans (without asking permission of the lender) and brings them current. The purchaser gets a grant deed signed by the seller and then owns the home and is responsible for the prior owner's mortgage payments, which remain in the prior owner's name. (A subject-to contract differs from loan assumption in that the mortgage remains in the original homeowner's name.) The seller gets a fresh financial start because the foreclosure was stopped, the loan was made current, and the seller's credit was repaired. The seller also gets cash for his equity from the buyer for, it is hoped, a new start.

If you are flipping your deal for a finder's fee, you can get your fee for the contract assignment at closing. If you're planning to hold the home, rehab it, and then resell it, your financial payback comes at that time.

It's a win-win situation for all parties!

The Options for Homeowners in Default

Homeowners in default don't always need to or choose to sell their home. As someone committed to helping these people, your job is to discover the real issues, explain all the options, and help find the best solution for *their* needs.

Experience shows that no matter what product or service you're selling, in order to close a deal—any deal—you first must overcome all objections, both spoken and unspoken. Even under a cloud of foreclosure, the same is true for a homeowner in default. The roadblocks don't disappear simply because you avoid discussing them.

> *To sit in front of someone days from being homeless and basically save their life is very powerful and wonderful.*
>
> —Bob Pratt, student of Alexis McGee's approach to pre-foreclosure investing

Following are some of the most popular options for homeowners in default. Keep in mind, though, that not every option is available to every homeowner. Individual situations and solutions vary.

Types of Home Financing

Here are a few home financing approaches. Many foreclosures are the result of homeowners purchasing homes they couldn't afford, using creative financing options.

- *Traditional fixed-rate mortgage.* Generally with a term of 10, 15, 25, or 30 years, the principal and interest payments are fixed for the life of the loan.

- *Nontraditional fixed-rate mortgage.* A 40-year term that differs from traditional fixed-rate mortgage in that it often starts with a low teaser fixed rate, then adjusts upward after a certain period of time.

- *Traditional adjustable-rate mortgage (ARM).* Typically offers fixed principal and interest payments for a period of time, with the interest rate and monthly payments reset annually (sometimes even monthly).

- *Nontraditional option payment ARM.* A negative amortization loan that allows the borrower to make monthly payments that don't cover interest costs, boosting the principal amount of the loan; after a certain period, payments adjust upward.

- *Interest-only mortgage.* Borrower pays interest only for a certain length of time, after which the interest rate is reset to the then-current rate and payments adjust to fully amortize to pay off the loan.

- *No or low down payment mortgage.* Allows most or all of the home purchase, including closing costs, to be financed.

- *Subprime mortgage.* Offered to borrowers who can't qualify for conventional financing because they have less than perfect credit (lower FICO/credit scores); has significantly higher points and interest rates than conventional mortgages; often involves low introductory teaser interest rates that, when eventually adjusted upward, financially cripple the homeowner and leave little option but foreclosure. Recent tightening of subprime mortgage qualifications by giant lender Freddie Mac and financial difficulties of major subprime lenders have eliminated this option for many homeowners.

Forbearance

Basically, forbearance is a borrower's second chance from the lender. With the payment of a lump sum or a schedule of payments over time, the delinquent loan is reinstated. Generally this is an option if a borrower fell behind in payments because of a temporary lapse of employment and is now reemployed. The lender may opt to allow the borrower to pay back the money through installment payments over six months or to pay a reduced monthly payment until he can get back on his feet financially. The borrower can then pay any remaining outstanding loan delinquencies in a lump sum.

The forbearance may be an oral agreement or written contract between the lender and the borrower. Generally these agreements will not exceed more than 12 months.

With the dot-com bust, Steven lost his high-paying job as CFO of a two-year-old e-company. Because he was young and had held the job for only two years, he had virtually no money saved. He had, though, recently bought a fancy home on the strength of his monthly income. When that income evaporated along with his job, Steven was left with a huge mortgage on a house with very little equity. Luckily, another company hired him after only a few months of unemployment. He was, however, a bit behind in his bills and needed some breathing room in the form of temporary relief from his big monthly mortgage payments. Steven went to his lender, explained the situation, and was able to work out a forbearance deal to give him the time he needed to get back on track.

Loan Modification

A change in the terms of the original note, this option is designed to assist a borrower through a temporary setback. At the discretion of the lender, modification can include a cut in the loan's interest rate, reamortizing the remaining balance, extending the term of the loan, or other options. Typically a lender will consider a loan modification when foreclosure is imminent and the borrower's income has been decreased, or he is unable to make the mortgage payments as is but can do so with the loan modification.

In Steven's case, he didn't need completely revamped terms for his mortgage—a loan modification—because his unemployment had been only temporary. His new job also paid him a sizable monthly income so once he caught up, he could afford the high monthly payment.

Refinancing a Mortgage

Generally open to borrowers who have a temporary financial setback and have shown outstanding credit history in the past, refinancing involves paying off the old loan plus fees, then get a new, bigger loan in exchange. A new lender allows borrowers to refinance the existing mortgage, wrap in any late payments and fees, and cash out part of their equity in the home so that they can regain control of a debilitating financial situation. However, borrowers must be able to prove they can make the new mortgage payment. That means they must show full documentation to the lender—including tax returns, pay stubs, bank statements, and verification of income and bank accounts—to fully qualify for the loan. Because the homeowner is in default this is a subprime or *hard-money* loan and therefore is at a much higher interest rate than for borrowers with good credit; it carries high points, too.

Remember Cliff, the homeowner in Chapter 2 who made some poor financial decisions and ended up in default? His compassionate mortgage broker helped him recognize that he had enough equity in his property and a credit rating high enough to refinance and avoid foreclosure on his home.

Second Mortgage/Home Equity Line of Credit

This financing option involves keeping the existing loan and adding a new one so that the borrower now has two payments per month—making a tight financial situation even tougher. Again, because the borrower is already in default, it's a hard-money loan or a subprime loan, both of which mean considerably higher interest rates than the going rate and substantial points or fees.

A new lender may offer a second loan or junior lien to a borrower in order to pay for any back payments, late fees, and other charges necessary to reinstate the loan. In exchange, the borrower must make an additional monthly payment to cover the principal and interest payments on the second loan.

For example, if rates on a typical first mortgage are 6.8 percent with perhaps 1 percent fees, a hard-money loan might carry a rate double that with perhaps 5 to 10 points in fees or 5 to 10 percent of the loan's value.

A note of caution with second mortgage/refinance: Not only are hard-money or subprime loans a costly way to play catch-up, but most homeowners fail to recognize that if they can't keep up the current mortgage payments, they will likely find it impossible to afford the new, higher payments. In addition, this kind of fix is often only a temporary solution to serious financial problems that eventually will force a homeowner to sell anyway.

In such cases, to avoid making a tough financial situation worse, you should strongly recommend that the homeowners talk to a mortgage person about whether they truly can afford a refinance or second mortgage, and not just whether they can get it. (Typically, no more than 40 percent of the potential borrower's gross income should go toward debt payments). Keep in mind, too, that you don't want to refer already-struggling homeowners to a lender who gives them too big a loan (and subsequent monthly payment) so that they end up with nothing left to live on, and strips their equity so that when they do sell they have nothing left.

A competent mortgage person often can help these homeowners realize they can't afford a new loan, and in turn can send them back to me to buy the house now—not later when it could be too late and they have no equity left.

Sale of the Home

If a homeowner in default can't work with the existing lenders or find new lenders to complete a loan transaction within a reasonable time frame—leaving at least three weeks before the auction—it's time to get serious about selling. Ideally, homeowners should list their houses for sale as soon as they run into financial trouble, so that they're more likely to get a full and fair market offer to purchase the home. (Depending on their resale market, it takes 60 to 90 days to find a home-buyer and then another 30 days to close a standard purchase) Some owners try to hedge their bets by shopping for a new loan at the same time they list their house on the market. But surprise! Mortgage brokers and lenders generally have strict policies that state if you put your house on the market, they will terminate your loan application.

If a foreclosure auction is at least 90 days away, it may make sense for the homeowner to contact a Realtor. If it's a hot market and the house is in good shape, finding a buyer may take only a few weeks. But even if the house sells, the risk is that the buyer still needs to get financing. That process includes credit approval by the lenders, an appraisal of the house, completing underwriting, title review, drawing up documents, and payoff demands. That adds up to a lot of variables. The closing process easily can take another four weeks or longer, assuming there are no problems or delays.

The reality is that most homeowners in default don't decide to sell early on. Instead, they hold out for that "pending" new loan or refinancing approval. By the time they learn they can't get the loan, it's usually too late to sell the house through the normal process and at the full appraised price.

Instead, these homeowners must rely on foreclosure investors who offer quick-closing, all-cash transactions in exchange for paying a discounted price for the property. The selling price is further discounted because, typically, the owner lacks the money to make necessary repairs to the home.

Keep in mind the benefits this approach can offer to homeowners. They get the loans on the property brought current, salvage their deteriorating credit, and retain any remaining home equity, which is converted to a cash payment at closing.

Let's break down the numbers on a typical deal for a home pre-foreclosure in which the best solution for the homeowner is to sell. The home has an appraised value of $400,000 after cleanup and repairs. The buyer uses subject-to financing—she assumes the seller's existing loan. The purchase formula calls for discounting 30 percent from the future value after property improvements, and another $12,000, which is the estimated cost to fix up the 1,200-square-foot home at $10/square foot. (We talk more about figuring out the numbers in Chapter 5.) The accompanying box shows how this scenario works out.

The outstanding loans of a borrower in default sometimes exceed the current

THE NUMBERS

Here's a look at typical numbers for a $400,000 home in pre-foreclosure:

- Value of home after rehab and repairs: $400,000
- Less 30 percent discount (includes 15 percent   <$120,000>
  for your profit plus 15 percent for buying,
  holding, and selling costs):
- Less estimated repair costs: <$12,000>
- Total discount: <$132,000>
- Total amount offered for home: $268,000
- Current mortgage in default: <$215,000>
- Total needed to bring mortgage current: <$13,000>
- Home seller walks away with cash in pocket at closing: $40,000

value of a home. In some cases, the lender may allow the borrower to sell the home, accept the *short* proceeds, and forgive the remaining debt. This is what's known as a *short sale*. We talk more about short sales and the problems/drawbacks associated with them in Chapter 11. A note of caution, however: If someone says he has a get-rich-quick-through-short-sales offer that sounds too good to be true, turn around and walk away. Short-sale schemes can involve fraud that includes duplicated sets of documents and books that are outright illegal. Also in a short sale, the homeowner will have to pay taxes on any loss the lender writes off.

Deed in Lieu of Foreclosure

As a last-ditch effort to avoid the negative consequences of foreclosure, a homeowner in default may voluntarily convey title of the property back to the lender. During the recession of the 1980s and 1990s, this happened frequently. Out of work and with no buyers for properties bought at top dollar, homeowners cleaned out their homes and walked away. With massive inventories, banks and lenders found themselves suddenly in the real estate business big-time.

Lenders state that there must be *no* second mortgage or junior liens on the property in order for a homeowner to qualify for a deed in lieu of foreclosure. Owners of properties with values exceeding the amount owed against the home (to include normal closing costs) should consider selling the property before voluntarily conveying the home to the lender.

Bankruptcy Filing

An option for people who owe more money than they can pay, bankruptcy involves either working out a plan to repay the money over time or wiping out or discharging most of their bills. The former case can be a Chapter 11, 12, or 13 bankruptcy, depending on circumstances; the latter liquidation is a Chapter 7. While in bankruptcy an individual, as well as his home, is immediately protected from creditors, and any foreclosure proceedings cease. It's not quite as easy as it sounds, though, and it has long-range negative implications.

The Federal Bankruptcy Code and the Federal Rules of Bankruptcy Procedure lay out strict guidelines about who qualifies, what bills are eliminated, the length of time the person has to pay back outstanding bills, the possessions that can be retained, and more. Keep in mind the long-term financial implications for homeowners in default who file for bankruptcy, too. Check out the U.S. Courts web site (www.uscourts.gov) from the federal government, and click on "U.S. Bankruptcy Courts" for more details, or try www.legalpub.com and click on *"U.S. Bankruptcy Code & Rules Booklet— January 2007 Black Line Edition."*

Bankruptcy petitions, schedules, and plans are public record. Generally speaking, a bankruptcy remains on an individual's credit report for up to 10 years and will be taken into consideration before any future credit is granted. No laws prevent or require anyone to extend credit to someone immediately after they have filed bankruptcy. Also, many homeowners in default who seek bankruptcy as the solution later realize they still can't keep their home and must sell it. Then, due to the bankruptcy, they often have trouble finding a rental property because landlords don't want them as tenants.

Pray for Auction Overbid

One of the last and least favorable choices for a homeowner in default is to do nothing and allow the home to go to foreclosure auction. Sometimes a home ends up on the auction block because the owners succumb to procrastination and denial, hiding from the world and hoping the problem will go away. With an auction, the problem does go away, but not in the manner hoped for.

At a foreclosure auction, the lender holds an involuntary sale of the home with the minimum bid as the amount of unpaid debt on that one loan. The property sells to the highest bidder. If there are no bidders, the lender wins the house by default and it is now a real estate-owned (REO) property. Generally, at that point, if the sellers aren't out yet, the new owner gets to evict them!

In some cases, before the formal foreclosure, a homeowner in default will get an anonymous letter from an investor who wants to bid for the home at auction.

The investor promises the homeowner more money if he allows the home go to auction because the "competitive bidding" will drive up the price. This sounds like a good scenario, but it's one that seldom materializes. In fact, bidders at an auction can be in collusion and will secretly agree *not* to bid against each other. They'll bid $1 over the minimum required bid and then split up their property deals after the auction. Yes, that constitutes fraud, but who is watching? The district attorney can't be everywhere. We talk more about scams and fraud in Chapter 9.

Even if a homeowner doesn't want to sell his property to you, be sure to warn them not to fall prey to this scheme. The effects can be devastating financially and emotionally.

The Trust Issue

Your ability to make money in this business and help homeowners in default depends on their willingness to trust you. Trust is, after all, the foundation for building relationships with others. That's true whether you're discussing the world with your best friend, trying to glean information in a business deal, or suggesting solutions to a homeowner's financial woes.

If as a foreclosure investor you want to gain someone's trust, forget the shark-in-a-feeding-frenzy approach. Preying on the fears of a homeowner in distress does not work, despite what anyone tells you and how much they want to charge you for advice. That doesn't mean you shouldn't tell the truth and be straightforward with the situation. It means you must take the time to earn the homeowner's trust. (More on how to gain trust in Chapter 8.)

Digging for the Truth

Remember that your goal in contacting homeowners should be to unearth the real circumstances surrounding their situation so that you can help them find a solution (which may or may not be to sell their house to you). You are, after all, in the solutions business. That means you must keep digging for the truth with open-ended, thought-provoking questions that expose the who, what, where, when, why, and how of their situation.

Expect people to disguise or embellish their situation and hide the truth. Getting an owner to talk to you boils down to asking the right questions in the right way and showing that you care about the people, not just their house and your profits. It depends on becoming very good at opening up people who have shut down, who have bottled up their worries, fears, and financial problems. You must get them to talk about themselves.

What would prompt you to discuss your problems with a stranger? Think about the answer to that question, and open yourself up to others. To get others to trust you, you must trust them. Without the capacity to trust and be trusted, you are going nowhere in this business.

Don't be put off if you need to ask the same question in several different ways before you get the *real* answer rather than a good answer. Never *assume* you understand a homeowner's needs, and never give advice prematurely. Every person is different and needs to be treated as such. Whatever you do, don't come across as a greedy investor who just left a get-rich-quick seminar! You're not charging for your advice. It's free. Also, be careful that you don't negotiate with lenders for a homeowner or provide legal advice. You're simply there to help someone better help themselves.

When a homeowner says the problem is "all taken care of," don't accept that response and move on to your next prospect. Instead, dig deeper. If he claims the problem is taken care of, ask how. The majority of the time, this simply is a brush-off answer, and you'll need to really dig to find the truth. If a spouse pays the bills, find out when the spouse will be home, and contact him or her.

Carlotta and Sam were facing foreclosure on their home. The couple had been married six years and had one young child. As far as Carlotta knew, things were going great. She and her husband both had good jobs, and Sam always seemed to have money when she needed it. Then the bill collectors started calling, and the mortgage delinquency notices began to arrive. Afraid and confused, Carlotta confronted Sam. It turns out he had been secretly gambling away the couple's income and savings. They had been living on cash from Sam's occasional winnings and checks he had written against their credit cards. The couple's bills were astronomical. Had a good foreclosure investor not identified Carlotta and Sam's property as a potential deal, persisted in trying to talk to Carlotta, and then persuaded her to listen to him and confront her husband, it's likely the couple would have lost their home and much more.

TALES FROM FORECLOSURE INVESTORS

In talking with a homeowner about why she signed a deal with me, she said that it was my calm demeanor and that I was the one person who, from beginning to end, didn't change my story. I wasn't afraid to be honest with her so that I could help her. Now I'm her best friend forever.

— Lou K., successful foreclosure investor

Critical Information

Of course, chances are the investor wouldn't have found the couple in the first place without access to up-to-date, accurate, and thorough information. You won't go anywhere in this business without information, whether it relates to prospecting for potential deals or working with actual homeowners in default.

Excited about getting started in foreclosure investing, Jan L. quickly learned the business and was ready to begin identifying potential pre-foreclosure properties in her target area. She figured it would be easy with the many web sites offering foreclosure listings for free as well as for sale. But Jan soon learned otherwise. Not all foreclosure lists are created equal. The first web site she went to didn't offer enough information about the properties for her even to determine if they were potential deals. At another web site, she found plenty of information but many of the property owners she called had already sold their homes or lost them to foreclosure. That's when she decided to invest the time needed to find the right sites to provide her lists. (See Chapter 4 for details on finding the best foreclosure lists.)

The good news is that sources of information are plentiful. The bad news, as Jan discovered, is that many sources—including many of those offering free information—are misleading, outdated, or inaccurate. Sometimes it's tough to tell if information is reliable until you've wasted valuable time running into dead-end after dead-end. Information pitfalls include homes that have already been sold or foreclosed on; wrong or nonexistent property owner names or addresses; costly lists that provide only sketchy data about the loan in foreclosure; inability to quickly and easily sort the information based on specific criteria; and more.

Sure, every list will include an occasional workout that's already under way. Even county title rolls aren't infallible as sources of information. But to be successful in this business, you must have information you can count on and numbers you can easily sort or cull to meet your investment objectives. If you aren't interested in the $500,000 homes in the area you're targeting for investment, you don't want to waste time going through them. If, instead, you want a list of scheduled foreclosure dates on entry-level homes with mortgages in default, all past foreclosure filings on those properties that have a minimum 30 percent equity and are in certain zip codes, then that's what an information list needs to provide you. You should also be able to print, export, or e-mail what you want, not what you don't want. (Figure 3.1 shows a sample page from a ForeclosureS.com list.)

You should expect all of that from anyone whom you pay for those services. And you can pay plenty, too—from a few dollars a month to more than $200 a month. What's surprising, too, is that top-dollar lists often only provide information on one small area rather than nationwide access.

FIGURE 3.1   Sample Foreclosure List
Check out all the information about a property in this one preliminary search list.
Source: www.ForeclosureS.com

By the way, don't expect your local Realtor association's Multiple Listing Service (MLS) to be your primary source of potential leads, either. More than 90 percent of the pre-foreclosure leads never make it to the MLS. Keep in mind that people in foreclosure don't seek to list and sell their homes, so they're not on the MLS. In short, there's no easy way to make the deals come to you. You have to go find them.

Many prospective foreclosure investors look to gurus for help. As we've mentioned a number of times, tread softly. Do your homework on a supposed expert before you plunk down your money—whether for advice, direction, or information lists.

You have to put in many, many, many tiny
efforts that nobody sees or appreciates
before you achieve anything worthwhile.

—Brian Tracy, world-renowned professional
speaker, author, consultant

Foreclosure Lists 101

The Basics

A good foreclosure list should, at a minimum, provide you the following to get started:

- Property address.

- Current owner(s) name and mailing address.

- Estimated market value of the property.

- Homeowner's equity in property (as a dollar amount and as a percent).

- Amount of loan in default.

- Origination date of loan in default.

- Type of property: single-family residence, multifamily, duplex, and so on.

- Size of property: square footage, bedrooms/baths, lot size.

- Default publication date.

Your Property Plans of Action

Every deal, whether it involves sale/purchase, refinancing, or some other financial bailout, has a point at which it does or doesn't make sense. It's the point at which the numbers do or don't add up. When you're working with a homeowner, together you two must find that financial point—that is, if a homeowner isn't already committed to another option. Sometimes the emotional attachment to a property, personal circumstances, or some other factor determines what happens. Your job, though, is to point out the financial options—current and future—and the pros and cons of each. That involves developing an action plan for the property. (If you end up buying the property, you must further lay out your own short- and long-term intentions for the property with your financial situation in mind.)

Arriving at the best financial approach involves valuing the property based on similar properties in the area; researching the title to make sure you're aware of all liens and the status of each (remembering that the first mortgage takes precedence); finding the money (whether yours, theirs, or an investor's); working out the contract details; and then making sure the deal goes through.

Laws are very specific about the documentation required. Different states have difference legal processes, and it's your job to know all of them and more. It may sound somewhat complicated and scary, but as you read on, you'll find it's not. Success is, after all, the natural consequence of consistently applying basic fundamentals, which we detail for you in this book.

TAKEaway

Some key points to remember:

- Not everyone is cut out for the foreclosure investing business. Recognize that, accept it, and if it's not for you, walk away *before* you unnecessarily spend thousands of dollars on that pseudo-expert or guru who promises you the moon.

- Buying a house in foreclosure or pre-foreclosure is very different from an ordinary home sale. The process typically happens in double time and takes special documentation and more. It's important that you know exactly what's required ahead of time.

- Homeowners in default almost always have options ranging from temporary workouts with their lender to getting a new loan, taking out a secondary loan, selling their home in pre-foreclosure, selling their property at auction, filing for bankruptcy, or offering a lender a deed in lieu of foreclosure. The best solution depends on a homeowner's individual situation.

- Make sure as an investor that you have solid, workable, current information and foreclosure data to use in compiling your potential deal lists. Not all information sources are equal or reliable, and a list's value often has little to do with its cost.

- Your success also depends on your ability to get homeowners and others to trust you, to recognize that you truly do care.

CHAPTER 4

All Foreclosures Are Not Created Equal

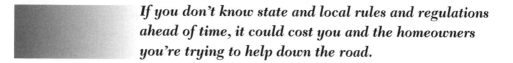

If you don't know state and local rules and regulations ahead of time, it could cost you and the homeowners you're trying to help down the road.

—Alexis McGee

The foreclosure process differs by state and sometimes by municipality or city. A foreclosure in California is not the same as one in Arkansas or Florida. Different states require different documents, legislate different procedures, and establish different time frames for various parts of the process that *must* be followed.

Not all foreclosures last the norm of 90 days. Some proceedings stretch on for months; others last mere weeks. In New York, for example, the foreclosure process usually takes 12 months or longer, while in Texas it's less than 30 days; and the list and the variations go on.

Some foreclosures are judicial in nature, involving the courts for up to several months; others are not. It's up to you to understand all the details and their ramifications in the geographic areas you cover. After all, your job is to help homeowners in default. In many cases, their ignorance of these details adds to their confusion and increases their vulnerability to the smooth talk and big come-ons from less scrupulous investors.

Different states have varying regulations that pertain to *foreclosure consultants* and *property purchasers*, too. Although you aren't and don't act as a foreclosure consultant, there's a fine gray line between you offering your advice free as a friend and confidant, and someone who comes along and wants payment to do whatever's necessary for the homeowner in default.

*Pay attention to the legal details or
you'll have to pay another way.*

—Alexis McGee

To protect yourself and your investments in the foreclosure business and to protect those you're trying to help, you must be aware of all state and local laws and regulations as they may pertain to you, the areas where you work, and the procedures you must follow. It's much better to comply with disclosure and other requirements up front than to pay the price of ignorance or deliberate noncompliance. It's a bitter pill to swallow if you're trying to make a deal with homeowners in default, and you end up losing your money or they end up losing their home because you didn't know the pertinent laws.

In most states, for instance, a lender can, depending on the details stipulated in the mortgage contract and by law, initiate foreclosure proceedings after only one missed mortgage (or deed of trust) payment. State laws detail the type of mortgage documents that can be used—deed of trust or mortgage—the foreclosure proceeding and time frames involved, homeowner rights to reclaim their property, and more.

Judicial Foreclosures

As mentioned earlier, there are two basic types of foreclosure proceedings, judicial and nonjudicial. A judicial foreclosure requires court action that begins with a lawsuit filing known as a *lis pendens*, meaning "litigation is pending." The real property ultimately can be sold at a foreclosure sale. The creditor generally also has the right to seek a *deficiency judgment*, which is the amount of money owed by the borrower after the mortgage holder forecloses on the property. Some states limit a deficiency judgment by what is called the *fair value rule*. That means the deficiency amounts only to the difference between the fair market value of the property as determined in a court hearing and the amount of the outstanding debt. If, for example, a court sets the fair value higher than the actual amount a lender could get when reselling the property, the lender is entitled to collect only the lower amount set by the court.

If a deficiency judgment is allowed by statute and sought by the lender, the property is sold subject to a *right of redemption*. That is, the property may be reacquired by the borrower within the redemption period (usually one year following the foreclosure sale) by paying the price paid at the foreclosure sale, plus

Important Words to Understand

Judicial foreclosure—a foreclosure that involves court action or a lawsuit.

Nonjudicial foreclosure—an action to take and sell a home, made possible by a clause in a mortgage or deed of trust that grants the lien holder the right to take the property if the terms of the lien are violated.

Lis pendens—a lawsuit that must be filed to begin a judicial foreclosure; the term means "litigation is pending."

Deficiency judgment—in judicial foreclosure, the right of a lender to collect additional cash from a property owner after foreclosure because the sale did not generate enough to pay off the loan. The dollar amount is based on the difference between the amount of the debt and the fair market value of the property; it varies by state, and amounts may be capped.

Right of redemption—the right of a homeowner, for a short period of time, to buy back her property after it has been sold at foreclosure. This is allowed only in certain states, and the time frame varies by state.

Source: ForeclosureS.com

interest, taxes, insurance, and similar expenses accrued during the redemption period. That means even after the foreclosure sale, you, as a foreclosure investor, can help displaced homeowners by contacting them and working out a deal to help them buy back their home. In turn they can sell the property to you. They get their equity and a new start in the form of cash, and you can pick up at a discount a property with plenty of potential to fix up, turn around, and resell at a profit.

Nonjudicial Foreclosures

Because of the time and expense involved in a judicial foreclosure, as well as the fair-value limitations on the amount of a deficiency judgment, the majority of foreclosures are nonjudicial. They do not involve a court action or lawsuit filing. Nonetheless, these foreclosures, too, are strictly regulated by state statutes. Ultimately, the real property can be sold at a trustee's sale or courthouse auction. Generally such sales occur because the borrower has signed a document, such as a deed of trust, which includes a *power-of-sale* clause preauthorizing a trustee to sell the real estate to pay off the debt if it's in default. Some power-of-sale clauses may contain instructions on the time, place, and terms of the sale, and more.

In most states, a nonjudicial foreclosure is initiated by a *notice of default*. As with most other aspects of the foreclosure process, state statutes are very specific about the details of what such a notice should contain, where it should be filed, how it should be displayed, who must be notified, the time frames involved, and more. Details vary by state, too. Among other things, the notice must contain an accurate statement of the nature of the breach of contract/mortgage. Without it, a foreclosure may be invalidated.

If applicable, the notice of default must also contain the reinstatement rights of a borrower in default—what that borrower can do to stop the foreclosure proceedings. A borrower has the right to bring his account current and avoid foreclosure by paying the past-due amounts plus certain permitted expenses. The amounts must be paid within a certain number of days (it varies by state) prior to the foreclosure sale. The borrower does not have to pay the full loan balance if he pays off or cures the default in a timely manner. After the time for reinstatement has passed, the borrower generally can stop foreclosure only by paying the entire amount of the debt, plus permitted costs and expenses. In some states, such as California, if two or more defaults have been recorded, a lender can refuse to accept reinstatement payment and demand payment of the loan in full.

Ariana, a single mom of three, had been in and out of default on her home several times. Each time, she found a bailout at the last minute. Once it was a quickie loan from her uncle; another time it was a cash infusion generated by racking up her charge cards; and still another time, a white-knight investor helped her work out creative financing that involved consolidating her bills. Each time, her lender accepted the eleventh-hour rescue. But the fourth time Ariana fell into default, the lender said no and proceeded with the foreclosure. Luckily, the same honest investor came forward and bought her house. Even at a discounted sale price, Ariana was able to walk away with some cash in her pocket for a new start.

Costs and expenses associated with foreclosure and reinstatement also are limited by statute. Even if the note or deed of trust provides for the recovery of costs and attorneys' fees, those fees and costs incurred in foreclosing are subject to the statutory limit.

Secondary or Junior Liens

The existence of junior mortgages or liens is determined as of the date the original loan was recorded. When a lender files foreclosure, all lien holders must be notified.

If a foreclosure is pending, a second lien holder may take action to prevent their lien from being wiped out. That could include advancing money to the first lender on behalf of the property's owner to stop the foreclosure and then adding that amount onto the secondary lien, or allowing the property to go to auction and then bidding on it.

Notice of Sale

Specific requirements for *notice of sale* for both judicial and nonjudicial foreclosures also vary by state. To give you an idea of what's involved, let's briefly consider the requirements of a few different states if a borrower fails to cure his default and a notice of sale is required.

- In California, the notice of sale is recorded no sooner than 90 days after the notice of default is recorded and stipulates that the property's auction will occur in 21 days. A copy is sent via certified mail to the borrower in default. The notice is also published weekly in a newspaper of general circulation in the county for three consecutive weeks prior to the sale date; and it's posted on the property as well as at the county recorder's office.

- In Alabama, with a judicial foreclosure in the absence of a power of sale, a lender may publish a notice of sale for four consecutive weeks in a newspaper published in the county, and then sell the property at the door of the courthouse of the county in which the property is located. For a nonjudicial foreclosure, if the details aren't stipulated in a power-of-sale clause, a notice of sale must be published weekly for four consecutive weeks in a newspaper published in the county in which the property is located. If no newspaper is published in that county, the notice must run in a newspaper in an adjoining county. The sale may not be held until 30 days from the last date of publication, and must be between 11 A.M. and 4 P.M. at the courthouse door as a public auction for cash to the highest bidder.

- In North Carolina, the notice of sale must be sent via first-class mail to the borrower, published weekly in a newspaper of general circulation in the subject county for two successive weeks, with the last publication date not less than ten days before the date of sale, and posted on the courthouse door at least 20 days before the date of sale. That state also allows bids on the property to be filed with the clerk of the court for ten days after the date of sale.

Are you beginning to get the convoluted legal picture? The lesson in all this is to know the laws that relate to what you're doing! The relevant statutes don't end on the courthouse steps, either. Remember, some states provide former homeowners the right of redemption. With the right amount of cash and within an allotted time, former owners can come back and reclaim their former property. We go into more of the details about auctions in Chapter 11.

Postponements and More

Foreclosure auctions can and will be postponed from the original filing date by mutual consent of both the borrower and lender. For example, the borrower asks for postponement, and the lender may or may not agree to grant it. If a postponement is granted, it's usually for only one week. But don't expect lenders to always okay a postponement request. After all, they want to recover their collateral on a loan and move forward to sell it. A bankruptcy filing by a borrower creates an automatic and immediate stay of the foreclosure process. It's not uncommon for a bankruptcy filing to precede the scheduled trustee's sale by hours (or, sometimes, minutes). As long as the bankruptcy proceeding is pending, a foreclosure cannot go forward unless the bankruptcy court permits it.

State Foreclosure Laws in Brief

Following is a brief look at basic provisions of some foreclosure rules and regulations in the different states. Keep in mind that those rules vary widely. For more details by state, visit ForeclosureS.com, click on "Tools" and then "Foreclosure Laws" in the drop-down box. You'll also find direct links to the individual state statutes that regulate a particular aspect of foreclosure law.

Alabama
Judicial foreclosure: Yes.
Nonjudicial foreclosure: Yes.
Security instruments: Deed of trust, mortgage.
Right of redemption: Yes.
Deficiency judgments: Yes.
Time frame: 30–60 days.

Alaska
Judicial foreclosure: Yes.
Nonjudicial foreclosure: Yes.
Security instruments: Deed of trust, mortgage.
Right of redemption: Nonjudicial foreclosure only.
Deficiency judgments: Judicial foreclosure only.
Time frame: Usually 90 days.

Arizona
Judicial foreclosure: Sometimes.
Nonjudicial foreclosure: Yes, most common.
Security instruments: Deed of trust, mortgage.
Right of redemption: No.
Deficiency judgments: Varies.
Time frame: Usually 90 days.

Arkansas
Judicial foreclosure: Yes.
Nonjudicial foreclosure: Yes.
Primary security instruments: Deed of trust, mortgage.
Right of redemption: Judicial foreclosure only.
Deficiency judgments: Nonjudicial foreclosure only.
Time frame: Usually 120 days.

California
Judicial foreclosure: Sometimes.
Nonjudicial foreclosure: Yes, most common.
Security instruments: Deed of trust, mortgage.
Right of redemption: Yes, judicial foreclosure only.
Deficiency judgments: Yes, judicial foreclosure only.
Time frame: 111 days or more.

Colorado
Judicial foreclosure: Yes.
Nonjudicial foreclosure: Yes.
Primary security instruments: Deed of trust, mortgage.
Right of redemption: Yes.
Deficiency judgments allowed: Yes.
Time frame: Usually 60 days.

Connecticut
Judicial foreclosure: Yes.
Nonjudicial foreclosure: No.
Security instrument: Mortgage.
Right of redemption: Court's discretion.
Deficiency judgments: Yes.
Time frame: Varies from 60 to 150 days.

Delaware
Judicial foreclosure: Yes.
Nonjudicial foreclosure: No.
Security instrument: Mortgage.
Right of redemption: No.
Deficiency judgments: No.
Time frame: Usually 90 days.

District of Columbia
Judicial foreclosure: No.
Nonjudicial foreclosure: Yes.
Security instrument: Deed of trust.
Right of redemption: No.
Deficiency judgments: Yes.
Time frame: Usually 60 days.

Florida
Judicial foreclosure: Yes.
Nonjudicial foreclosure: No.
Security instrument: Mortgage.
Right of redemption: Yes, brief and subject to court procedure.
Deficiency judgments: Yes.
Time frame: Usually 180 days.

Georgia
Judicial foreclosure: Yes.
Nonjudicial foreclosure: Yes.
Security instruments: Deed of trust, mortgage.
Right of redemption: Yes.
Deficiency judgments: Yes.
Time frame: Usually 90 days.

Hawaii

Judicial foreclosure: Yes.
Nonjudicial foreclosure: Yes.
Security instruments: Deed of trust, mortgage.
Right of redemption: No.
Deficiency judgments: Yes.
Time frame: Usually 60 days.

Idaho

Judicial foreclosure: No.
Nonjudicial foreclosure: Yes.
Security instrument: Deed of trust.
Right of redemption: Yes.
Deficiency judgment: Yes.
Time frame: Approximately 150 days.

Illinois

Judicial foreclosure: Yes.
Nonjudicial foreclosure: No.
Security instrument: Mortgage.
Right of redemption: Yes, limited.
Deficiency judgments: Varies.
Time frame: Usually 210 days.

Indiana

Judicial foreclosure: Yes.
Nonjudicial foreclosure: No.
Security instrument: Mortgage.
Right of redemption: Yes.
Deficiency judgments: Yes.
Time frame: Usually 150 days.

Iowa

Judicial foreclosure: Yes.
Nonjudicial foreclosure: No, but deed in lieu permitted.
Primary security instrument: Mortgage.
Right of redemption: No.
Deficiency judgments: No.
Time frame: Usually 150 days.

Kansas
Judicial foreclosure: Yes.
Nonjudicial foreclosure: No.
Primary security instrument: Mortgage.
Right of redemption: Yes.
Deficiency judgments: Yes.
Time frame: Usually 120 days.

Kentucky
Judicial foreclosure: Yes.
Nonjudicial foreclosure: No.
Security instrument: Mortgage.
Right of redemption: Yes.
Deficiency judgments: Yes, with restrictions.
Time frame: Varies.

Louisiana
Judicial foreclosure: Yes.
Nonjudicial foreclosure: No.
Primary security instrument: Mortgage.
Right of redemption: No.
Deficiency judgments: Yes.
Time frame: Usually 60 days.

Maine
Judicial foreclosure: Yes.
Nonjudicial foreclosure: No.
Security instrument: Mortgage.
Right of redemption: Yes.
Deficiency judgments: Yes.
Time frame: Usually 90 days.

Maryland
Judicial foreclosure: Yes.
Nonjudicial foreclosure: Yes.
Security instrument: Deed of trust, mortgage.
Right of redemption: No.
Deficiency judgments: Yes.
Time frame: Usually 90 days.

Massachusetts
Judicial foreclosure: Yes.
Nonjudicial foreclosure: Yes.
Security instruments: Deed of trust, mortgage.
Right of redemption: Yes, in foreclosure by possession.
Deficiency judgments: No.

Michigan
Judicial foreclosure: Yes.
Nonjudicial foreclosure: Yes.
Security instruments: Deed of trust, mortgage.
Right of redemption: Yes.
Deficiency judgments: Varies, case by case.
Time frame: Usually 60 days.

Minnesota
Judicial foreclosure: Yes.
Nonjudicial foreclosure: Yes.
Primary security instruments: Deed of trust, mortgage.
Right of redemption: Yes.
Deficiency judgments: Yes.
Time frame: Usually 60 days.

Mississippi
Judicial foreclosure: Yes.
Nonjudicial foreclosure: Yes.
Security instruments: Deed of trust, mortgage..
Right of redemption: No.
Deficiency judgments: No.
Time frame: Usually 60 days.

Missouri
Judicial foreclosure: Yes.
Nonjudicial foreclosure: Yes.
Security instruments: Deed of trust, mortgage.
Right of redemption: Yes.
Deficiency judgments: No.
Time frame: Usually 60 days.

Montana
Judicial foreclosure: Yes.
Nonjudicial foreclosure: Yes.
Security instruments: Deed of trust, mortgage.
Right of redemption: No.
Deficiency judgment: Judicial foreclosure only.
Time frame: Usually about 150 days.

Nebraska
Judicial foreclosure: Yes.
Nonjudicial foreclosure: No.
Security instrument: Mortgage.
Right of redemption: None, after confirmation of sale.
Deficiency judgments: No.
Time frame: Usually 180 days.

Nevada
Judicial foreclosure: Sometimes.
Nonjudicial foreclosure: Yes, most common.
Security instruments: Deed of trust, mortgage.
Right of redemption: Judicial foreclosure only.
Deficiency judgments: Yes.
Time frame: Usually 120 days.

New Hampshire
Judicial foreclosure: Yes.
Nonjudicial foreclosure: Yes.
Security instruments: Deed of trust, mortgage.
Right of redemption: No.
Deficiency judgments: Yes.
Time frame: Usually 60 days.

New Jersey
Judicial foreclosure: Yes.
Nonjudicial foreclosure: No.
Security instrument: Mortgage.
Right of redemption: Yes, limited.
Deficiency judgments: Yes, restricted.
Time frame: Usually 90 to 120 days unless contested.

New Mexico
Judicial foreclosure: Yes
Nonjudicial foreclosure: No, except commercial properties.*
Security instrument: Mortgage.
Right of redemption: Yes.
Deficiency judgments: Yes.
Time frame: Usually 120 days.

New York
Judicial foreclosure: Yes.
Nonjudicial foreclosure: Yes, but rarely used.
Security instruments: Deed of trust, mortgage.
Right of redemption: No.
Deficiency judgments: Yes.
Time frame: Usually 12 to 19 months.

North Carolina
Judicial foreclosure: Yes.
Nonjudicial foreclosure: Yes.
Security instruments: Deed of trust, mortgage.
Right of redemption: Yes.
Deficiency judgments: Varies case by case.
Time frame: Usually 60 days.

North Dakota
Judicial foreclosure: Yes.
Nonjudicial foreclosure: No.
Security instrument: Mortgage.
Right of redemption: Yes.
Deficiency judgments: Yes.
Time frame: Usually 90 days.

Ohio
Judicial foreclosure: Yes.
Nonjudicial foreclosure: No.
Security instrument: Mortgage.
Right of redemption: Yes.
Deficiency judgments: Yes.
Time frame: Usually 150 days.

---

*Nonjudicial foreclosure is available only for commercial or business properties valued at $500,000 or more.

Oklahoma
Judicial foreclosure: Yes.
Nonjudicial foreclosure: Yes.
Security instruments: Deed of trust, mortgage.
Right of redemption: None, upon confirmation of sale.
Deficiency judgments: Yes, with time limitation of filing.
Time frame: Usually 90 days.

Oregon
Judicial foreclosure: Yes.
Nonjudicial foreclosure: Yes.
Security instruments: Deed of trust, mortgage.
Right of redemption: Yes, but only with judicial foreclosure.
Deficiency judgments: Yes, but only with judicial foreclosure.
Time frame: Typically 120 to 180 days.

Pennsylvania
Judicial foreclosure: Yes.
Nonjudicial foreclosure: No.
Security instrument: Mortgage.
Right of redemption: No.
Deficiency judgment: Yes.
Time frame: Usually 90 days.

Rhode Island
Judicial foreclosure: Yes.
Nonjudicial foreclosure: Yes.
Security instruments: Deed of trust, mortgage.
Right of redemption: Varies by process.
Deficiency judgments: Yes.
Time frame: Usually 60 days.

South Carolina
Judicial foreclosure: Yes.
Nonjudicial foreclosure: No.
Security instrument: Mortgage.
Right of redemption: No.
Deficiency judgment: Yes.
Time frame: Varies.

South Dakota
Judicial foreclosure: Yes.
Nonjudicial foreclosure: Yes.
Security instruments: Deed of trust, mortgage.
Right of redemption: Yes, but various time periods.
Deficiency judgments: Varies on case-by-case basis.
Time frame: Usually 90 days.

Tennessee
Judicial foreclosure: Yes.
Nonjudicial foreclosure: Yes.
Security instruments: Deed of trust, mortgage.
Deficiency judgments: Yes.
Right of redemption: Yes, nonjudicial foreclosure.
Time frame: Usually 60 days.

Texas
Judicial foreclosure: Yes.
Nonjudicial foreclosure: Yes.
Security instruments: Deed of trust, mortgage.
Deficiency judgments: Yes.
Right of redemption: No.
Time frame: Usually 60 days.

Utah
Judicial foreclosure: Yes.
Nonjudicial foreclosure: Yes.
Security instruments: Deed of trust, mortgage.
Right of redemption: Yes.
Deficiency judgment: Yes.
Time frame: Varies.

Vermont
Judicial foreclosure: Yes, in strict foreclosure process.
Nonjudicial foreclosure: Yes.
Security instruments: Deed of trust, mortgage.
Right of redemption: Yes.
Deficiency judgments: Yes.
Time frame: Usually 210 days.

Virginia

Judicial foreclosure: Yes.

Nonjudicial foreclosure: Yes.

Security instruments: Deed of trust, mortgage.

Right of redemption: Varies.

Deficiency judgments: Yes.

Time frame: Usually 60 days.

Washington

Judicial foreclosure: Yes, but not commonly used in Washington.

Nonjudicial foreclosure: Yes.

Security instruments: Deed of trust, mortgage.

Right of redemption: Available only in judicial foreclosure, and very rare.

Deficiency judgment: Yes, but only in judicial foreclosure.

Time frame: 190 days.

West Virginia

Judicial foreclosure: Yes.

Nonjudicial foreclosure: Yes.

Security instruments: Deed of trust, mortgage.

Right of redemption: No.

Deficiency judgments: No.

Time frame: Usually 60 days.

Wisconsin

Judicial foreclosure: Yes.

Nonjudicial foreclosure: Yes.

Security instruments: Deed of trust, mortgage.

Right of redemption: Yes, if no court confirmation of sale.

Deficiency judgments: Yes, unless waived.

Time frame: Usually 90 days, but may be one year.

Wyoming

Judicial foreclosure: Yes.

Nonjudicial foreclosure: Yes.

Security instruments: Deed of trust, mortgage.

Right of redemption: Yes.

Deficiency judgment: Yes.

Time frame: Usually 90 days.

Laws Pertaining to Consultants

Beyond the rules and regulations that govern foreclosure processes and procedures by state, rules exist that regulate *foreclosure consultants*, too! You should *not* act as a paid foreclosure consultant. But when you work with someone on how to resolve a bad financial situation and no property purchase is involved, you could unwittingly violate a law and face serious consequences as a result if you cross the line of confidant/friend and become a paid consultant. You should not give legal advice or ever collect a fee for services. All you can do is offer to help homeowners as their friend. Don't make calls to lenders or other organizations on a homeowner's behalf. What you can do as a foreclosure investor is be someone who helps direct the homeowner down the right path.

Consider the California case of *Onofrio v. Rice*. Evelyn Onofrio was delinquent on the first and second mortgages, in bankruptcy, and her home was in foreclosure. Enter Marshall Rice, who approached Onofrio saying he was a real estate broker specializing in foreclosure properties and that if she called him, he could help her. Subsequently she contacted him and Rice arranged a loan by his wife to cure the existing defaults. The disclosure statement that accompanied the loan indicated a 35 percent annual interest rate. Although Rice did nothing beyond the usual broker activity in closing a loan, he qualified under California law as a foreclosure consultant. In the end, in return for his wife's $21,000 loan to Onofrio, Rice was held liable for what amounted to almost $350,000! On a positive note, however, Onofrio didn't lose her home.

If you live in California, commit the following definition to memory. Check out similar regulations in whatever state you live or do business. It's the better-to-be-safe-than-out-big-bucks approach.

> A *foreclosure consultant* is anyone who makes a solicitation, representation, or offer to any owner to perform *for compensation* or who, *for compensation*, performs any service in which the person in any manner represents that they will do any of the following:
>
> - Stop or postpone a foreclosure sale.
> - Obtain any forbearance from any beneficiary or mortgagee.
> - Assist the owner to exercise the right of reinstatement of a mortgage.
> - Obtain any extension of the period within which the owner may reinstate his or her obligation.
> - Obtain any waiver of an acceleration clause contained in any promissory note or contract secured by a deed of trust on a residence in foreclosure.
> - Assist the owner of a property to obtain a loan or advance funds.

- Avoid or ameliorate the impairment of the owner's credit resulting from the recording of a notice of default or the conduct of a foreclosure sale.

- Save the owner's residence from foreclosure.

The category of foreclosure consultant does not include a Realtor, attorney, lien holder, financial institution, title insurance company, or a nonprofit housing counselor, among other things (although laws may apply to those people, too).

Don't dismiss the idea of laws regulating foreclosure consultants as merely a California phenomenon. Other states have such laws, too, and they're very specific.

Still More Legal Hurdles

Yes, you need to know still more rules and regulations pertaining to the business of foreclosure. But don't be scared off by it all. As discussed in Chapter 3, once you know the fundamentals, the legal aspect of this business can be pretty smooth sailing.

Here's a brief look at some legal concerns that easily can be overlooked, resulting in costly mistakes for foreclosure consultants and the homeowners they hope to help. (These are more reasons to be careful that you don't qualify as a foreclosure consultant!)

- *Legal documents*. Pay attention to the forms of contracts, deeds, mortgages, notes, leases, and other legal instruments used in your area. Special forms could be required for licensed real estate agents that may also apply to you. Learn how to custom-tailor the forms for your needs, and then have them checked by a knowledgeable local real estate attorney. Check out your state's statutes as well as ForeclosureS.com, and consult a competent local real estate attorney. Forms available for a fee from USLegalForms.com (www.uslegalforms.com) or are included in ForeclosureS.com's Home Study course.

- *Recording rules*. Know where the legal documents you need must be recorded, and be cognizant of any filing fees and taxes associated with them. Be sure your documents are in the correct format, too. Contact your local title company or the county recorder's office for information.

- *Disclosure laws*. As touched on previously, pay attention to disclosure laws even if you think they don't apply to you. Also, if you're planning to sell or rent a property to someone, you will be required by law to make certain disclosures about the property to prospective buyers or tenants. That could include information about lead, asbestos, or even convicted sex offenders living in the neighborhood. You can usually find out what must be disclosed from a local Board of Realtors member.

- *Licensing laws.* Be aware of licensing laws for real estate agencies in your area. Check with your state licensing agency for more information. If you are rehabbing homes, pay attention to building regulations and licensing rules for contractors, too.

Correcting Past Mistakes

We all make mistakes. Homeowners in default and people like you and me who want to help them are no exception. You must convince homeowners (and yourself) that if you make a mistake, you can and should do all you can to correct it. If a homeowner ignores a notice of sale until a week before the auction, yes, that's a mistake. But solutions to the problem exist nonetheless.

Remember Ariana's plight, earlier in this chapter? Her lender denied her the chance to cure her default and stop her home's foreclosure. But even her plight wasn't hopeless. A white-knight investor came forward to help. Actually, he gave her and her family a new life. Without the financial noose of her house around her neck and with cash from the home's sale, she was able to pick up the pieces of her shattered financial life and start over.

And what about Cliff from Chapter 2? He made financial mistakes. He overlooked and ignored the legal process available to help him and almost lost his house. But with the help of a compassionate mortgage lender, he worked out a way to save his home, his dignity, and his financial life.

With so many legal details involved in the foreclosure and investing processes, you *will* make mistakes. Accept that, brush yourself off, and keep on striving for your goals.

You can help the homeowner *if* he lets you and *if* you believe in yourself. If you go back for follow-up and the loan commitment fell through, perhaps the homeowner will change his mind and reach out for your help. It's the same if the homeowner overlooked filing a form or a lender turned down the homeowner's request for a workout. Perhaps you can help. You won't know if you don't try.

If you're not a sales pro or a legal expert, fear not! Countless sources of information are available if you know where to go and what questions to ask. Turn mistakes—yours and those of others—into learning experiences. It's that power of positive thinking yet again. Go for it.

TAKEaway

Some key points to remember:

- Different states have varying regulations that pertain to foreclosure consultants, property purchasers, the foreclosure process, necessary documentation, and more. You must know and understand all of them to protect yourself and the homeowners you help.

- You should not act as a foreclosure consultant, provide legal advice, or negotiate with a lender on behalf of a homeowner. Remember, you are offering your knowledge free as a friend and confidant.

- Costs and expenses associated with foreclosure and curing a default may be limited by law.

- If you take over a mortgage or buy a property outright, check the records to make sure you're aware of any and all liens against the property.

CHAPTER 5

What about Money?

Money isn't the issue. Knowing how and where to get it is.

—Alexis McGee

Rule number one in this business: Don't fret about having the cash to get started. It's out there when you know where to find it. Pre-foreclosure investing is an opportunity for anyone, period. You don't have to be independently wealthy or have a fat bank account to be successful in this business. In fact, you don't need good credit to get started, either. It's better not to use your own money or credit on your first deals, anyway. As mentioned earlier, if you're dealing with a property pre-foreclosure, we recommend either *subject-to financing*, in which you take over the existing loan of a homeowner in default, or *contract assignment*, where you land deals and then pass them on to third-party investors in exchange for a finder's fee.

All you need to get started in the foreclosure-investing business is the know-how to structure deals so your investors—the cash cows—will stick with you. Plenty of deep pockets are available, ready, and willing to cough up the cash and pay you handsomely for generating the deals. After all, the big double-digit returns on a pre-foreclosure or foreclosure investment done right can be far greater than the single-digit returns typical of most ordinary investments.

When ForeclosureS.com coach Sarah Garlick was getting started in the business, she tried foreclosure investing on the side in addition to her day job. "I'm a little conservative and I didn't want to quit my job. My goal was to match my corporate salary in the first year," says Garlick.

With the help of other investors' money (she picked up finder's fees for those deals) and subject-to financing, Garlick did four deals that first year, working at it only part time. "I took home about $200,000 doing this part-time, and decided the corporate job was costing me money," she says.

Let's look more closely at your options and the choices best suited to your particular goals.

Why Not Your Own Money?

By starting out in this business with someone else's money, not only do you limit your risk but your efforts are validated in the form of a finder's fee at closing. Although the monetary reward may be less than if you invested your own money, the personal reward of helping someone in financial need adds to the satisfaction of banking a healthy finder's fee. A paycheck from your investor for $10,000 to $30,000 and up when the purchase deal goes through provides an immediate and ample reward for you without the hassles or risk associated with holding, rehabbing, and reselling a property.

In fact, some veterans in this business such as Garlick prefer the cost-effectiveness of contract assignments because they are quicker, cleaner, and create fewer headaches. It's a matter of identifying highly motivated sellers, putting together a deal they agree to, passing off that deal to an investor with deep pockets, and picking up your finder's fee. "I can do an assignment in two weeks and make a $20,000 finder's fee," says Garlick. "Or I can spend seven months to take title to a property, rehab it, put it on the market, sell it, close the deal, and get a $70,000 paycheck. That breaks down to $10,000 a month. That's a long road to a little house."

Money has a time value to it, says Garlick. "As an investor, you must ask yourself, is the money more valuable to you as cash on hand now or if you speculate on cash in the future?"

The answer to that question depends on your personal preference.

Contract assignment, in which you receive a finder's fee in exchange for providing an investor with a pre-foreclosure deal, is the closest thing to instant gratification in the foreclosure-investing business.

—Alexis McGee

Subject-To Financing Works!

For some new investors, subject-to financing works well the first time around. Karl B., a career military officer, had for a long time thought about getting into the real estate investing business after retiring. Because he had spent so much time away from family and home over the years, he had had plenty of time to dream of big investments and big successes. The only problem: His colonel's retirement pay wasn't quite enough to fund the reality of his dreams.

Then he read about the white-knight approach to making money in foreclosure investing. Karl liked the idea of being able to make a comfortable living for his family and was accustomed to putting the safety of his soldiers ahead of his own. So he figured this investing approach that emphasizes the importance of helping others would be a good way to profit from and capitalize on what he knew was one of his strengths.

Using other investors' cash to get started appealed to Karl, too, because it provided him entry into the investing business. Some of his former colleagues had already moved beyond the military and become quite successful, and they were always looking for investments. He figured it wouldn't be too hard to find other investors to provide the necessary cash.

So after he retired, Karl attacked his new endeavor as he would any assignment. He studied the business, decided on a geographic area where he would concentrate his efforts, and learned the ins and outs and nuances of the laws relating to what he wanted to do. After only three months and plenty of telephone calls and research to contact property owners, Karl had already closed two deals using his investors' money. Those investors purchased the deals he put together on pre-foreclosure properties at a 30 percent discount. They took over the seller's mortgages (subject-to financing) and then repaired, cleaned up, and were in the process of reselling the properties at a large profit.

Karl's finder's fees, both received at the closings, totaled $45,000. Not bad for three months' work! Too, his advice had saved three other homeowners from losing their homes to foreclosure. Karl was thrilled that he could provide so much help and relief to others simply by understanding the legalities and ramifications of their situations.

*Showing a profit means touching something
and leaving it better than you found it.*

—Jim Rohn

Ed K. banked on subject-to financing, too, when he started in the foreclosure investing business, but his path to success wasn't quite as smooth as Karl's. A veteran construction worker, Ed was out on the job sites and working hard come rain, snow, sleet, or shine. The work was physically demanding, but it was what he knew how to do and he was good at it—that is, until he injured his back. Unable physically to handle the grind anymore, Ed decided to try foreclosure investing. He was still young and single, and had saved a chunk of money. What a great way to make more money, he figured, especially with his background in construction. He could use his cash to buy houses in pre-foreclosure for discounted prices, repair them himself, and turn them around for big profits.

Despite cautions not to use his own money, especially because he was out of a job and had no steady income, Ed forged ahead. He used his savings and bought his first house with subject-to financing, then got busy with the rehab so he could turn it around, sell it quickly, and get a paycheck.

Unfortunately, Ed hadn't done his homework thoroughly. He miscalculated his costs for repairs, which amounted to double his estimate. He also failed to adequately figure his costs for a prolonged hold period before the rehabbed house sold. Not only did his local real estate market turn cold right after he bought the property, but Ed priced the house too high. As a result, the property failed to move quickly, Ed ended up overextended financially, and he almost lost the house. It sold eventually but at a reduced price, and Ed walked away with a loss. If, instead, Ed had turned to other investors for cash to pay for the deal in exchange for a finder's fee, he would have maintained his savings, suffered fewer headaches, and walked away with a fair amount of cash at closing.

Undaunted but wiser from the experience, Ed tried again. He knew he was good at rehabbing homes because of the skills he'd learned on the job in construction, and he knew he could succeed in foreclosure investing if he took the right approach. For his next few deals and until he had built up his own sizable cash supply, Ed counted on other investors' money. That was three years and 28 deals ago. Today, Ed regularly taps a small portion of his comfortable nest egg to purchase pre-foreclosure properties, rehabs them, and then resells them at a healthy profit.

The lesson you can learn from Ed's successes and failures, as well as Karl's successes, is to do your homework thoroughly. Before you start in this business, assess your strengths and weaknesses and recognize how to deal with them. Then research your markets, your laws, and your options. Pay attention to what's happening in the community where you're looking to acquire properties. No matter what anyone says, real estate markets don't suddenly collapse without any prior indication. Most of all, whether you think you have the money to do it yourself or not, get started with someone else's cash!

Financing: Comparing Your Options

It's easy to see why subject-to financing makes timely sense for foreclosure investors. Here's a brief look at what's involved in obtaining various types of financing:

Conventional Financing

This is generally a normal full loan package, not including money for home repairs. Average time to closing: 20 working days.

- Review comparable sales and estimate repairs.
- Sign purchase agreement.
- Submit loan application.
- Lender performs credit checks.
- Provide two years' federal tax returns.
- Provide three months of bank statements.
- Lender verifies applicant's employment.
- Lender verifies applicant's bank account(s).
- Get home appraisal.
- Conduct home inspection.
- Get termite report (clearance on Section 1, which involves repairing any damage already done to property).
- Get preliminary title insurance review.
- Get lender's underwriting approval.
- Lender and escrow agent draw up loan documents.
- Sign closing documents in escrow.
- Close escrow.

Private Investor or Hard-Money Lender

These are the typical requirements for funding your purchase and repairs. Average time to closing: 10 working days.

- Review comparable sales and estimate repairs.
- Sign purchase agreement.
- Get termite report with bid for work (clearance not required).
- Get bid for repairs from licensed and bonded general contractor.

(Continued)

Financing: Comparing Your Options *(Continued)*

- Obtain preliminary title insurance review.
- Obtain data on three to six comparable sales in the last 90 days within a quarter-mile radius of property.
- Meet investor or lender at the property.
- Get investor approval.
- Lender and escrow agent draw up loan documents.
- Sign closing documents in escrow.
- Close escrow.

Subject-To Financing
Average time to closing: 5 working days.

- Review comparable sales and estimate repairs.
- Sign purchase agreement.
- Get preliminary title insurance review.
- Escrow agent draws up documents.
- Sign closing documents in escrow.
- Close escrow.

Subject-To Options

Let's look more closely at subject-to financing. Bottom line, it's about not needing a lender's permission to buy a house. Such permission essentially is required when you take the typical approach to home financing, whether with a new loan, refinance, or loan assumption. You must fill out a credit application, provide your tax returns, and gather verifications of employment, bank accounts, and so on. If you've ever bought or refinanced a house or condo, you know the drill and how long it takes. You spend countless, frustrating hours preparing to qualify for a loan before you can even write an offer to purchase a property. Once your offer is accepted, you spend more time and energy getting fully approved and funding the loan for your purchase.

Forget all that! With pre-foreclosures, you don't have time for this drawn-out approach. Instead, opt for subject-to financing. That's a clause in a property deed that transfers title from a seller to a buyer *subject to* the existing liens. The lender's remedy for nonpayment is limited to foreclosure.

A typical sales agreement with *subject to* financing includes the following:

Seller agrees to sell and Buyer agrees to buy the described property (as listed in the contract) for the sum of . . . (equity amount minus deductions as listed as part of the contract) and to take title subject *only* to those existing encumbrances listed (include specific trust deed as well as terms per month and at what interest rate) *not in excess of* . . .

In most cases, you the buyer or your investor gives the seller cash for his equity and then takes over his existing loans and liens at closing. You'll need enough cash at closing to bring the loan current and out of foreclosure, plus enough cash to give the seller his or her equity/moving money. Remember the home we talked about in Chapter 3 with an appraised value of $400,000? In that case, the investor paid $13,000 to bring the loan current and paid the seller $40,000 in cash.

Risks of Subject-To Financing

Subject-to financing sounds so simple, yet it does carry risks. In some cases, when the lender discovers the property has been sold, it has the right to call the loan and demand that it be paid in full. Usually the lender has that right because of an *acceleration* or *due on sale clause*, which is a provision in most mortgage documents stipulating that the lender can demand payment of the remaining balance of the loan when the property is sold. However, this clause is a contractual obligation, not a civil or criminal law. That means that if title to the property is transferred, the bank may (or may not), at its option, decide to call the loan due. (If you don't pay them quickly, they can file a Notice of Default which is then recorded against the previous property owner's name, but secured by what is now your house. You then have a certain amount of time—in California, for example, it's 111 days—to refinance or sell the home.)

Most lenders, however, don't bother to call the loan because you have brought it current. As long as you keep the loan payments coming and all other requirements of the loan—property taxes, insurance, and so on—are met, the lender will be happy and leave you alone.

Subject-to financing is not currently illegal. The right of a lender to call a loan—demand that it be paid in full— is a contractual right, not a law.

Of course, before you buy or finance any pre-foreclosure or foreclosure property, do as Cliff did in Chapter 2: Make sure you know your state laws and ask the legal advice of a good real estate attorney. That can save you from making easily avoided mistakes.

How Much Should You Offer?

Let's look at the $400,000 home that sold with subject-to financing for $268,000 (see Chapter 3). The purchase offer was discounted by $132,000. At first glance, you might think that's a rip-off for the home's seller. But let's examine how the buyer arrived at her offer and how it benefited both her and the seller's needs.

The $400,000 was the appraised value for the home *after* it was thoroughly cleaned and fixed up. In this instance, the buyer estimated repairs at about $12,000, or $10 per square foot. This is a good ballpark price for simple cleanup with paint and carpet. If more repairs are required to bring a home up to neighborhood standards, you should figure $15 or more per square foot. Luckily the buyer was pretty close in his estimate (it ended up costing $14,000), but it just as easily could have and often does cost thousands of dollars more. At one time or another, we've all decided to fix something in our own homes, only to find that we ended up spending much more money—and time—than we had planned.

The buyer faced plenty of other risks, too. What would have happened if the former owners had decided to trash the home before they moved? Unfortunately, that happens occasionally if a homeowner loses the home at foreclosure auction and is especially disgruntled. Or what if, while the home was vacant and under repair, it was vandalized? All those unexpected expenses must come out of the buyer's pocket. What about the costs to the buyer for the monthly payments, insurance, and more before the house even gets back on the market? And a big variable: What if the home doesn't sell quickly? What if the market goes cold? The average buy, fix, and sell time in a hot market runs about three to four months. In a cold market, that time climbs to six to nine months. Many foreclosure investors fail to predict and accurately figure into their purchase price offer the cost of holding the property until it sells. Don't forget the $40,000 cash the buyer paid to the seller for his equity, either, and, of course, the $13,000 required to bring the defaulted loan current.

That all adds up to a lot of expense and risk with the possibility of little gain. Think about the fact that a real estate agent in a standard residential deal earns 6 percent of the purchase price for no risk at all. For all the variables and gambles a foreclosure investor takes, his profit should be at least double that—12 percent to 18 percent of the resale of the home. For costs other than repairs associated with a purchase and holding the property (closing costs, mortgage payments, carrying

A Few of the Risks to Buyer/Investor

Any pre-foreclosure property purchase comes with plenty of variables/risk for the buyer, including:

- Cost overruns associated with repair and rehab of the property.

- Costs associated with previously unnoticed or unknown defects and damage to the property.

- Changing local real estate market conditions that affect the time it takes to resell the property as well as selling price and profit, if any.

- Getting the owners out quickly after the closing.

- Variables related to costs of holding a property, including closing costs, mortgage payments, carrying costs, and selling expenses.

- Possible increased cost of cash required to bring loan current and pay seller for his equity.

costs, and selling expenses), I deduct another 15 percent to determine my final offering price.

In other words, the amount of money you can afford to offer homeowners in default for their property should reflect approximately a 30 percent discount off the appraised value of the property *after* it's cleaned up and fixed up, minus your estimated costs to make those repairs. (More on determining your offer price in Chapter 10.)

It's fair. It's equitable. Remember, the seller walked away from the deal with a check for $40,000 to start over, and his credit, which had been nonexistent, was now repaired because his mortgage had been brought current. From an investment standpoint, the 30 percent discount is enough to attract solid investors, too. On that $268,000 deal, the buyer rehabbed the property and then resold it six months later for $390,000. Not quite the $400,000 appraised, but by pricing the property below market in a cool market, she sold it relatively quickly. After all her expenses, she walked away with $50,800. Given that the property's seller walked away with a check for $40,000, the deal was a true win-win.

How fast you sell a property and the amount you
sell it for can make the difference between an
unbelievable deal and a marginal dog.

—Alexis McGee

You determine whether that kind of return is worth it to you for a six-month project. If all it takes is intensive work on your part up front and a little effort later on, then it is. If it takes loads of work for six months, the deal becomes less appealing, and you can see that, as the buyer, an offering price of $268,000 is too high. Holding costs as well as marketing and seller incentives—if your market demands them—can add up and affect your offer price, too. You must do your homework up front. Check recently sold comparable homes in the market. Consider current and anticipated market conditions and whether you'll have to discount your selling price or offer buyer incentives to move your home fast.

If a home's original owners decide to sell to you, work with them to determine how much money they truly need and will accept for their new start. As the deal maker you must be creative and find out what will work best to meet a home-

---

THE NUMBERS AT A GLANCE

The actual selling price was $390,000 (originally valued at $400,000).

Amount Paid for Home

Cash needed to close:

Cash to stop foreclosure (reinstate loan in default):	<$13,000>
Cash to seller at closing:	<$40,000>
Total	<$53,000>
Existing financing (use of subject to financing)	<$215,000>
Total amount paid for home	<$268,000>

Soft Expenses (Buy, Hold, Sell Costs)

Closing costs (buying and selling)	<$7,800>
Total mortgage payments:	<$16,600>
Costs to carry property (includes taxes, insurance, utilities):	<$5,900>
Real estate commissions and selling expenses:	<$26,900>
Total soft expenses	<$57,200>

Hard Expenses

Repairs and cleanup	<$14,000>
Total expenditure (purchase, soft and hard expenses)	<$339,200>
Total net profit (selling price minus all costs)	$50,800

owner's needs in the context of your needs, too. That means ask questions—many of them. Help the homeowners understand the difference between what they want and what they need to start over.

If they want you to buy their home, your goal is help them so that if you or your investor purchases the house, everyone walks away in win-win mode. At first, a couple may demand $100,000 for their equity to sell their home, but that may not be what they really need or what they will settle for. Keep asking, and keep them realistic about what they *need* versus what they *want*.

It's essential, too, that you define the dollar amount at which you can't afford to help them. In every deal, there is a limit to what you can pay, and if they insist that you exceed it, you must walk away from the deal. When a homeowner who wants you to buy immediately says he needs 100 grand to get going, your response may be, with a big grin, "I need $100,000, too!"

You're responsible for working with the homeowner to change his mind-set to one of reality, not dreams. You are trying to help him make the best of a very difficult financial situation. You cannot pay him full resale value because you're not going to live in the house to recoup any lost money. You will have costs associated with any deal and need to make a profit, too. This shouldn't surprise the seller. Make sure he also knows that you're not operating as a nonprofit organization.

Finding Other Investors' Money

There's more than enough money out there. I know, you're thinking, "Yeah, right!" Well there is, if you know where and how to find it. Just start by asking businesspeople you know if they would be interested should you discover where and how to find a house 30 percent below market value. Watch them beg for more information. Everyone with money looks for great deals. The problem, though, is that they rarely have time to find the deals. You might already know solid sources of cash, as was the case with Karl, the retired soldier. He tapped his former military buddies, and a successful business was born.

In your quest for cash, start by finding the money before you need it, and then keep a Rolodex or similar file of available sources. That way, if a deal comes up and you need the money immediately, you can get it without having to scramble.

The classified section of a newspaper is a good source of potential investors. Generally, the classifieds will have a heading like "Money Available," often right beside the real estate listings. Another solid source is the online web site Craigslist (www.craigslist.com); look for similar listings of "Money Available," "Investments Wanted," or "Cash for Real Estate."

Classifieds proved an awesome source of money. I had many more investors than I had deals, and that was when I just started out and had no track record. I now just pick and choose the money partners I want to work with. Someday I'll be the investor for someone else who finds the deals. I can't wait!

—A now successful ForeclosureS.com graduate

Another way to find money partners is to Google "hard money" and your city name, which will bring up a number of hard-money lenders and their web sites. A *hard-money loan* is industry jargon for a loan funded privately (not through a banking institution) based on the equity in a property, not an individual's credit-worthiness.

You also can advertise on Craigslist and in your local newspapers, too. An ad could read, "Have house 30 percent below market. Need money partner ASAP."

Real estate message boards like those on Creative Real Estate Online (www.creonline.com) and ForeclosureS.com (www.foreclosures.com) are another great source of investment cash. More message boards include:

- Real Estate Forums (www.realestateforum.com)
- BiggerPockets Forums (http://forums.biggerpockets.com)

Start blogging. You'll be surprised at what you can find.

Protect Yourself

As we've said, add to your Rolodex the names and contact numbers of those people who come to you with money to invest. Of course, thoroughly check out anyone you contact or who contacts you. Google their names; check them out with the Better Business Bureau (www.bbbonline.com); check your county recorder's grantee-grantor index (an official index of deeds with related information, and listed alphabetically by the grantee or property owners' name) to make sure they have no liens against their names. Also check their names against complaints in your state's secretary of state's office as well as with your state's attorney general, the state real estate commission, or the local district attorney's consumer fraud unit. If your potential investors have any professional designations, check them out with those licensing organizations, too.

When the time comes that you need the cash, call the investor and give him no more than a few hours to get back to you with a yes or a no. Then go on to the next person in your Rolodex. You must get a fast answer in order to move on your deal. A person may be a great potential money partner, but if he's on vacation, so what? Call the next name on the list. You can't afford delays at this point in a deal.

Have a backup plan, too. If you're working with a new money partner or haven't really established your credibility yet, have a backup investor ready and waiting in case your would-be partner gets cold feet.

Insist on getting your finder's fee at closing through escrow. Don't let investors talk you into waiting to get paid until after they buy the house or when they resell the property. You've done your job, regardless of when the property sells or for how much. Your check needs to be part of the proceeds paid out at the time of purchase. You get paid when the seller gets paid. You should not carry the risk of repairing or reselling the property. That's why you chose to assign the deal to someone else in the first place—to remove that risk.

What About Your Money Needs?

If you don't have cash of your own or don't plan to use your own cash, can you afford to get started in foreclosure investing? You can't afford *not* to. But you must ask yourself if you're willing to quit your current job and get going. It's all about how your time can be best spent. Early in my foreclosure investing career, I actually had no income one year. That's right—no money came in for an entire year.

But that was before I learned the ins and outs of the business and how to insulate myself from market ups and downs with the right approach and skills. I hope this book teaches you that approach—the approach that sets you apart and helps ensure your success.

If you're trying to figure out whether you, too, can afford to get started in this business, ask yourself these questions:

- Are you willing to do the work necessary to get the biggest return for the investment of your time and energy?

- Are you looking for a way to profit from foreclosure real estate investment honestly and ethically?

- Do you want to create your own business that taps your personal talents and fuels your passions?

If you said yes to all of the above, and if you want to make great money and wake up every day knowing that you can use your expertise to help others, then this is the new career for you. Don't sweat the money. Instead, get out there and get going!

Tips on How to Make the Career Change Work

If you are the sole breadwinner for your immediate and extended family and worry about how to make foreclosure investing work for everyone in the beginning, consider involving everyone in the process. This is a research-intensive business up front. Your 12-year-old could do Internet research for you, and so could your mother-in-law. If Mom isn't computer savvy, she can organize your office and check phonebooks for you. How about having your spouse make some calls to track down leads and background information on potential homeowners? More, as in information, is better in this business and can lead more quickly to better rapport with potential homeowners in default.

Sondra T. had an extremely successful home-based sales business. She was excellent at dealing with people, and the business was so successful that the divorced mother of two quite easily and comfortably supported her immediate family, her parents, and even an aunt. They all worked for her, too. But Sondra was bored and wanted more satisfaction in her work. So she decided to try foreclosure investing even though, she figured, it would mean her aunt and parents would have to support themselves initially. She agonized about "turning them out on their own" until she realized they could help with the details and information management necessary in the foreclosure-investing business just as they did with her sales business.

Fast-forward six months into her new business: "I love it," says Sondra. "Dad tracks down the initial potential leads; Mom keeps track of who I have to contact when; I do the follow-up; and the kids do the filing. And my aunt feeds us all regularly. It's a great income, a family endeavor, and we all feel so good about what we do. Why did it take me so long to get started in this business?"

TAKEaway

Key points to remember:

- Even if you have your own money, when you start out in this business it's generally best to count on other investors to provide cash to purchase properties. You can flip your deal to another investor for a finder's fee. Although the financial returns are not as great, your risk is minimal and the financial rewards immediate.

- Look to subject-to financing when buying pre-foreclosure homes. That means you or another investor take over payment on the seller's loan. That expedites the time involved for you to purchase the property, brings the seller's loan current, and repairs and improves the seller's credit so he can buy another home in the near future.

- Subject-to financing is currently *not* illegal. A mortgage agreement is a contractual obligation, not a civil or criminal legal issue.

- You must determine ahead of time how much you truly can afford to pay a homeowner for his or her property. This is, after all, your business, and you have to pay your bills, too.

- There is a difference between the price a homeowner in default needs and the price she wants for the property she has agreed to sell. It's up to you to separate the two.

- The decision to quit your day job in favor of foreclosure investing depends on your commitment to your success and the time you are willing to devote to it. You can succeed if you believe in yourself and are willing to work accordingly.

- If you're the breadwinner for your immediate and extended family, why not make your new venture a family endeavor? Involve everyone in the business.

CHAPTER 6

Finding Potential Deals

There are deals in every real estate market everywhere in the country. No matter where you go, there are folks with financial difficulties. You just have to know how to find them.

—Alexis McGee

Forget what the foreclosure gurus teach about how and where to find potential property deals. Mailers, roadside advertisements, billboards, and the like simply don't work. Those methods are oversold, out of date, and virtually useless as far as getting property owners facing foreclosure to contact you.

The best deals are not found at auctions or at trustee sales on the courthouse steps, either. You'll find far more success, as we've discussed, if you focus on properties in pre-foreclosure. That's when you can truly help homeowners in trouble and—if it's the best solution—buy their properties.

That means you must learn to identify, get the attention of, and generate interest from homeowners whose properties are in default *before* their homes end up on the auction block. Finding those homeowners requires the right research in the right places. After you've located a prospective seller, you learn what you can about him or her *before* picking up the phone to make a connection. There are no shortcuts.

If you suffer from a case of phone phobia, you'll have to get over it. To succeed in foreclosure investing requires that you learn how to talk easily to strangers about the personal matters that caused their predicament. You must be a combination of television talk show self-help gurus Dr. Phil and Dr. Laura. As Dr. Phil, you draw out the truth; as Dr. Laura, you have the answers. Unfortunately, you don't have the advantage of either's celebrity and are likely to hit a few roadblocks along the way. But none of those obstacles should stop you unless you let them.

If you're genuine in your caring and persistent in your personal contacts, you will win big at this game. We've already told you why, but it's worth repeating: Homeowners in foreclosure are scared by their situation and overwhelmed by investors who want to take advantage of them. Showing that you are an honest, caring person who truly wants to help with no strings attached—free of charge-will set you far apart from the pack.

You can offer homeowners in default multiple benefits, too, depending on their unique situation. Those benefits include:

- Stopping the foreclosure.
- Improving the homeowner's credit.
- Cash for the equity in the home. (The homeowner likely would lose it all at auction.)
- Privacy and discretion. (An auction is public information.)
- A new chance at a comfortable place to live.
- Stopping the bill collectors from hounding the homeowner.
- Giving the homeowner a fresh start.

This is all about the win-win situation we strive to create for all parties involved. Remember, though, not every homeowner wants or needs to sell the property to avoid foreclosure. Often, all that's required is to get control of a bad financial situation, as with Cliff in Chapter 2, who simply needed to sit down with a lender and put together a workout solution for his loan in default. Your job is to show people their options and help them identify what will work best for their needs.

Where to Look

Let's assume that by now you've decided foreclosure investing is in your future. The next step is finding homeowners in default with properties that potentially can be cleaned up, fixed up, and resold easily. That means the best potential properties are not the most expensive homes in a neighborhood or the one-of-a-kind floor plans targeted to a very small audience. Shoot for middle-of-the-road, in-demand properties—especially the entry-level homes (perhaps with about 1,400 square feet maximum) that most people can afford to buy. No matter market ups or downs, there's always a ready buyer for an entry-level property that's priced right. People always need a place to live.

You should also look for homeowners in default who have enough equity in their homes—generally 30 percent or more—so that working with them also works financially for you. If a property owner has too little equity, the numbers won't add up and the deal could cost you too much to generate the necessary profit. (See the chart in the accompanying box.) From a property owner's viewpoint, that minimum 30 percent equity represents something tangible and worth protecting beyond the sometimes abstract concept of a *credit rating* that's jeopardized if a property ends up in foreclosure.

The search for your target homeowners can be labor-intensive and time-consuming if you don't know where to look. Public sources of information online and off can yield valuable data about properties and their owners, including bankruptcies, liens, court filings, contact names and addresses, neighbors, family, and friends.

WHEN THE NUMBERS DON'T ADD UP

Here's an example of a potential pre-foreclosure property purchase in which the numbers don't add up for a potential investor.

Selling Price of Fixed-Up Home		**$360,000**
(actual appraised value: $400,000)		

Amount Paid for Home

Cash needed to close:		
Cash to stop foreclosure (reinstate loan in default)		<$23,000>
Cash to seller at closing		<$20,000>
Total		<$43,000>
Existing financing (use of subject to financing)	<$245,000>	
Total amount paid for home	**<$288,000>**	

Soft Expenses (Buy, Hold, Sell Costs)

Closing costs (buying and selling)		<$7,800>
Total mortgage payments:		<$20,000>
Costs to carry property (includes taxes, insurance, utilities):		<$7,900>
Real estate commissions and selling expenses:		<$26,900>
Total soft expenses		**<$62,600>**

Hard Expenses

Repairs and Cleanup		<$14,000>
Total expenditure (purchase, soft and hard costs)		**<$364,600>**
Total net profit/(loss) (selling price minus total cost)		**($4,600)**

Where to Find Local Pre-Foreclosures Lists

- Ask at your county recorder's office or courthouse whether there is a local research firm that collects and sells subscriptions to the notices of default and auctions or lis pendens, complaints, clerk's certificates, and final judgments. This is the best way to find a localized source of leads.

- Check the classified section of your local newspapers for foreclosure notices posted there.

- Visit your county recorder's office to collect data as it is recorded. However, it's usually more time- and cost-effective to hire someone to do that for you.

- Find a newspaper online that provides local area classifieds.

- Check out ForeclosureS.com for listings.

Start first by finding a pre-foreclosure listing service. National providers like ForeclosureS.com generally offer more searchable information in their databases. Smaller listing services will often require more hand work on your part, but they can still save you some time. The key to weeding these lists is to pull out only those leads in which the homeowners have substantial equity in their properties. Equity is the difference between the fair market value of the property and its total secured debt (loans and liens). The greater the equity, the greater the profits for you.

Here's a handy four-step approach to weeding potential property leads:

1. To find your target area, start by property zip code—perhaps where you live—and then expand outward in a 20-mile radius or so.

2. Cull or eliminate any properties listed that are not one- to four-unit residential. That generally means you consider single-family homes, duplexes, triplexes, fourplexes, townhomes, and condominiums.

3. Determine the range of your target resale value for the area. It's generally near or just under the median home price in your county.

4. Look for the amount of equity in a property by comparing its market value with the amount of the loan in foreclosure. You should get the market value information free from your listing service. Or, if you don't, you can get look it up for each property on free sites such as Zillow(tm) (www.zillow.com), HomeGain(tm) (www.homegain.com), and Trulia Real Estate Search (www.trulia.com), as well as other sites around the Web.

Weeding Your Leads

Here are a few things to keep in mind when it comes to weeding pre-foreclosure leads.

- Search by location. You should be able to weed your list of leads by state, county, zip code, or even street name. The key is to be able to limit your search to those properties in your specific target area.

- Search by equity. You should further limit your search by homeowner equity in their properties and be able to do that quickly and easily. Since you're not doing short sales, you'll need to qualify your leads by looking for those with a minimum 30 percent equity based on the information you're given.

- Pay attention to default publication dates. That's the day the default became public record. If it's longer than several weeks ago, you should find out if a cancelled notice of default was filed on the property. You can check that at the county recorder's office (which takes time and effort), or good listing services will provide that extra level of information. Some properties may have been sold or refinanced out of a default, so you need to make sure any potential property lead is still in foreclosure before you make your telephone calls.

- Make sure your list includes pertinent information about the trustor—the person who signed the loan and against whom any default is recorded—and the current owners (sometimes they're not the same). The current owner can sell the house. In subject-to financing, the trustor's name remains on the title.

- Delinquency amounts should be included, too, along with loan amount, loan document numbers, and the document number of the notice of default, or notice of trustee sale. You'll need those numbers to find related documents or, in the case of a public sale, to get minimum bid information from the trustee.

- Look for the square footage of the property, the lot size, and the year in which a property was built, too, as a way to eliminate properties that are not "entry level." If you concentrate on small, affordable homes in established neighborhoods, you won't have to compete in the crowded, overpriced new-home market.

The Numbers

Pre-foreclosure investors should target properties with a loan-to-value ratio of 70 percent or less. The equation to determine this is as follows:

$$\frac{\text{Amount of loan in default}}{\text{property resale value}} = \text{loan-to-value ratio (expressed as a percent).}$$

Sample equation:

Property market valuation range: $230,000 to $270,000

Property resale value: $270,000 (the value after it's repaired)

Loan value in default: $170,000

$$\frac{\$170,000}{\$270,000} = 63\%$$

Conclusion: Property's loan-to-value ratio is 63 percent, which is less than your 70 percent maximum, so the property owner has enough equity for you to consider it as a potential deal.

Anything with a loan-to-value ratio of 70 percent or less is a keeper. For example, let's assume that a $170,000 loan is in default on a property that has a market valuation range of $230,000 to $270,000. Figure the property's resale value at $270,000 (the high end because at resale the house will be fixed up). Divide that resale value ($270,000) into the amount of the loan in default ($170,000). The answer is 63 percent. That means the property has a loan-to-value ratio of 63 percent. It's less than 70 percent, so keep this property on your list as a potential deal.

> *Reputable Internet foreclosure lists—local and national—*
> *can simplify your search for potential property leads.*
> *But be careful. Not all lists are created equal.*

Reputable sources of pre-foreclosure lists are available at a reasonable price and can help you locate properties with loans in default, and then initially sort or weed those leads based on the very specific criteria you select. If, for example, you want to see only entry-level homes with a minimum 30 percent equity in zip codes within a 20-square-mile radius of your own home, ForeclosureS.com's web site (www.foreclosures.com) will do the electronic legwork for you.

Remember, too, that your local Realtor's MLS listing is *not* a reliable source for finding pre-foreclosure properties. Most pre-foreclosure property owners do not want to sell their homes, so they rarely call a Realtor to have the home listed on the MLS. Instead they wait for other solutions to keep their house. Those solutions often fail to materialize, and the property owner ends up with a quick sale to an investor as the only option to foreclosure.

As a general rule, don't bother driving through neighborhoods looking for deals, either. Your time is better spent culling your pre-foreclosure lists via computer and filing system, reserving your neighborhood visits for qualified appointments.

But don't close your eyes to what can be obvious sources of potential deals. If a home is empty and in obvious disrepair but isn't for sale, its owner could be about to go into default. Ditto if you pass a house with tall grass, oil-slick driveways, cracked windows, dirty yards, and graffiti. It pays to check out neglected homes, and the resulting deals can be diamonds in the rough.

That's what Arnie B., a new foreclosure investor who hadn't yet quit his day job, discovered early in his career. Five days a week en route to that day job, Arnie drove down the same street, past the same rundown house. For weeks, maybe months, he'd paid little attention to it other than to wave to the elderly gentleman wandering around outside, smoking his pipe.

But one day Arnie realized he hadn't seen the man for quite some time and the home appeared a bit seedier than usual. A light bulb blinked in his brain, and it occurred to Arnie that something might be up with the property. Arnie checked it out on his pre-foreclosure list and discovered that a notice of default had been filed. So he dug further. It turned out that the elderly man wasn't the owner at all, but a tenant. The absentee owner, Burt, had run into some financial trouble; the home's loan was in default, and a foreclosure auction was scheduled. Burt, who also had solid equity in the property, was a motivated seller. So Arnie contacted him to see if he could help him understand his options and perhaps offer to buy the house.

Arnie was undeterred by a few initial rebuffs, and his persistence paid off. He learned that Burt had bought the house on a whim several years earlier, thinking it would be a good rental property. But he lost his tenant—the elderly gentleman with the pipe had died—and his job at about the same time, and hadn't been able to keep up the mortgage payments. Burt planned to let the house go to auction and hope for the best. He hadn't realized, as Arnie pointed out, what a foreclosure on his record might do to his credit. Burt was thrilled with the prospect of a buyer and the fact that he could walk away with his equity and with his credit intact. Arnie purchased the house for $88,000, cleaned it up, then turned around and sold it after only six weeks for $142,000. His profit on the deal: $21,300 for what he figured was a total week's worth of work! (See the sidebar on the following page.)

Here's a look at the numbers in Arnie's deal to purchase Burt's home.

Appraised value of fixed-up home	**$142,000**	
Less 30 percent discount (15 percent for holding costs, 15 percent profit)		<$42,000>
Less costs to repair home ($10/square foot for 1,200-square-foot home)		<$12,000>
Purchase price	**$88,000**	
Financing the $88,000 Purchase		
Existing loans taken over subject to:		<$41,000>
Cash paid at closing to bring loan current:		<$5,000>
Burt's cash for equity payment at closing:		<$42,000>
Arnie's profit on the deal (15 percent of $142,000)	**$21,300**	

Choosing Where to Look

Arnie's is a great story and a win-win situation for both him and Burt, but, admittedly, that's not how you consistently find property leads. A better long-range approach: Start by deciding what geographic area you would like to cover. Bigger is not better; it's often just more cumbersome. Choose a familiar area or, at least, one that you can readily and affordably access. It doesn't make sense to select a place too far from where you live or work, because you'll likely make numerous visits to the neighborhood once you find prospective properties, especially if you end up buying one and rehabbing it for resale. Obviously, if you live in a small town with limited properties, you may have to expand your coverage area.

If you live in San Francisco, California, don't look to Tampa, Florida, for pre-foreclosure properties unless you plan to move there. However, if you live in Tampa, it might not be a bad idea to target an area in nearby St. Petersburg or Clearwater.

Ellen W. was a retired mail carrier who decided to get into foreclosure—investing as a way to make money and keep busy. After all, for 27 years she had delivered her mail route rain or shine, and she definitely didn't like the idea of retirement. Ellen chose to concentrate her foreclosure investment efforts on the same area where she had delivered mail because, she said, "I know the neighborhoods. I know these people, and I know I can help them."

She was right. At last count, after only a year in so-called retirement, Ellen had already earned finder's fees from three deals she put together for an investor, and had helped a half-dozen other homeowners out of their foreclosure nightmares. By the way, her investor was another of her former mail customers!

Do Your Homework

Once you've identified where you want to concentrate your efforts geographically, you're ready to do that lead-weeding we've discussed. Look to reputable lists of properties in default. Before you pay for any information, thoroughly check out the site and its organizers or owners—Google it, read real estate blogs, check with the Better Business Bureau (www.BBBOnLine.org), your secretary of state's office, and even the Federal Trade Commission (www.ftc.gov).

Decide which types of properties you're interested in identifying. Again, entry-level first homes are an excellent way to generate solid income because—no matter what the market conditions or real estate ups and downs are—ready buyers are always available for these homes. You can be as specific as you like in your search.

Pay particular attention to the default dates of filings. If a notice of default was posted eight weeks ago and the property sounds like a promising deal—good location, plenty of equity, a low default dollar amount—chances are the owners already think they have found a solution to their financial problems. Make sure you check to see if they are still in default or not. Again, top listing services provide that information for free. Otherwise you can check your county recorder's grantee-grantor index. If you find a "Canceled Notice of Default" filed, move on to the next prospect. Depending on the list you decide to use, even if it's the old-fashioned, time-intensive search for your pre-foreclosures, eventually you will end up with your own list of fairly solid leads.

Now comes the fun part. Other investors and students would, in this order:

1. Send a mass mailer to everyone on the list.
2. Send another mailer in about a month, if they remember.
3. Drive by the properties and wonder what to do next.

Of course, what you should be doing is none of the above.

Get Connected!

Forget mailers. No one, especially someone in foreclosure, reads junk mail, even if it's delivered as certified mail. Folks in financial distress are buried with bill collection notices, credit card offerings, and refinancing options every day. They have quit reading their mail by the time the notice of default is filed. In fact, when they are sent a copy of their notice of default via certified mail, they often refuse to accept the delivery. Mail has become the place to get more financial bad news, so they simply ignore it.

Forget driving through neighborhoods first. Your list isn't short enough yet to afford you the time to go door-knocking. Reserve that for well into the process when you've identified the best prospects by telephone and have already tried extensively to contact the homeowners.

Instead, *get on the telephone*. That's right, put on your friendly face, and start dialing for information about those prospective homeowners and properties. You can't help someone solve their financial problems unless you know:

- What the problems are.
- How they developed.
- What someone is doing to solve the problems.
- What's going on in that person's life now.

You must talk to neighbors and relatives of a property owner first. They can be valuable sources not only for a homeowner's telephone number but of information—and yes, gossip—that can help you learn about and understand a situation. Doing your homework ahead of time can mean fewer angry sellers hanging up the phone on you because they think you don't understand them. Show them you do!

The Friendly Approach

- Don't interrogate friends, neighbors, or family members of homeowners.
- Consider casually asking for their help.
- Keep it simple and be curious.
- Avoid giving details of why you need to speak with the person.
- Pay attention to your surroundings. They may offer clues that can be of help in developing a rapport with that friend, neighbor, family member, or even the homeowner in default.
- Sample dialogue: "Hi, I was hoping you could help me. I am trying to get in touch with your neighbor (name). He seems to be hard to reach. Can you help me?"

After you've gathered some information about the homeowner, you're better able to contact him or her. Before you pick up the phone, though, remind yourself that the objective of the call is to find out how you can help, what the homeowner is doing to keep the home, and how they ended up in default.

Now it's time to get the owner on the phone and get personal. You can't make recommendations to help someone out of financial difficulty unless you know their whole story.

Daryl White recounts the story of one home seller—we'll call him Roger— who had agreed to sell Daryl his property and then introduced him to his wife as a longtime friend. It turns out the wife had no clue the couple had any financial problems. "I had never thought to ask if the wife knew they were in default," says White. "It was a simple question, but I never bothered to ask it."

When Roger's wife was out of the room, White discreetly told him that he needed to discuss the situation with her, and that he would call him later. White then quietly left.

The deal did finally go through but only at the last minute. It seems that when Roger told his wife, she was so upset that she wouldn't even discuss signing a deal. She finally agreed to sign just days before the auction after realizing they had no other options. "It could have gone so much smoother if I had asked Roger a month before if his wife knew what was going on," says White.

"I learned my lesson," he adds. "I now ask those questions and dig for the whole truth up front."

The twin killers of success are impatience and greed.

—Jim Rohn

It's up to you to get the scoop—from neighbors, family, the homeowner, and anyone else with relevant information. It's your job to find out where the property owners stand physically and financially, how they got there, why they ended up in default, and where they would like to be. Find out what they would do differently if they could do things over. Then you can truly help them solve their problems.

Sources of Information

By now you're probably saying, "Yeah, it all sounds great, but how do I find all these people and get their phone numbers, too?"

The Internet has changed our lives. Just as it simplifies your search for defaults and foreclosures, it also yields a goldmine of personal and property information. You will be amazed at the information out there and how easy it is to access—much of it free of charge. Find neighbors, owners, family, and even properties with the help of Google (www.google.com) or DogPile (www.dogpile.com) searches, information directories, online court and county records, reverse directories that locate someone by address, and more.

Check prison and inmate lists, too. A few sources include state web sites (look up "Department of Corrections"), Skipease (at www.skipease.com, click on "Inmate Searches"); and USA People Search (usa-people-search.com). Skipease is also a site to find military personnel (click on "Military Locator").

Want telephone numbers? Skipease (www.skipease.com), Yahoo's People Search (http://people.yahoo.com/), Infospace.com (www.infospace.com) and other Internet white pages directories like Anywho.com (www.anywho.com), WhitePages (www.whitepages.com), and Searchbug (www.searchbug.com/peoplefinder/) are solid free sources.

To find neighbors who may be able to help you get a property owner's phone number, and even share the gossip about a property owner in default, try WhitePages.com or 411.com (www.411.com), and follow the links to "Reverse Address" or "Find Neighbors." (With these two searches, I generally turn up the phone number for a homeowner about 25 percent of the time.)

At many of these sites, you can even find potential relatives. Try phoning people with the same last name as a prospect and see if they are related to the person you're trying to reach. If they are, ask them for help in reaching your property owner. Most likely they will take your phone numbers. The worst they can do is say no.

These aren't long, drawn-out calls, either. You're simply trying to gather information about a potential property owner in default and his or her situation. If you have to leave a message for someone, spare the details. Make it casual, use first names, and just say you're trying to get in touch with so and so.

Another option is ZabaSearch (www.zabasearch.com). That site links to tons of free state, national, and even international databases loaded with information. ZabaSearch makes it easier than ever to find comprehensive personal information on anyone. Additional personal information—including aliases, bankruptcy records, and tax liens—is available from data brokers, but access typically requires a fee.

Public Access to Court Electronic Records (PACER), at http://pacer.psc.us-courts.gov, another good source, allows users to get case and docket information from federal appellate, district, and bankruptcy courts, and from the U.S. Party/Case Index, a national index for U.S. district, bankruptcy, and appellate courts. For example, the site can provide or direct you to information on whether a homeowner is involved in litigation; enable you to check out documents filed for certain cases; look for contact names, and more. It also has a complete listing of home pages for various courts (http://www.uscourts.gov/links.html).

The Homeowner Call(s)

Once you get a homeowner's phone number, try again and again and again to reach him by phone. Don't leave detailed messages and don't be put off if he doesn't answer the phone. After all, many homeowners in default are hounded by bill collectors—if you were in their place, chances are you wouldn't answer the phone, either. That's why you are calling their neighbors and relatives, too. You are trying to reach them in any way possible. Be persistent. Your honesty and genuine concern are what count. If, after many telephone attempts, a homeowner still won't answer, drop off a short note scribbled on a piece of paper (business cards are too intimidating) that asks him to call you, but don't give a reason why. Don't leave any other message, and don't mention their financial problems because you don't know who will be reading the note. (More details on honing your communication skills in Chapter 8.)

Treat homeowners in default as you would like someone to treat you if you were in the same situation. Don't patronize or be judgmental.

—Alexis McGee

When you finally do talk to the homeowner, don't be insulting or offensive with patronizing comments such as "How did you get into such a mess?" or "Why in the world did you do *that*?" You must develop rapport as a friend and treat the homeowner as you would your own family members. Serve them first. It's okay if you don't buy their house. If you do end up in a deal together, it will be a win-win proposition.

Remember, if you take the position of serving the seller first, treating him with respect and dignity, and doing what you would want someone to do for you in a time of need, you will end up buying homes below market value and making friends at the same time. That's what I consider living the life of a successful foreclosure investor.

Do's and Don'ts of Contacting a Homeowner

Do:

- Contact neighbors, family, and friends first.
- Learn all you can about a homeowner's personal situation from anyone and everyone he may know. Get the gossip first.
- Check out the homeowner with online searches via court records, Google, ZabaSearch, and more.
- Contact the homeowner by phone initially.
- Offer to help them understand their options.

Don't:

- Leave detailed voice messages.
- Send out mailers or leave long notes on a homeowner's door.
- Emphasize how much money you can pay the homeowner.
- Knock on the door without first trying to contact the homeowner by telephone.
- Give up easily or take no for an answer.

The Wet-Noodle Approach

Be patient, too. This business takes the noodle-on-the-wall approach—seriously! It's like throwing buckets of wet noodles on a wall. Most fall off, but eventually some will stick. That's what identifying potential deals is like. You must do your research and make countless phone calls to find neighbors, relatives, and others to help you glean tidbits of information before you ever even reach a homeowner. You will probably talk to dozens of homeowners, too, before ever getting your first deal.

Remember, you will need to make an average of 100 calls a day to buy 8 to 10 houses a year. That doesn't leave much time for busywork that gets you off the phone.

Instead, you could simply put a sign on your car, or send out e-mails or fliers, or post notices, or erect billboards announcing that you buy houses for investments. You could also drive your car into a brick wall. The result would be the same: a dead-end.

This is a people business. You build rapport, gain trust, learn someone's life situation, and then provide solutions. It doesn't happen by posting signs and operating behind a big business storefront.

You are a combination of Dr. Phil and Dr. Laura. You are not afraid to get personal. It's your job to probe with open-ended questions and get to the bottom of a homeowner's situation. Sure, homeowners won't be in a good mood. They're angry about their situation. You must understand that and forgive them. In the end they will be your friend. The worst that can happen is that they hang up the phone or slam the door in your face. But you must try to help them anyway. The alternative for them is far worse than your clear questions when asked with the goal of helping them solve their problem. They have nothing to lose and everything to gain by talking to you.

Knowing How to Help

As we discussed in Chapter 3, some or all of the following avenues might be available to a property owner in default, depending on his situation:

- Working with a Realtor to find a homebuyer if this occurs immediately after the financial crisis becomes apparent. Selling a home conventionally can take many months, so if foreclosure is around the corner, this is not a viable option.

- Working out a plan with their present lender to cure the default. Again, this depends on the ability of the homeowner to requalify with the current lender and make the workout plan payment. If the homeowner is unemployed, this is not an option.

- Working with a mortgage broker to get a new loan. This option depends on the ability of the homeowner to fully qualify to make new payments; if they're unemployed, it's not an option.

- Filing bankruptcy to defer the foreclosure. A bankruptcy filing can have serious long-term ramifications. The wisdom of choosing this option depends on whether a homeowner truly can't afford a property or his debts and has exhausted all other options to pay off debts (tightened bankruptcy laws have made filing bankruptcy more difficult).

- Doing nothing and losing the home at foreclosure auction. If this route is followed, the homeowner loses the roof over his head and all his equity, destroys his credit, is evicted by the sheriff, and walks away with nothing, not even dignity.

- Selling the home to an investor before the foreclosure auction. This depends on the outstanding debts on a home and the amount of equity in the property; without enough equity, an owner could end up with nothing in a sale.

As the white knight, your responsibility is to help homeowners determine what's best for their situation. You must point out each and every option available to the homeowner, as well as the pros and cons of each. Some homeowners may be able to choose from all of the preceding options; others may be limited to only two—losing their home or selling it. Still other homeowners may be so far in debt and so desperate financially that bankruptcy is the only way to protect the roof over their heads. Selling the property to you or anyone else isn't necessarily the best course.

That doesn't mean, however, that you don't run the numbers to determine whether a deal would work for both you and the homeowner. Sometimes the best solution for a homeowner is to sell the property; sometimes it isn't. Sometimes you'll find that you just can't afford to buy someone's home. No matter how much you would like to help, their debts are simply too high and their equity too low to make the numbers add up for you. In this business, the goal isn't to drag you down; the goal is to lift both you and the homeowner. The target is win-win for everyone.

It's the difference between coming up with a solid solution for a homeowner or simply slapping a bandage on their financial difficulties, adds ForeclosureS.com coach Sarah Garlick. "A homeowner trying to borrow their way out of a problem often is just circling the drain. Their income has to at least match their outflow. If it's lopsided, the problem only worsens and down they go."

Art and Marie had a ton of equity in their home of eight years. But both had been laid off from work, and their mortgage had fallen into default. Desperately they tried to refinance to give themselves some breathing room, but without luck. In reality, refinance made no sense since both were unemployed. It only would have dug them deeper into the debt pit. "These were nice salt-of-the-earth people who basically just fell on hard times and needed to begin anew," says foreclosure investor and ForeclosureS.com coach Tim Rhode.

When the couple realized that selling their home was the solution, they asked Tim to buy it. "I had to convince them, though, that I had to be assured of my minimum profit. I had to tell them, 'This is how I earn my living, and I will not buy the house if I can't get it at my price.' I let them know that in exchange for this I would push the sale through quickly, and unless I got hit by a bus, the deal absolutely would close as I had written it."

Art and Marie went ahead with the sale and ended up with a $75,000 check for their equity, enough for their new start. The house was in great shape and needed only a few repairs, so Tim was able to clean it up, turn it around, and resell quickly. "We netted about $30,000," he says. "It makes you feel great when you make a profit and help good people get on with their lives at the same time."

When to Walk Away

You can't help everyone. Period. Not all property owners truly want your help; not everyone can benefit from your help, either. You must realize and accept that. We don't get into this business to be abused. Sure, people get mad at us; they resent our intrusion into their private lives, and many of them initially tell us to get lost. But the majority of people you approach actually want and long for your guidance. However, you have to learn to recognize the difference between those people and the people who genuinely do not want your help.

Experience and your gut instinct usually will tell you when to walk. Obviously, if you are ever concerned for your safety, run, don't walk, away. But use common sense.

Lawrence J. had done his homework on a potential property but couldn't reach the homeowner, so he headed out to door-knock. When he drove up to the house, it was in disrepair but appeared relatively clean. A number of not-so-ordinary-looking people were mingling outside. You know the picture—cars parked at weird angles everywhere, including on the lawn, and people sitting around doing nothing. Lawrence figured he was safe enough outdoors in broad daylight, so he walked up to the house and starting chatting with the people about the day, the weather, and so on. Despite his first impression, the group was very friendly, so Lawrence asked to see the owner. "Is Joe in?"

Lawrence carefully avoided looking or sounding like a bill collector in any way. In fact, when one of the people asked if he was "after the money," Lawrence, who was dressed in jeans, a T-shirt, and sneakers so he would fit in, looked at his own clothes, laughed, and then responded, "No, but I know about Joe's problems, and I can offer some advice to help him."

It was the right approach and the right timing. Joe, it turned out, was the man who had asked Lawrence if he wanted the money. A conversation ensued, and eventually Lawrence was able to build up a rapport and, ultimately, help Joe avoid losing his home.

"I didn't go inside the home right away," said Lawrence. "And besides, if my reception hadn't been pleasant, I would simply have walked away."

In deciding whether to work with a homeowner or avoid a property, here are some questions to ask yourself:

- Does the owner have enough equity in the property to make it worthwhile for you? That's a must, and something you should already know from weeding your lists.

- Do you feel safe in the neighborhood? If you feel there is crime or drug activity, it's generally not a good idea to knock on an owner's door.

- Is the property overbuilt—larger and nicer than anything else close by—for the area in which it's located? If so, you will have a tough time selling it, so it's best to walk away now.

Do-Not-Call Registry

As someone trying to help people, don't sweat whether your telephone calls fall under the purview of the National Do Not Call Registry (www.donotcall.gov). The registry, with well over 107 million numbers listed, targets solicitors—people peddling products and/or services for a fee. You're not a peddler. So, until there's a legal precedent from a court case or an amendment to the existing law, you, as an individual who helps people and without a real estate license, are not affected by the registry. (Licensed real estate agents and brokers do fall under the law's purview as directed by the National Association of Realtors' legal counsel.)

We call homeowners in default to offer free advice and assistance to help them figure out how to keep their homes from foreclosure. We do not collect a fee to stop their foreclosure—we talked about that and foreclosure consultants earlier—nor are we soliciting the owners to sell us their homes. We're not attorneys or accountants, either, so we don't offer legal or tax advice.

Personal and Confidential Information

We need to and do find out personal and confidential information about homeowners in conjunction with potential deals. It's important to remember that even though it's public record, the information is personal. Would you like your neighbors to know all your financial problems? Absolutely not, so use common sense and be sensitive to an individual's privacy.

This is a prime time for that Golden Rule approach. You can get the gossip from the next-door neighbor without giving any explanation of why you're calling other than, "It's personal. I just need to reach (name). When was the last time you saw him?" Do not pass on any gossip you've picked up or the financial blow-by-blow of someone's problems. If your mortgage was in default, you wouldn't want your 10-year-old child to face the thought of being homeless. If a child answers the phone, simply ask for the homeowner and avoid the grim details. If she wants to know why you're calling, simply say something like, "I'm trying to get in touch with Daddy. When will he be home?"

What you give comes back to you.

—Alexis McGee

If purchasing an owner's home does end up being the best option for both of you, the great thing is that by buying directly from that person, chances are you have an exclusive deal. No matter what anyone else says, when you do things the right way, and establish trust and empathy for a person's situation first, rarely does an owner in default look to the competition when you contract to buy their home.

TAKEaway

Important points to remember:

- If you have phone phobia or don't like talking to strangers, you need to get over it or find a different business. You have to be able to connect with people via phone and in person to establish the rapport necessary to be a white-knight foreclosure investor.

- Don't interrogate or be judgmental when talking with others. Treat them as you would like to be treated in the same situation.

- The Internet is your ticket to finding out phone numbers and information about prospective homeowners in default and even their properties. Start with Google and go from there. And don't overlook the good old phone book—online or in print.

- Your responsibility is to help each homeowner understand his options and determine what's best for that unique situation.

- Until there's a court case that says otherwise, the National Do Not Call Registry does *not* apply to you. You are not soliciting business for a fee. You are trying to talk to someone as a friend to help them.

- Be cognizant that even though the information you deal with is public record, it's personal. Treat it that way.

CHAPTER 7

Who Are These Homeowners?

There is no typical homeowner in default. Anyone can make a financial mistake and their home end up in foreclosure.

—Alexis McGee

Foreclosure isn't the sole purview of alcoholics, drug addicts, divorcees, the deceased, the unemployed, or the underemployed. Property owners in financial distress come in all shapes, sizes, ages, and walks of life. To be successful in this business, you must understand and accept that fact without being judgmental. You must also learn to recognize different personalities, different sets of problems, the different paths to financial distress, and the different ways you might be able to help. Although homeowners may share various hardships, pains, and problems, each situation is unique.

Cliff, whom we heard about in Chapter 2, was a businessman who simply made a few poor financial decisions. Ariana's default situation was the result of a divorce and a deadbeat ex who failed to pay child support. Art and Marie, who almost lost their home in Michigan, were casualties of economic fallout after drastic job cuts by the nation's automakers. Steven, a high-powered computer whiz with a high-powered job, banked on future earnings when he bought his top-dollar dream home. Then came the dot-com bomb, and he found himself overextended with mega mortgage payments and no job. The latter situation, luckily, proved brief and he was able to rescue his home.

A list of foreclosure victims and their stories could fill volumes. As someone well versed in the business of foreclosures, you can help at least some of these people with honest, straightforward information and guidance if you understand all the aspects of their situations.

This business is about making profits and, at the same time, making a difference in someone else's life. That demands you pay attention to the life details and nuances of the person with whom you're dealing. Probe and prod for the answers, but do so with grace and with respect for that person's dignity. Always treat the homeowner the way you would like to be treated if you were in the same situation. There's the Golden Rule yet again.

How do you deserve a fortune? Render a fortune of services.

—Jim Rohn

Let's take a closer look at exactly who ends up facing foreclosure.

The Numbers

The American Dream of homeownership is alive. The good news is that an estimated 69 percent of Americans owned their homes as of year-end 2006, with 75.6 million housing units occupied by their owners, according to the most recent data from the U.S. Census Bureau.

The less positive news is that, in 2006 alone, close to 1 million people filed for foreclosure in the United States, according to numbers from ForeclosureS.com. That's up more than 51 percent from just over 640,000 foreclosure filings in 2005. Neither year's total includes the hundreds of thousands of homeowners who, like Cliff, Steven, Ariana, and others, found last-minute reprieves to their mortgage default woes.

Early payment defaults on subprime loans through mid-2006 more than tripled the rate of early 2005, according to Freddie Mac, the congressionally chartered private mortgage market investor. Delinquency rates on all its mortgages at commercial banks totaled 1.91 percent in the fourth quarter, the highest level in nearly four years (see Economic & Housing Outlook, March 8, 2007, "In Like a Lion . . . ," by Frank Nothaft, Amy Crews Cutts, Calvin Schnure, and Nela Richardson at www.freddiemac.com/news/finance/pdf/Mar_2007_FRECOM_Outlook.pdf).

A total of 4.95 percent of all mortgage loans on residential properties (one to four units) were delinquent in the fourth quarter of 2006, up from 4.67 percent in the third quarter, according to the Mortgage Bankers Association's National Delinquency Survey. A breakdown of percentages of loan delinquencies by type of loan:

- Prime mortgages: 2.57 percent delinquent in the fourth-quarter of 2006, up from 2.44 percent in the third quarter of 2006.

- Subprime loans (those made to individuals with no or poor credit): 13.33 percent delinquent versus 12.56 percent in the third quarter of 2006.

- FHA loans: a record 13.46 percent delinquent in the fourth quarter 2006 versus 12.8 percent in the third quarter of of 2006.

- VA loans: 6.82 percent delinquencies in the fourth quarter of 2006 compared with 6.58 percent in the third quarter of 2006.

Subprime mortgage lenders have felt the hit, too. In March 2007, the New York Stock Exchange suspended trading in shares of one of the nation's largest subprime lenders, California-based New Century Financial Corporation (NYSE: NEW), after the company said it no longer could pay its bills or make loans; in April the company filed for Chapter 11 bankruptcy protection and slashed its workforce by more than half, laying off about 3,200 staff.

Also in March, Countrywide Financial Corporation (NYSE: CFC), the nation's largest mortgage lender and another big lender in the subprime market, announced it would no longer offer no-money-down home loans.

In other subprime mortgage market news, California-based Fremont General Corporation, also among the nation's largest subprime lenders, was forced to lay off employees because of double-digit drops in its stock. And in February, Freddie Mac, the congressionally chartered private mortgage market investor, announced tougher subprime lending standards to lessen the risk of future defaults. Among other things, the mortgage investing giant will no longer buy subprime adjustable rate mortgages (ARMs) unless a borrower qualifies at the fully indexed, fully amortizing rate. In other words, it's no longer enough that a buyer simply qualify for a loan at a low teaser rate.

The end result of all these and more clampdowns, subprime market pullouts, and financial difficulties is that homeowners in default are now faced with even fewer options to keep their homes. More properties will end up sold to private investors, on the auction block, or as bank-owned (REO).

No state, it seems, is immune to foreclosures, either. Predictably, major metropolitan areas with employment losses are hard hit, but so are more rural areas in the nation's heartland. States such as California, Texas, Florida, Illinois, Michigan, and Colorado are among the leaders in numbers of foreclosures. So are Massachusetts, Ohio, Georgia, New York, New Jersey, and Nevada.

The Culprits

The culprits, also predictably, can be job cuts, a cooling economy, spiraling costs of living, and so on. But even more to blame, many Americans, no matter their income or education, regularly buy homes they can't afford. They do so by counting on creative financing and banking on future income. That financing, as we discussed in Chapter 3, often includes nontraditional and adjustable rate mortgages ranging from no money down to interest-only and 40-year terms.

Each time the number of foreclosures increases, a different set of circumstances is to blame, says Marsha Townsend, vice president and co-founder of ForeclosureLink Inc., Fair Oaks, California–based foreclosure trustees. "This time we're faced with the creative loans. People are just in over their heads," Townsend says. "What we're seeing this time around, too, is that the sellers have at least two mortgages on their property," she adds.

For some of those people who looked to nontraditional financing, their anticipated future jobs or higher salaries never materialized. Many of those homeowners don't understand the realistic financial ramifications of what will happen to their monthly living expenses when their mortgage payments adjust upward—which they will, and they do. Sometimes, after the initial teaser period, the payments increase on a regular basis.

An interest rate increase of only 1 percent can make a big difference in monthly payments, especially to someone already stretched financially. Let's assume you have a standard 30-year $200,000 mortgage. At a rate of 6 percent, your monthly payment (not including taxes and other fees) might run about $1,193. If that rate goes up only 1 percentage point to 7 percent, your monthly payments jump $129 to about $1,322. If you took out that same loan at a low teaser rate, perhaps 3 percent for three years, the monthly payment starts out at only $840. At the end of those three years, however, that upward adjustment of almost $500 to $1,322 a month is huge!

The Effects of a Rate Increase

Here's a comparison of the monthly payments (not including taxes and other fees) on a standard 30-year $200,000 loan that starts with a low introductory interest rate of only 3 percent for three years, and then adjusts upward to market rates:

Introductory interest rate of 3 percent	$ 840
Interest rate 6 percent	$1,193
Interest rate 7 percent	$1,322
Total difference	$ 482 a month

The result: Many overextended homeowners end up in default or foreclosure, facing the reality of losing the roof over their heads. Often they're afraid, confused, uninformed, unsure, and ignorant of their options. Your job, of course, is to understand them and offer them the options that best work for their individual situations. And, as the numbers indicate, even if a homeowner in default can figure out a way (with your guidance) to come up with the extra cash every month, staying in the home over the long haul may or may not be a wise option. Again, it's that income versus outflow equation, and if it's lopsided, something has to give.

After five years of hard work, Ranata and Charles finally bought their first home. By most people's standards, it was modest, even small, at only 1,000 square feet. But to the newly married couple, it was a palace. Both had grown up in the projects of inner cities, so their home truly represented the American dream to them. Unfortunately, they bought at the height of the price appreciation frenzy and paid top dollar for their home. Adding to the problem, they listened to an overzealous mortgage banker who talked them into an interest-only ARM. "It will be easy," he told them. "By the time the ARM adjusts upward—in five years—you'll both be making twice as much money at your jobs."

Thrilled by the concept of homeownership, the couple jumped at the chance to buy more home than they truly could afford. With purportedly "cheap" financing, they could buy new furniture, too. You can finish the story. The economy, along with the couple's salaries, nose-dived; the housing bubble burst; home price appreciation stagnated; all other costs of living, including the couple's health insurance, jumped significantly; and the couple could no longer afford their dream. Bill collectors hounded them, so they turned off the phone and refused to open the mail, including the certified mail with the notice of default from their lender.

Luckily, Mel C., a white-knight foreclosure investor, found the property and connected with the couple before it was too late. With his help and guidance, the couple—both gainfully employed—contacted their lender and were able to work out terms to make up the back payments on their loan. They were able to keep their home for now, but for how long is hard to say. Mel may hear from them again in the future if their incomes don't catch up to their lifestyle soon.

Storybook endings, as you know, aren't the norm. In the 1990s, I was at an auction on the courthouse steps. A middle-income woman was there with her children. Their home had ended up in foreclosure because the husband had ignored several foreclosure notices. I remember talking with the woman before the auction. She was excited about "all the money" the family would get from the auction and that it would be enough to pay off all their bills. She was clueless that the family could very well end up homeless and lose all the equity in their home. It was gut-wrenching to watch as the house sold for just $1 over the balance of its loan in default. The family lost everything. It was too late to help her.

Had a white-knight investor approached her earlier and gotten personal with questions and answers, chances are he could have helped her solve her financial problems.

Typical Homeowners

Never jump to conclusions about a solution for a homeowner in foreclosure until you know *all* the facts. That's standard procedure. Also standard procedure, as we've mentioned, is to look for motivated sellers—there are literally thousands for every investor. Many of these are the folks who have already made those down payments, qualified for loans, used up all their credit, and are now in default. As you weed your pre-foreclosure lists, you can select them by the amount of equity they have in their property. If your local foreclosure list doesn't calculate that for you, remember that equity is the difference between the market value of a home and the value of the primary mortgage minus the balance of any other liens and mortgages secured against the property.

When you're weeding your leads for those motivated sellers early on, you will also learn to recognize some basic types of homeowners and their behaviors. Let's examine a few of the most common.

The Habitual Defaulter

A variation of the motivated seller, these homeowners have been in default before. By researching past foreclosure notices (hopefully you're getting that information free from your listing service), you can see how often a homeowner has been in default. These people are good candidates for potential deals because they've probably exhausted their options for getting additional cash to bail them out of their financial mess again. Also, with multiple defaults, lenders are less likely to renegotiate their loan or give them a new one, which further reduces their options to keep their property.

But just because they've been in default before doesn't mean they know the routine, the ramifications, or their choices. All that is up to you to explain.

If you contact a homeowner who isn't ready to sell yet, find out what he has done to date about the default, and talk with him about the available options. Make sure you keep the door open for future discussions, too. You never know when someone might decide it's time to sell. If they do decide to sell, you want them to think of you. Until then, you can further cement your relationship through follow-up contacts and visits. The number one reason why many investors fail to buy a pre-foreclosure home is that they simply don't bother to follow up with motivated sellers. Don't make that mistake.

The It's-All-Taken-Care-of Owner

"I don't need to take care of it. It's all fine," is their typical comment. In fact, when dealing with most homeowners in default, chances are you'll hear this at least once.

If you hear that, jump in feet first and start asking questions—in a noninterrogatory manner, of course—about how they took care of it. In most cases, the "taken care of it" is only a smokescreen. Don't let them brush you off! Let the homeowner answer each question, but always respond with another question. You want the homeowner to know that you know the business—the details, fallacies, and complications. Your goal is to win his trust and help him understand that you want to help him. Some of the questions you may want to ask include:

- How have you taken care of it?
- Who did you talk to?
- What options did they say you have?

   Homeowners fall back on the "taken care of" tack because:

- They don't want to talk about their situation.
- They're afraid.
- They're confused.
- They don't know what else to say.
- They don't know what they're going to do.
- They are in denial about their situation.

The Angry Homeowner

This guy blames the whole world for his financial miseries, especially a pending foreclosure, without ever taking a look at himself. "It's that crook who sold me this house." "It's that lousy liar of a lender who promised me, but didn't deliver." "It's that creep of an ex who lied to me." Those are only a few of their typical comments. Never will you hear anything from these homeowners about how they made a mistake or messed up. It's always the other guy.

Sometimes you can get through to this type of homeowner by trying to get beyond the blame and examining the issues with positive solutions instead.

The My-House-Will-Sell-at-Auction Owner

"I'm not worried. I'll get full market value at auction" is the refrain of these homeowners. They think that selling their home at a foreclosure auction is the magic pill to cure their financial ills. But they're quite mistaken and often end up homeless and close to penniless, like the woman and her family mentioned earlier.

The fact that other, more appealing options exist can be a tough sell to someone brainwashed by the convincing tale that they'll get full market value from selling their house at a foreclosure auction. They may even consider you a crook who's trying to rip them off because you offer to buy the home at a discount as opposed to "all that cash we'll get at auction."

You must work hard to try to help these homeowners understand the real ramifications of their decision and the importance of looking for other options—including selling their home quickly before the auction to lock in cash for their equity. If you don't, they stand to lose so much and end up with so little. You may not be able to buy their home—it might not make financial sense for you or the homeowner—but you can educate them on reality.

The Scared-and-Hiding, a.k.a. I-Don't-Want-to-Talk-about-It Homeowner

Also known as the "If-I-ignore-it, it-will-go-away" type, these people truly don't understand what's going on and sometimes don't even realize their home has been sold at foreclosure auction until afterward with the knock on the door and the order to vacate. They definitely don't realize that, in many cases, if they talk with their lender when their financial problems begin, that lender may be willing to work with them.

A variation of this homeowner is the "Totally-Confused/Has-All-the-Facts-Wrong" type. It's often tough to get through to this particular homeowner because he has just enough information—or misinformation—to think he has all the answers. He doesn't understand the foreclosure process or timeline. Often he thinks that sending in a partial payment will stop the foreclosure. It won't. But once you help him see what the actual facts and options are, he's often so appreciative that he will want to work only with you. That is our goal!

The This-Is-My-House! Owner

We're all familiar with this homeowner. His home is his home, period, and no one else—especially not the bank—can have it. In some ways, this is a hybrid of the I-Don't-Want-to-Talk-about-It and the Totally-Confused homeowners. They're in the dark on the issue, their rights, and their responsibilities, and they won't let go of their home no matter how far behind they've fallen on their payments. The extent of their refusal to accept the situation is tragic—especially if you could easily help them if only they would let you.

Some of these homeowners still seem to be living in another world when it comes to their foreclosure situation even after you've delicately tried to explain their options. Their response: "It's my house; I am not going to sell it to anyone."

At some point you have to hit them with the brutal truth: "You agreed to and signed a contract with your lender. Now you're not living up to your contract, so the bank is not asking you; they are selling your home to pay off what you owe them. The question is, what are you going to do to stop this? It's your choice."

We try to be kind in this business, but from time to time you do have to say things you wish you could avoid. Don't cop out and evade the issue. Be bold, brave, honest, and kind. Treat the homeowner as you would your brother or sister—but tell it like it is.

The Shopping-for-Investors Owner

You know this type, too. He shops around for investors with the aim of selling his home to the highest bidder. Who can blame him? That's a great concept. The only problem is that this homeowner has no idea how to shop for integrity in a buyer and is clueless about the scams as well. Often he will end up taking the hard-sell bait of big promises, only to end up out in the cold—literally.

With this group, all you can do is be persistent, consistent, honest, and always follow through on what you say you are going to do. Hold your integrity high. In the end, that's really what counts.

The Big-Fat-Liar Owner

You need to know when to walk away from these prospects, too. Every time you call, their story changes. No matter how hard you try, or how deep you dig, you can't get to the truth. And if you can't get to the truth of their situation, you can't help them.

You can try compassion and consistency, but at some point you may have to rephrase all their lies back to them. I do that by starting out acting confused—it's the TV detective Colombo persona: "What do you mean? I don't get it."

Make the homeowner explain it all again. Then, at some point you will have to ask them, "Now I really don't get it. Which one of your stories is the real one?"

Don't back down. Don't fall prey to the lies. They and others may actually believe their stories, but you must be skeptical and keep asking the same questions in pursuit of the real truth. Again, be bold!

The Flake Homeowner

This group can be incredibly frustrating to deal with. They may say they understand their options and agree with your suggestions, but somehow they never do what they say they will. Even taking care of the smallest details that could easily stop their foreclosure is beyond them. They seem to be in a flurry of activity, but nothing ever gets done. You'll likely go nuts as you watch them lose their home to foreclosure. Don't fall victim to the what-ifs or if-onlys. You can only do your best to try to educate and direct.

You have to be especially bold with this group. If a homeowner doesn't listen to you and do as you suggest, all you can do is watch as he loses his home.

The Bottom Line

In dealing with homeowners, you must develop the right mix of compassion for them, their family, and their dilemma, along with an awareness of the reality of the situation, their choices, and the practicality of what can be accomplished. Only then can you arrive at the best solution to their financial troubles. Every situation is different, as is every homeowner.

With practice, you can master this delicate balance with ease and satisfaction. Think about how you would feel and like to be treated if you were in a similar situation, and look for win-win solutions for everyone.

We talk more about what to say and how to say it to homeowners in the Chapter 8.

TAKEaway

A few points to remember:

- All kinds of people—from businessmen and women, to single parents, young couples, singles, retirees, and more—can fall into default on their mortgages.

- Recognize that new homeowners often get intoxicated by the idea of owning a home and fail to realize the financial ramifications of meeting that monthly mortgage payment.

- Learn to recognize categories of traits that certain homeowners in default have in common, yet do *not* jump to conclusions when it comes to offering advice.

- Patience, compassion, and consistency in your approach will go a long way toward helping you help all kinds of homeowners in default.

CHAPTER 8

The Art of Communication

You don't know what you don't know.

—Alexis McGee

The ability to communicate successfully with others is fast becoming an art lost in cyberspace and sabotaged by video waves. I-Pods are replacing eye contact; text-messaging and e-mail are replacing conversation with its content in context.

But knowing how to formulate and convey your message in person and then understanding the reactions of others is essential to success in the business of buying and selling foreclosures. You have to be able to communicate accurately and consistently with property owners, lenders, investors, and potential buyers. A pinpointed high-dollar marketing message means nothing if no one bothers to look at or listen to it. Your perfectly scripted phone call is worthless if the homeowner won't pick up the phone or, if he does, slams it down the moment he hears your scripted voice.

Even if you're already a good communicator, you can hone your skills. We all can work harder to improve our message, its delivery, and its acceptance. We can become more sensitive to the pitfalls of miscommunication and misunderstanding. We can learn to reach out to others in ways they recognize and understand.

The rewards of effective communication cannot be overstated. People will know that you are genuinely concerned about their well-being. They will realize that you honestly want to understand their personal issues, and they will want to sell their homes to you at your price when it's the best solution to their situation.

Beyond Words

Communication is conveying a message. But it's much more than simply what you say. It's how you look and act, your tone, your approach, body language, eye contact, and interaction with others. It's what you say as well as what you don't say, and what you do and don't do, too.

Try this simple experiment. Walk into a room to initiate a conversation with a friend while holding your arms casually at your sides. Most likely that person will glance up briefly, smile, and the conversation will proceed as planned, without any confrontations or expectations of argument. Now try it again, only this time walk into the room with your arms folded across your chest as they might be if you were angry. Notice a difference in the other person's reaction to you? This time he or she probably tenses up and is expecting you to be confrontational in tone or content. Your friend expects you to attack and therefore gets ready to defend.

Let's try another exercise to help you understand the effect of body language. Flip through television channels during prime-time newscasts, and notice the demeanor and body language of the anchors. Generally, their arms and bodies are relaxed; they're at ease and open to you. For more poignant stories, the brow furrows. Their expression often is sympathetic.

Then try watching the Sunday morning debate shows with an eye to body language. Chances are you can figure out who is ready to pick a fight and who is on the defensive just from how they sit, talk, or act. For an even more striking awareness of body language, hit your TV's mute button as you flip through the newscasts and debate shows. You don't even need to hear the TV personalities to read their meaning.

How We Communicate

The message you convey in everything you say and do results from much more than the words themselves. Among factors that affect your message:

- Tone of voice.
- Body language.
- What you wear.
- Your physical appearance.
- Your eye contact or lack there of.
- What you don't say.

The Business of Body Language

Next time you talk to someone, keep in mind a few basics of what body language can convey.

- Arms folded across your chest: stay away from me.
- Stooped shoulders: lacking self-confidence.
- Standing while others are sitting: intimidating.
- Lack of eye contact: afraid and insecure.
- Tilting your head slightly: open to what others have to say.
- Doing something else at the same time: I don't care about you.
- Personal space: too close and you're infringing on someone's space; too far away and you're being standoffish.

Impressions Count

It's no different when it comes to talking with homeowners in default, their neighbors, and their families. If you want to develop rapport, you must start out by being open and accepting, compassionate and understanding. Whether a homeowner knows it or not, he will be reading your body language and picking up signals about your intentions.

Even the simple act of listening to someone's problems or hardships demands a physical response. Let the person know you're paying attention with a positive nod of the head, a verbal "uh-huh" or "okay," or a furrowed brow. Folding your arms in front of your body—as in our experiment—is a closed position that signals to others we are mentally turned off to their words and aren't willing to listen. Instead, when you're talking with a homeowner keep your hands at your sides or on your lap—both receptive, listening positions. Other body language no-no's, obviously, are glancing at your watch, avoiding direct eye contact, and appearing to study the home rather than the homeowner, or being condescending in your approach.

When you listen, you have power.
When you talk, you give it away.

—Voltaire, French philosopher

If you are unsure of or worried about how you come across to others, try having a friend or family member videotape you in a mock conversation with a homeowner, then study the tape. You may be surprised by the effect of the smallest gesture or what you thought was your most innocuous approach. Next time consciously try to correct those wrong moves.

Great Listeners Make Great Property Buyers

One of the greatest psychological needs people have is for other people to listen to them without bias—to totally listen—not just listen waiting for a chance to argue a point or jump in and resume our talking . . . When we fill this need for people, they'll unconsciously want to fill our needs, and the best way for them to do that is to listen to us without bias.

—Ron Willingham, author and founder
of Integrity Systems, Inc.

Great property buyers develop the ability to hear what their sellers, their Realtors, and their buyers are really saying. In doing so, they understand the other's needs and know how to meet those needs while buying and selling property for profit.

The two biggest communications hurdles to overcome for new foreclosure investors are the need to talk about themselves and what they do, and the inability to listen carefully to the sellers' answers. Rather than try to impress or overwhelm the homeowner, buyers must take the time to listen and then respond directly to property owners with open-ended questions about them and their situation.

How great a listener are you? No matter how proficient we think we are, most of us can improve our listening ability. Consider the following ways to hone your own listening skills.

- *Turn off the self-talk*. You cannot hear what someone else is saying if your own thoughts are in the way. Most people talk to themselves while others are talking to them. The rate of speech in your own head is about 600 words per minute, while most of us speak aloud at a rate of only 150 words per minute. So slow down; focus on the other person's words; listen to their needs, and stop thinking about your own.

- *Actually hear what the other person is saying.* Often we allow our mental filters to interpret and change what someone else says. We've all experienced it—those misunderstandings that we commonly pass off in our everyday lives. Our filters are the culprits. They become barriers to actually hearing what someone else is saying. When you're thinking ahead to your next response, your own bias, background, culture, and even your education can all act as filters. Great property buyers eliminate all filters to hear the seller's message clearly.

If your mouth is moving, your ears aren't open.

—Sarah Garlick, ForeclosureS.com coach,
successful foreclosure investor

How to Listen to Property Owners

Do:

- Be attentive.
- Let the other individual know you're listening, with a nod of the head or other occasional acknowledgment.
- Be genuinely concerned.
- Be curious about them and their situation.
- Keep your body relaxed, arms at your sides.
- Respond to a homeowner with open-ended questions about themselves and their situation.

Don't:

- Be critical.
- Look at your wristwatch.
- Talk about yourself.
- Try to impress the other with how much you know.
- Take a condescending approach.
- Study the home rather than the homeowner.
- Ask questions about the home only.

Tone and Trust

If you sincerely focus on the homeowners and not on yourself, they will actually find comfort in talking with you. When you are genuine and caring in your approach, you will connect with homeowners and be successful buying and selling property.

Aspiring foreclosure investor John J. tried the following script to initiate a conversation with a homeowner. See if you can tell why it didn't work.

> Hi, (name). Based on public record information, you are in foreclosure on your home. If you do nothing, you are going to lose your home. I am an investor who pays all cash and can close quickly. What are your loans? What is the equity in your home? Where will you be moving to? How much cash would it take to get this done today? When can we meet?

The script did *not* work because the property, the deal, and the money that the investor would make took center stage, not the homeowner and his problems. Remember, the homeowner doesn't care about you. He cares about himself and how you can help him. Leave the money conversations for later, after you've built rapport.

The approach John should have taken is one that encourages a person in trouble to talk about his woes, puts the emphasis on the homeowner, demonstrates John's empathy, and leaves the door open as to how he can help.

Put yourself in the homeowner's shoes. This is the prime time to consider the old adage: What we sow is what we reap. Be friendly in your tone of voice, line of questioning, and demeanor. On the telephone, people can hear if you're smiling or frowning.

John should have tried this approach instead:

> Hi, (name). This is John Jones. I understand you're having a tough time with your house, and I wondered how I could help . . . How did this happen? . . . What have you been doing to keep your home?

Whoever asks the questions is in control of the conversation. If a homeowner asks you a question, answer it briefly, and then end your response with another question for the homeowner.

—Alexis McGee

What to Say (and Not Say)

Once you've introduced yourself to a homeowner, he will inevitably have dozens of questions to challenge you and your expertise. Don't crumble. Your goal, instead, should be to maintain control of the conversation. Keep in mind that whoever is asking the questions is in control. That means you must learn to briefly and honestly answer a homeowner's questions but always tack another question onto your answer. This is not a way to evade the issues; it's a way to work with property owners so you can truly understand their situation and help them determine the solution that's right for them. Consider the following conversational gambit:

Owner: "Who are you and why are you calling me?"

Investor: "Oh, I'm sorry, this is X. I live nearby in Z, and I help folks in situations like yours. So, how did this happen?"

Note how the investor answered the question, and then ended his response with another question. This is a tough one to master, but you must learn to do it so that you're in control of the conversation and leading it toward answers that can help you help that homeowner.

After you've asked those questions, though, pause and listen for the homeowner's response. Don't answer questions for them, and do not guess what their answer will be.

Don't be put off by typical protestations or objections, either. A few include:

- "No thanks. I've taken care of it."
- "I don't know what you're talking about."
- "You've got the wrong number/person."
- "My spouse is handling it."

That last response can be especially frustrating because, as crazy as it sounds, many people assume their husband or wife is handling everything when, in fact, they're not. Believe it or not, many couples end up without a roof over their heads because of this "don't ask, don't tell" attitude.

Let homeowners speak for themselves. As much as you think you know what they are about to say, let them say it! Never answer for them or make assumptions.

—Alexis McGee

Be conversational in your questions and in your tone to gain a homeowner's trust. Homeowners will respond to you if you actually listen and don't assume you know what they want or that your money will solve all their problems—which, of course, it won't. That's a guarantee.

There is something about a well-worded question that
often penetrates to the heart of the matter and
triggers new ideas and insights.

—Brian Tracy

When the issue of the loan default comes up, and the homeowner's response is, "I've taken care of it," don't back off. Consider instead a response something like, "How have you taken care of it? I'm concerned. I see no record of it at the county recorder. What did you do? When did you send in the money?"

Here's another red flag that the homeowner probably hasn't done anything about his default:

Investor: "What have you done about the default?"

Homeowner: "I'm sending them the money."

Investor: "How? I'm a bit confused here. You haven't had the money to pay the lender so far and now you're going to mail it to them? What's changed?"

In all these scenarios, it's about being inquisitive, skeptical, bold, and not accepting the standard comments made hastily to get rid of you. Note also the continued use of questions and curiosity to help get to the truth about a homeowner's situation.

Improve the Connection

Pay attention to personalizing your communications with property owners, friends, their relatives, and anyone else you work with, too. It's a simple concept and goes a long way toward overcoming someone's doubts about you and your intentions. It also helps to create familiarity and forge a bond.

How do you personalize communications with strangers? In talking with homeowners, use that gossip from the neighbors or your online background research as a way to connect, to form the beginnings of a bond. If your Internet search of military personnel sites revealed that the property owner was a veteran of the war in Iraq and you're a veteran, too, that's a connection. Capitalize on it. Or perhaps a check of local obituaries reveals that the homeowner's mother died this year. Mention it, offer your sympathies, and if you've recently lost your own mom or she's aging, talk about it. This is how you develop rapport with a homeowner, and it will separate you from all the others and put you in a different league. Don't be shy about really getting to know a homeowner, because that's the only way to create a win-win situation for all parties.

That doesn't mean you sugarcoat reality or avoid the issues. It's just that you are there to help, not hurt or take advantage of someone in distress.

Remember Anna, the white-knight investor from Chapter 1 who helped Joaquin and his family keep their home? Even though Joaquin had turned away everyone else, he listened to Anna because she gained his trust. She didn't approach him with a preprogrammed solution or jump to conclusions about how she could help, and she especially didn't go into the situation grubbing for money. She genuinely listened to Joaquin's needs and, in turn, was able to help him come up with the right solution for his particular situation.

You will be able to do the same *if* you start with honesty and persistence, and continue with trust and caring for each person as an individual with a unique set of circumstances. Only by careful listening will you be able to determine what those circumstances are. If you aren't genuine, a homeowner will know it and won't deal with you.

Find out what's most important to a homeowner—
keeping the home, starting over, or whatever—
and then see if you can make that happen.

—Tim Rhode, ForeclosureS.com coach,
successful investor and broker

Appearance Matters

Our physical appearance plays an important role in our ability to communicate successfully. Remember in Chapter 6 when Lawrence, the foreclosure investor, walked up to that seedy home with the rough-looking people outside? Quite deliberately he had thought ahead to the neighborhood he was visiting, the people who lived there, and their likely attire. He dressed accordingly—faded jeans, a T-shirt, and sneakers. That's not to say he looked like a slob. His jeans and T-shirt were clean; his sneakers weren't grimy or hole-y. But he consciously dressed so he would fit in, which is an essential ingredient to building rapport with strangers. How would the people outside that house have confronted Lawrence if he had driven up in a Lexus (which he could easily afford) and wearing a designer suit, starched shirt, and impeccable shoes? Probably not too favorably.

Dress to blend. In this business that means you need to fit in appearance-wise with a neighborhood. That includes your means of transportation. Leave the flashy car at home!

—Alexis McGee

You must think about these things, too, as part of the message you communicate to others. If you're not sure of what to wear to meet a homeowner, drive the neighborhood first. See what fits in, and dress accordingly. (Forget the business cards, too. They're intimidating.) After all, your approach to foreclosure-investing is not to intimidate but to work with homeowners in trouble as their friend, confidant, and guide.

More Tips

If you have to leave a note for a homeowner you don't know, be honest but vague. The less they know, the more likely they are to be curious and call you back. For example: "Hi Bob. Call me as soon as you can. This is Alexis, 555-5555."

When you do reach a homeowner, to help make sure you understand exactly what he—or anyone else—is saying to you, try paraphrasing his statements back to him. Repeat key words to verify what he said. For example, if a homeowner explains a loan issue, respond with, "So, if I understand you correctly . . ."

Stop, listen, and don't end someone else's sentences, either. Jumping to conclusions too quickly can easily derail a conversation.

Recognize, too, that the blame for misunderstandings isn't all on your shoulders. We don't always say what we mean. That's particularly true when you're starting out in this business, as well as for homeowners under the stress and duress of a very public pending foreclosure.

Also, in cases involving default, people aren't always honest the first, second, third, or fourth time you ask the same question. Be persistent and keep asking the question in different ways. You'll know when you hit the truth. The bottom line is that the more you ask, the more likely you are to eventually learn the seller's true story and be able to help accordingly.

Don't get tripped up by questions asked of you, either. So many investors go cold when they ask a question and are hit with a question in return. For example, if you ask a homeowner about his plans for his house, he might snap back, "I don't know. Why are you calling me?" Again, don't wilt. Ask a question right back and stay in control. Why not respond with something like, "Because I can help you as I have countless others in situations like yours. So how did this happen? Are you working?" (Note that the response ended with yet another question!)

Keep in mind what we said earlier: Whoever asks the questions is in control of the conversation, and your goal is to be in control.

Hone Your Communication Skills

ForeclosureS.com coach Sarah Garlick suggests these essentials to enhance your communications skills with homeowners:

- Don't make assumptions. Start with a blank slate. You may think you know why a homeowner is or isn't doing something, but if you assume that, you will miss out on what's really happening and thereby not be able to provide the right solution.

- Think of yourself as a doctor—a highly trained specialist to whom people turn when they're really sick. Homeowners in default are financially sick, and you can help them. Like a doctor, don't diagnose the problem until you know all the facts. You wouldn't want to make a misdiagnosis.

- Don't answer your own questions. No matter how nervous you are on the telephone or in a face-to-face visit, once you ask a question, be quiet, and allow the homeowner to answer. Especially don't offer multiple choice answers. If you do, the homeowner simply will pick a convenient one.

- Let the homeowner do 95 percent of the talking. That means when you're interviewing him, you provide only 5 percent of the conversation.

- Be honest. If what a homeowner tells you doesn't make sense, it's your responsibility to tell him so—gently, but don't be too compliant and polite. This isn't the corporate world. You are your own boss. You have a license to speak the truth.

- Follow the old sales adage: People don't care how much you know until they know how much you care.

Don't ask confrontational or condescending questions, either, or you'll come across as an interrogator and repulse a homeowner rather than attract him. Start your conversations with simple questions that build rapport and trust, and then work your way to the tougher financial ones that ultimately must be answered.

A Drill for Improvement

Here's another exercise. Put a tape recorder on your desk or in the top drawer and record your next 10 telephone conversations. Then listen to what you said, keeping the following thoughts in mind:

- How many questions did you ask?
- How many questions did you answer without a follow-up question?
- Try to identify one element of your listening and questioning skills that needs improvement. Then, every day, focus on changing it. Once you see results, start working on the next skill that needs improvement.

At some point, you will become a great listener, and, of course, that means you'll be a great property buyer, too!

Getting to the Closing

As we've discussed, building rapport with and learning about a property owner is essential to the success of your efforts. This must be your first goal when you initially contact a property owner, whether on the telephone or in person. You must radiate your urge to help them and get them to trust you so they eventually will listen to your recommendations.

To help you determine if selling a property to you is in a homeowner's best interests, be thought-provoking in your questions. Some possible questions:

- What do you hope to have happen?
- Have you talked to your current lender?
- Have you tried to get a loan?
- If so, why hasn't it closed yet?
- Where will you move to, and how much is your new rent?

Try using questions the sellers would be able to answer after they have sold their property to you—questions that mentally throw them into the future and assume the deal is already done.

Asking questions is an art and takes a lot of practice. And remember: Once you've proposed to purchase a property, *be quiet*. The next person who talks will *not* own the property!

You won't close them all, but if you actively pay attention to your communication skills along with developing the right prospects, you will start closing sales. At first it may be only 1 out of 20, but don't despair. You will simply have room for improvement.

> *Once you've pitched a purchase deal to a homeowner, be quiet. The next person to talk will not own the property.*
>
> —Alexis McGee

Power to Motivate Others

Renowned motivator, author, and speaker Jim Rohn suggests two personality powers that you can develop to increase your charisma and ability to influence others: purpose and self-motivation.

Men and women with charisma and personal magnetism almost invariably have a clear vision of who they are, where they're going, and what they hope to achieve. Leaders in sales and management have a vision of what they want to create and why. They focus on accomplishing some great purpose and are decisive about every aspect of their lives. They know exactly what they want and what they must do to get it. You can increase your charisma and magnetism by setting clear goals for yourself, making plans to achieve them, and working on your plans with discipline and determination every single day.

The second personality power is self-confidence. Men and women with charisma have an intense belief in themselves and in what they are doing. They are usually calm, cool, and composed about themselves and their work. Your level of self-confidence is often demonstrated in your courage and your willingness to do whatever is necessary to achieve a purpose you believe in. People are naturally attracted to those who exude a sense of self-confidence, those who have an unshakable belief in their ability to rise above circumstances to attain their goals.

You can demonstrate self-confidence by assuming that people naturally like and accept you and want to do business with you. For example, one of the most powerful ways to close a sale is simply to assume that the prospect has decided to purchase the product or service, and then go on to wrap up the details.

Believe in yourself and what you do. It's what
motivates others to believe in you, too.

—Alexis McGee

Think about how increased self-confidence and power of purpose can help you communicate with homeowners and help them solve their financial dilemmas while generating profits for yourself.

Beware the Fatal Mistakes

Master foreclosure investors recognize the importance of guarding against five critical mistakes when it comes to negotiating and discussing solutions with homeowners in default. Pay attention to these deal busters, and you'll buy more properties, make better deals, and feel more comfortable about the entire process.

Do Not Defend or Attack

Be open to understanding a property seller's situation and beliefs. Consider his proposals as options, and then talk about other possible solutions to the problem. When you are defensive about your suggestions or attack a potential seller verbally, you lose credibility, rapport, and the sale.

If the seller attacks you verbally, try to understand the intention behind the attack. Understandably, people in pre-foreclosure often feel vulnerable and stigmatized. Ask yourself what they hope to gain or are trying to protect themselves from. When a person launches an attack, he expects a counterattack. Responding in kind and attacking the other party usually only escalates the situation and makes that person more defensive. If you attack or counterattack a seller, he will defend his position, no matter how untenable, rather than run the risk of seeming weak by giving in to you.

Instead of offending or defending, be curious. Curiosity is a valuable tool to defuse anger, learn more about a situation, and discover creative solutions to problems. Remember the earlier scenario of the homeowner who, when asked his plans for his house, came back with the challenge, "Why are you calling me?" The investor, instead of defending his presence as expected, simply explained he could help, and then turned curious with the question, "So how did this happen?" With enough questions and polite, gentle persistence on your part, a homeowner may begin to open up and talk with you so that you can help. Most likely it won't be on the first call and probably not the second call, and maybe not even the third. But if you can establish rapport and convince homeowners that you care, they will remember you and come back to you for help. Then if they decide to sell the home, it will be to you.

Avoid Insults

Stay focused on your intended outcome—closing the deal. Do not try to gain leverage by putting down the other person. If someone insults you, don't respond in kind. Treat the insult instead as an attack on a problem that you both face and both want to solve.

In this business, you often find yourself working with and buying properties from people who do not have good people skills. The tenuousness of their situation can make them more insecure, insensitive, or short-tempered. Don't fall victim to exchanging insults with them. That damages the relationship, sidetracks the negotiation, and will cost you deals. Simply understand and forgive them.

Avoid Blame and Do Not Accuse

Placing blame seldom helps resolve conflict and never helps make a deal. If a problem arises, address it as an opportunity to find a solution. If you try to assign blame for the situation the seller is in, it's the same as if you attacked him. He will likely become defensive and not sell at all.

Instead, from the beginning be clear about your goal. Is it to find a workable solution and make a deal, or do you want to force the seller to admit he made a mistake and is at fault? Obviously, it's not the latter.

Do Not Give Too Many Reasons or Justifications

Provide the homeowner with only a few reasons for your proposed solution or sale. Most people won't listen to lengthy justifications, anyway. Besides, you may need a little ammunition in the form of additional justification later to seal the deal with a homeowner.

Figure on the "rule of three." Give one to three main reasons for your proposal, and then let the other side evaluate your reasons. Present your most compelling reasons first. If the seller agrees with you, move on. If he disagrees, try to understand the objections before offering additional arguments.

Avoid Poker Tactics

Successful master sales negotiators in the foreclosure investing business do not use tricks or manipulation. Avoid bluffing or misleading your prospect. Do not use emotional outbursts to try to manipulate the other party, either. Be honest and sincere.

First-Deal Jitters

Picture this. You've been on the phone with a homeowner many times trying to help resolve his financial nightmare. You have tried to get the existing lender to do a workout plan for the homeowner. You have asked the seller to call family and friends to see if anyone can bail him out. You even had the seller call your mortgage broker for a refinance or a new junior loan. You've guided the homeowner through the process of listing the house through an agent or doing a "for sale by owner" (FSBO). But for whatever reason, you now are facing a homeowner who can't make any of these solutions work. He turns to you, and says, "Hey, I'm sick and tired of trying to save this house. Why don't you just buy it from me?"

Whoa! What do you do now? You had better know the answer to that question ahead of time, because this will happen to you. If you treat a homeowner with dignity and respect, he or she will look to only you for help.

This scenario actually happened to Mary Kay on her first deal. After an initial panic, she regrouped her thoughts, crunched the numbers, wrote the contract, opened escrow, reviewed title, found and negotiated with a contractor to rehab the home, and created a plan to sell the property. "You were honest with me," the homeowner told her later. "You were the only one I trusted to help me."

The deal went through; the homeowner walked away with cash in her pocket and clean credit, and Mary Kay later resold the property for a handsome profit.

You can do it, too!

TAKEaway

Key points to remember:

- Communication is much more than just words. Pay attention to the message conveyed by your body language, appearance, and tone of voice.

- Your goal should be to come across as open and accepting, compassionate and caring, yet honest and straightforward, too.

- Great listeners make great property buyers. Truly hear what the other person is saying.

- Look for common ground or other ways to establish rapport with the other person.

- Turn off the self-talk. A homeowner wants help with solving his or her dilemma and really doesn't care what's happening in your life.

- Whoever asks the questions is in control of the conversation.

- Don't be offensive or defensive in your communication. If under verbal attack, try to understand why. Be curious. You'll be surprised at how much you'll learn from a conversation.

- Personalize your communications. One size—as in the same pat, memorized approach to conversation—does not fit all.

- Do not bluff or mislead a homeowner. It's all about that Golden Rule, one more time: Treat someone as you would like them to treat you if you were in similar straits.

CHAPTER 9

Recognizing Fraud and the Scams

If someone is going down the wrong road, he doesn't need motivation to speed him up. What he needs is education to turn him around.

—Jim Rohn

The headlines read "Foreclosure Scams on the Rise," "Mortgage Loan Fraud," "Lenders in Trouble," and "Scammers Target Homeowners." In these stories, the victims are usually homeowners and banking institutions. The stories, however, fail to mention an often hidden victim: would-be investors who are lured by the siren song of some self-proclaimed gurus. As foreclosure numbers have skyrocketed, so have the numbers of certain gurus who will charge potential investors hefty prices for their exclusive *secrets* to foreclosure buying and tremendous wealth.

Who are these people and what do they mean to you? Many are very good salespeople capitalizing on the latest hot trend. They know how to develop multi-level marketing systems that collect plenty of money from ordinary people interested in improving their financial footing by getting involved in foreclosure investing.

Other gurus are more slippery and the results more ominous for those potential investors who adopt their approach and for the homeowners they target. These salesmen tout hush-hush marketing techniques to invest in foreclosures that are often unethical, dishonest, and illegal. They actually teach potential investors how to perpetrate fraud against homeowners, lenders, and others. The fraud may involve two sets of contracts, hidden agendas, usurious loans, bait and switch, and outright lies. Some of these gurus aggressively market directly to consumers through fliers on telephone poles, late-night infomercials, and spam pop-ups on your computer screens. These gurus promise instant riches if only you hand over the cash.

Government Agencies Get Involved

We talked about these numbers earlier: Home ownership is up, foreclosures are up, and mortgage loan fraud is up, too. In fact, the latter is spiraling upward at a mind-boggling pace. The number of suspicious activity reports (SARs) relating to mortgage loan frauds was up a whopping 1,411 percent between 1997 and 2005, with 2006 numbers showing no sign of slowing down, according to the Financial Crimes Enforcement Network (FinCEN) of the U.S. Department of Treasury. FinCEN is the government organization charged with keeping abreast of and tracking financial crimes. As the fraud numbers have skyrocketed, so have the numbers of victimized homeowners forced into foreclosure as a result—from Florida to Massachusetts to Colorado to California.

Fraudsters use public records to locate homeowners in default on their mortgages and then contact them, often presenting themselves as rescuers who will help distressed homeowners keep their home in exchange for a fee. But these people send a warning signal that it's essential to heed: They advise homeowners *not* to communicate with their lender or an attorney. In fact, those are the first people a homeowner *should* contact when trouble looms.

Another Kind of Victim

Although FinCEN and other organizations tally the numbers of homeowners and lenders hurt in these scams, it's much more difficult to track the victims of self-proclaimed foreclosure-investing gurus. Many well-meaning investors spend tens of thousands of dollars on the promise of making big money if they fork over the cash.

Unfortunately, the gurus seldom deliver.

Misleading Messages

The messages of these so-called experts echo with phrases such as "secrets," "true stories, true successes," "guaranteed," "instant cash," "get rich," "click here to be a millionaire," and other far-fetched promises. Their messages perpetrate myths and misconceptions about foreclosure investing. Here's a look at a few of the come-ons and the truth behind the rhetoric.

You Can Get Rich Overnight!

Success in the foreclosure-investing business, as we've emphasized, takes hard work and know-how. The financial and emotional rewards can be huge. But to achieve such rewards, you must learn to use the tools and ethical systems necessary to build your business—something that doesn't happen overnight.

You Can Get a House for Only $1,000!

A homeowner doesn't hand over the keys without getting something in return. An honest investor structures win-win deals so that the homeowner gets cash for some

Check It Out

To find out more about the scams and frauds out there, check out any of the following:

- ACORN: Association of Community Organizations for Reform Now (www.acorn.org).
- Federal Trade Commission Bureau of Consumer Protection (www.ftc.gov/bcp/consumer.htm).*
- FinCEN: Financial Crimes Enforcement Network of the U.S. Department of the Treasury (www.fincen.gov).
- Inman News (www.inman.com).
- Justin Leonard's Infomercialscams.com (www.infomercialscams.com).
- National Consumer Law Center (www.consumerlaw.org).
- Rip-off Report.com (www.ripoffreport.com).
- Scam.com (www.scam.com).

*The FTC does not resolve individual consumer problems, but your complaint helps them investigate fraud and can lead to law enforcement action.

of the equity and a fresh start. The investor, of course, gets a great deal on a home that he can fix up, turn around, and then sell for a profit.

You Don't Have to Work That Hard!

Success takes arduous work, persistence, and follow-up. But ask those successful white-knight investors if the hard work is worth it, and they'll resoundingly say yes. There's nothing quite like fulfilling your financial and emotional dreams.

The Different Approach

As you've read, the white-knight approach to foreclosure investing *is* different. The so-called secrets, which really aren't, are compassion, honesty, persistence, and common sense. White-knight foreclosure investors are honest and aboveboard. They make money, but they also try to help countless owners in default resolve their financial dilemmas in a positive manner.

Let's briefly look at some of the fraud schemes that FinCEN and other organizations and institutions have uncovered.

Sale-Leaseback

This is touted as the easy deal: Persuade the homeowner to hand over the deed to his house for little or no money with the promise that he can stay in the home and lease it back with the option to repurchase in one year. The owner in default gets to keep his house and his embarrassing secret to himself. It sounds great, but there's a catch. The new monthly rent payment is higher than the old mortgage that the homeowner couldn't afford in the first place. When the former owner—now tenant—misses a month's rent, the investor evicts him and sells the house.

A variation on this theme is that the former homeowner stays the year and makes his monthly rental payments but still can't get the house back. The option to buy after his term ends has now somehow vanished.

Let's look at the numbers in this kind of a deal using as the example a $100,000 house in foreclosure with a $50,000 balance on the mortgage. The homeowner is behind $5,000 in mortgage payments, so the investor agrees to make up the back payments in exchange for taking title to the home. He then leases back the home to the now former homeowner and gives him an option to buy it back for $100,000, the home's fair market value.

It sounds okay, but again there's a catch, one that leaves the investor out in the cold. Often these former homeowners will go to court and claim that the sale/leaseback was really just a disguised loan. Their attorney will ask the court to recharacterize the transaction as a loan and place title to the property back in the *original* homeowner's name. The court often agrees that the loan is illegal because it's *usurious*—it carries a higher interest rate than permitted by law. In our $100,000 scenario, the investor has *loaned* the homeowner $5,000 at 1,000 percent interest. The investor basically gave the homeowner $5,000, and the homeowner must repay $50,000—the $100,000 option price minus the $50,000 mortgage balance. The consequences to the investor: He loses the house and the $5,000, too.

If this happens and an investor gets caught making usurious loans on a regular basis, it's a criminal offense and the penalty is prison.

Predatory Lending

These are lenders who offer loans to folks unable to make a single payment. If the homeowner has any equity, these lenders will take it in the form of exorbitant loan fees, usurious interest rates, and unconscionable prepayment penalties. New laws have been passed to prohibit predatory lending practices, but it is still not difficult to find people who are willing to loan money to an owner in default using these practices. They simply can't resist all the money up front, and then they get to own the house and sell it for a big profit.

TALES FROM FORECLOSURE INVESTORS

A struggling young couple paid a man who they thought was an honest mortgage broker $12,000 to help them refinance. He promised them $40,000 in the deal; they got $8,000! He also locked them into a 15-year mortgage which shot their already too-high monthly payments beyond affordability altogether. Adding to their woes, the same broker promised $500 for any referrals, so the couple referred a family member. The family member, too, was misled and ended up with an unaffordable mortgage.

Read Up on Predatory Lending

Good sources of information and direction related to predatory lending include:

- Association of Community Organizations for Reform Now (ACORN): www .acorn.org.
- Consumers Union: www.consumersunion.org.
- U.S. Office of Housing and Urban Development: www.hud.gov/buying/localpred lend.cfm.

Some of those predatory lending practices include:

- Frequent loan refinancing with no benefit to the borrower and simply to generate lender fees.

- Equity stripping, as mentioned earlier: persuading a homeowner to take out a loan beyond his ability to repay.

- Bait and switch, in which a lender advertises one set of rates and fees that suddenly zoom upward at closing.

- Inflated appraisals up front force larger loans at higher rates; a homeowner can't refinance the total loan amount later because the home's value is less than the loan amount.

Organizations such as the Association of Community Organizations for Reform Now (www.acorn.org), the Consumers Union (www.consumersunion.org), and the U.S. Department of Housing and Urban Development (www.hud.gov) offer valuable insight into predatory lending and what can be and is being done to combat it.

Loss Mitigation

Also known as "I Stop Foreclosure (for a fee)," these guys offer to help people keep their homes, and they collect an up-front fee for doing so. Red flags should go up on this one! The rescuer calls the lender on the homeowner's behalf and magically gets the lenders to do a loan modification or workout plan so the owner can keep his home.

The *rescuer* gets paid no matter what. Unfortunately, many homeowners don't realize that if they run into financial trouble, the very first thing they should do is call their lender themselves. They don't need this third party to broker the deal. But they're afraid to call the lender on their own because most delinquent borrowers see the lender as another bill collector who doesn't care. As we mentioned earlier, these homeowners simply won't pick up the phone and tell the lender their story.

Freddie Mac, together with Roper Public Affairs and Media, part of GFK Customer Research NA, surveyed delinquent borrowers in 2005 and found that more than 6 in 10, or 61 percent, of late-paying borrowers were unaware of workout options for short-term financial difficulties. Oddly enough, 75 percent of those delinquent borrowers recalled being contacted by their mortgage-servicing company. Consider some of the reasons why these delinquent borrowers said they didn't contact their mortgage servicer, according to the survey:

- There was no reason to talk to their servicers: 28 percent.
- They could take care of the payment problems without any help: 28 percent.
- Only 7 percent said they didn't call because they didn't have the money to make the payment.
- Embarrassment was a reason for not calling: 6 percent.
- Fear was the reason for not calling: 5 percent.
- They didn't know who to call about their problem: 5 percent.

An earlier Freddie Mac survey (2004) concluded that if only homeowners in default would talk to their lenders, repayment plans could lower the probability of home loss due to foreclosure by 80 percent among all borrowers and 68 percent among low- to moderate-income borrowers. This is just one more reason why you can do so much to help so many people if you approach this business with an honorable attitude.

List and Sell, or I'll Buy Your House

This scheme is being sold to real estate agents and brokers who want another income stream. The idea is for the agent to make an appointment for a listing presentation with an owner in default whose auction is 60 days away. As part of the listing agreement, the agent offers the homeowner a guarantee to sell the house or else he will buy it. On the surface, this sounds great for the owner. But here's the kicker: The agent overprices the house on the MLS so that no one wants to buy it. Then he offers to buy it for substantially less than the listing price.

Did the agent *really* try to sell the house or was it priced so it wouldn't sell and he could step in and buy it on the cheap? What was the agent's true intention—selling the house or buying it? It's tough to prove or disprove good faith on the agent's part.

That's one reason why it's important to wear only one hat when you meet with the owner. Help him either list or sell the home, or else refer the owner to another agent to list and sell. That way, if the homeowner needs an investor, you are available without having to worry about any potential or perceived conflict of interest.

A note of caution: If you're a licensed real estate agent or loan broker as well as a foreclosure investor, you're bound by two sets of laws—those that cover foreclosure investing in your state as well as your state's Department of Real Estate rules. Beware of conflicts of interest, too. If you wear multiple hats, you must be conscious of good-faith effort and more.

Bait-and-Switch Bully

Timing is key here. The scammer shows up at the end of the foreclosure process and promises the homeowner top dollar to buy the house. If it's already in contract, no problem. He'll pay $5,000 more if you cancel that contract and sign with him. Sounds good, right? Wrong. The rescuer drags out escrow until the very last minute before auction, and then tells the homeowner that his original offer was too high and he must pay substantially less for the house. The poor homeowner is cornered by the foreclosure deadline and has no other alternatives. The owner must accept the offer or lose the house at auction.

To ensure that the deal goes through, the would-be buyer adds a hint of threat with statements such as, "The sheriff will be here in just a few days to throw you out." Of course, that isn't quite true, but the homeowner most often doesn't know his state's foreclosure laws.

Hide It in the Contract

Hiding bombshells in the contract works like the bait and switch, but instead of waiting until the eleventh hour to renegotiate the deal, the scam perpetrator hides his true intentions in his contract with the homeowner. The contract is fat and cumbersome anyway, and a homeowner in default often has no idea what he is signing. Such homeowners rarely have the resources to go to an attorney for legal advice, either. So, at close of escrow, the buyer suddenly realizes all those "repair deductions" built into the contract ended up costing much more than expected. But there's no time now to verify or negotiate such line items, so the homeowner is stuck. He either signs at closing or loses his house to foreclosure.

A Note on Property Flipping

Property flipping is a term we hear frequently these days when it comes to buying and selling real estate. The media bandy the phrase about all the time. Unfortunately, it means different things to different people in different contexts, and the result is confusion.

Actually, every time someone buys a property—wholesale, retail, lease-option, or owner-financing—and then sells it, they're *flipping* it. It's either a quick flip or a slow flip, but it's a flip nonetheless.

Obviously, buying and selling a property isn't illegal. What is illegal is the *illegal* buying and selling of property. That means transactions involving false appraisals that artificially inflate or deflate the price of a home, duplicate contracts, and more. FinCEN, the agency of the U.S. Treasury, describes fraudulent property flipping as "purchasing property and artificially inflating its value. The fraud perpetrators frequently use identity theft, straw borrowers, and industry insiders to effect property-flipping schemes. Ultimately, the property is resold for 50 to 100 percent of its original cost. In the end, the loan amount exceeds the value of the property and the lender sustains a loss when the loan defaults."

To protect yourself, the homeowners, and the sellers whom you're trying to help, and even potential buyers of any property you may flip, pay attention to federal and state laws that address buying and selling—and flipping—of properties.

No matter what the intentions, you must avoid the following illegal activities:

- Do not pay an appraiser to overvalue your property so you can get a bigger loan for your buyers or your refinance.

- Do not create side deals with your buyers so they don't have to put up the lenders' required minimum down payment.

- Do not modify lender-required documents to get your buyer approved when your buyer would not be approved if the lender were aware of the true situation. An example of this is giving the lender phony tax returns showing inflated income to get the buyer qualified.

- Do not change lease agreements (for instance, back-dating them) to create a track record of payments that weren't actually made so you can refinance.

Anytime an actual situation or circumstance differs from what is presented to the lender, a fraud is being perpetrated—no matter how many people engage in the process. And when you defraud a financial institution, that can mean a long stay in a federal penitentiary!

TAKEaway

Key points to remember:

- As a foreclosure investor, you must pay attention to red flags. If something sounds too good to be true—for you or a homeowner—it usually is, especially when it comes to foreclosure investing.

- Whether it is a homeowner hoping to keep his home or an investor hoping to make a difference, anyone involved in foreclosure investing needs to temper their compassion with a healthy degree of skepticism.

- Homeowners in default need to be aware of how easily they can be scammed. Those headlines in the news tell the story. Mortgage and foreclosure scams happen every day. Unsuspecting and vulnerable homeowners living with the threat of homelessness fall victim all the time.

- Foreclosure investors get scammed, too. Never give away your money until you have thoroughly checked out a teacher or guru. You wouldn't choose a family doctor, buy a car, or pick a college without first checking it out or Googling them. It should be the same when it comes to the foreclosure investing business.

- Property flipping is *not* illegal if you do it right. That means pay attention to laws that may relate to it, and document your improvements and expenses involved.

CHAPTER 10

Tips, Timing, and Math

The key factor that will determine your financial future is not the economy; the key factor is your philosophy.

—Jim Rohn

Your expertise and commitment are paramount in being financially successful in this business and helping homeowners resolve their foreclosure woes. But expertise isn't the whole story. Timing, tenacity, and charisma play key roles, too.

Do your homework, pay attention to details—especially the laws—stay focused, consider the other guy, and never allow yourself to become discouraged. You must be ready to seize any and every opportunity to help people save their homes. In the process, you will maximize the chances of finding great deals that lead to your own personal financial gain as well.

Nothing Is Easy!

If you question whether you can do all this and keep your sanity, too, consider the tale of ForeclosureS.com coach Mary Kay. She is now a successful foreclosure investor, but she didn't start out that way. It took her four weeks of dead-end leads, tears, and self-doubt before she purchased her first pre-foreclosure home.

From the curb, the house looked abandoned, nearly engulfed by a tangle of overgrown bushes, trees, and weeds. The front door was barely visible, and no car was in the driveway. Pushing aside vegetation and spider webs, Mary Kay rang the doorbell and knocked several times. No answer. Hearing music and voices next door, Mary Kay fought her way across the yard to see if the neighbors could help her connect with the homeowner.

The neighbors were very friendly but spoke little English. With their six-year-old acting as an interpreter, they finally understood that Mary Kay wanted to reach their neighbor. One of them crawled through a broken section of the backyard fence and emerged a few minutes later with the homeowner—we'll call her Anita.

Anita must have sensed Mary Kay's sincerity because she took her back through the fence and into her home, which definitely needed work. In fact, as Anita showed her the house, Mary Kay thought to herself: "Do I really want to tackle this project even if we can work something out?" The kitchen and bathrooms showed extensive water damage and would need to be replaced entirely. Stains on the ceiling indicated a leaky roof, and Mary Kay wondered if the wiring had been affected. Virtually every window but the front one was broken and boarded with plywood, and the back yard was even more of a jungle than the front. Then Mary Kay stopped herself. "I'm supposed to be helping Anita save her house before I even think of buying and rehabbing it!"

As Mary Kay talked with Anita, she discovered that Anita had been given the home by her father when he fell ill. When Anita lost her job, she fell behind on the payments and couldn't make necessary repairs. But Anita was reluctant to call the lender, explain the situation, and ask for a loan modification or forbearance (temporary financial relief) because she was so embarrassed by the property's disrepair and circumstances. Even though she now had another good job, she didn't want anyone to see her home as run-down as it was. It turns out that Anita also had a drug habit that she desperately wanted to kick.

Mary Kay immediately worked with Anita to contact the lender. Unfortunately, with the trustee sale only 40 days away, the foreclosure process was in full swing. Anita didn't have enough income to cover an increase in monthly mortgage payments, and the lender said no to any loan modification or forbearance. Refinancing was out, too, because Anita had been in her new job only four months, which was too short a time to qualify for a new loan. Anita had already talked to Realtors about selling the home conventionally but was discouraged by the extensive repairs they said were necessary. Besides, she felt humiliated at the prospect of people tromping through her home.

Fast-forward several weeks: With the phone disconnected for nonpayment, the power due to be disconnected in three days, and the notice of trustee sale posted on the door, a desperate and afraid Anita called Mary Kay from a pay phone. She wanted her to buy the home. The two talked about what Anita needed and what Mary Kay could afford, then settled on a fair price they considered a win-win for both of them. Anita would get enough cash to start over and her credit would be brought current because the deal would involve subject-to financing. Mary Kay could afford to have the repairs made and then resell the house for a profit. Everything should have been smooth sailing, but an unforeseen snag almost scuttled the deal.

"Although Anita and I settled on a fair price which would give her a good start at a new future, we had a big problem," says Mary Kay. "Turns out the home's title from Dad to Anita had not been done through an insured transaction from a title company. That situation had to be corrected so I could get clear title. Dad, naturally, lived out of town, so I jumped on a plane Sunday morning and traveled to Dad's to get the necessary document. Plus, on a Sunday, mind you, I had to find an interpreter who was also a notary to get Dad's signature notarized. Then back on the plane Sunday night with the documents, and off to the title company Monday morning to stop the sale scheduled for Tuesday. Thank goodness for a fantastic escrow/title officer who worked the Saturday before the sale to help me out with the details. Without her I would have lost the deal!"

Anita, at last able to have enough money to pay for a drug treatment program and a new start, was as happy as Mary Kay with the deal. Mary Kay gave her two weeks to move out but promised a bonus if she moved out sooner. Three days later Anita called Mary Kay and said everything was out of the house. The two of them traveled together to get the closing statement and final payment.

"I had bought my first notice of default property," Mary Kay recalls. "I thanked the next-door neighbors with a check for $1,000, and they used it to finish the remodel on their home. Anita took her money, kicked her drug habit, and went back to nursing school. She located a safe apartment for herself and her daughter and bought new furniture and a far better car."

The remodel—every bit as extensive as Mary Kay had thought it would be—took her contractor more than a month to finish but turned out beautifully. Mary Kay decided to try selling the property "by owner." With the help of dozens of strategically placed signs directing traffic to the newly refurbished home, she sold it the first weekend on the market.

"Anita, the neighbors who helped connect us, the contractor, the escrow/title company, and the new owners all profited from this deal," Mary Kay says. "When I collected my check from escrow after resale, I knew this path was the right decision. I had been able to help so many people that my heart sang aloud, and my pocketbook was full to the brim."

Mary Kay hasn't looked back since. You can make the same choice she did. With the right approach to foreclosure investing, you will help others as well as yourself.

Let's look at a few more tips to help ensure your success at this rewarding way of making a difference.

What Makes a Deal Work

Real estate is a people business. You must be comfortable with talking to people and asking thought-provoking, open-ended questions that are relevant to them. The owners will answer only what you ask, and if you don't ask, you will never get to the truth. Of course, as we've mentioned, you must be sensitive in your approach and listen to what homeowners have to say. Don't answer your own questions.

If you assume you know the answers, you aren't genuinely asking questions, and when you're not asking the questions, you can't get to the truth. Without the truth, you cannot help someone find the right solution, nor can you offer them a beneficial reason for accepting your suggestions. When you can't offer a solution and show its benefits, you don't have a deal.

There's no point in offering someone cash to walk away from their home unless you can show that person how and why the cash will benefit them. If buying the house makes the most sense, you must answer the following questions to put together a deal that works:

- What does the homeowner need the cash for?

- How much do they really need to make a new start? That means money left over after paying off debts.

- How does your offer benefit the homeowner in dollars and cents? Break it down so that the individual can see the actual gain.

Let's look more closely at these questions and how they relate to Mary Kay's deal with Anita:

- Anita needed the cash to start her life over, get off drugs, go back to school, get a new apartment and car, and pay off credit cards and personal debts.

- To make a new start she needed $25,000 in cash after paying off her debts.

- The deal's dollar-and-cents benefits included:

  - Having enough cash to buy food for herself, her child, and her pets.

  - Purchasing a reliable car so that she could get to work (because she had trouble getting to work in her old car, her job was in jeopardy).

  - Getting professional treatment for her drug problem.

HOW THE NUMBERS ADDED UP FOR MARY KAY

Here's a look at the numbers in Mary Kay's deal with Anita. To determine her offering price, Mary Kay used comparable sales and market prices of properties in the area as well as figuring in the estimated costs of repairs and more. Her timing was right, too. The local market soared between the time she purchased the property and resold it.

Estimated market value at time of purchase	**$200,000**	
Actual purchase price:		
Subject to first deed of trust/liens/taxes		$86,000
Cash to Anita at closing		$25,000
Total purchase price		**<$111,000>**
Cost of repairs to property after purchase		<$40,000>
Buy, hold, and selling costs		<$16,000>
Total invested before resale		**<$167,000>**
Actual resale value	**$242,000**	
Net profit	**$75,000**	

Ten Commandments of Prospecting Property Sellers

We've already detailed the basics of finding pre-foreclosure properties, how to cull those preliminary lists of properties, and the importance of getting on the phone to identify the very best prospects. Here are a few more things to keep in mind when working your leads. If you follow these "Ten Commandments of Prospecting Sellers," chances are you will hit pay dirt and your business will overflow with prospects.

1. *Make an appointment* with yourself each day to review new foreclosure-owner leads. Prospecting requires discipline.

2. *Be prepared* before you make your calls. Before you can prospect, you must weed your leads for those properties with 30 percent or more equity, on the one loan in default. (Don't get stuck doing full title research on a property before you make calls.) Remember, if a homeowner has that equity in a property, he will want to salvage it either by selling or doing something proactive to save the house.

3. *Have a supply*—at least one month's worth-of qualified leads on hand at all times.

4. *Make the phone calls*—as many as possible. Because you already defined your target market when you weeded your leads, you need to call your prospects. Set a goal to spend 20 hours a week or more on the phone.

5. *Make the most of your calls*—don't hurry people. It takes time to get some-one to open up and give you their full attention. Your goal for the call is to get to the truth, not make an appointment. Only then can you offer the homeowner sound advice just as you would if he were a member of your family.

6. *Work without interruption.* Don't take other calls or allow yourself to get sidetracked during your prospecting time. The more calls you make, the bet-ter those calls become. Interruptions disrupt the quality flow.

7. *Prospect during off hours* when you're more likely to reach homeowners. Con-ventional business hours are 9 A.M. to 5 P.M. Make your calls earlier in the morning, during the typical lunch hour, after 5 P.M., or on Saturdays. Don't al-ways call at the same time, either. Try different times and different days.

8. *Be organized.* Use a contact management system (electronic or print) that al-lows you easily to record follow-up calls whether tomorrow, the next day, or three months from now.

9. *Visualize the end* before you begin. Establish a goal and then develop a plan to work toward that goal.

10. *Don't stop.* Persistence is a key virtue for success in this business.

Math Matters

For Mary Kay to put together that win-win deal for Anita and herself, she had to figure the numbers correctly. That meant knowing ahead of time the local resale market and her anticipated expenses, including the cost to repair Anita's home and to hold the home until its resale.

One of the biggest—and costliest—mistakes new foreclosure investors can make is failing to figure accurately their own expenses in a deal. If, for example, the average time on market for resale of a like home in a specific area is eight weeks, you must determine what it will cost you to hold on to a home—and pay its bills—for eight weeks. You must also figure the cost to repair the property to neighborhood standards (we talk more about that in Chapter 13). It's not good enough to guesstimate the cost of repairs unless you are a contractor and already know what repairs cost. You must know how to identify needed repairs and up-grades, and then determine the actual cost to make those improvements to the property.

Your Offer Price

Most new investors really don't know what to pay for a foreclosure property. They think if it's in foreclosure, they'll just give the seller as little as possible and take over their loans, right? Wrong! You must know how to structure win-win deals to give your sellers the most possible so that they say yes to your offer and you can buy more houses and make more money. So where do you start?

My offer formula is really simple. As in any business, first determine the re-sale value of the product, then deduct your costs—in this case buy, fix, hold, sell, and profit. What's left is what you can pay for a property. Figuring into the equa-tion, too, are the seller's needs—the amount of cash payment he needs at the end of escrow so that the deal is win-win for both of you. To be a viable deal, the seller needs to have enough equity (existing loans and liens must be substantially less than what you want to pay for his house) so you can do the deal.

Be conservative in your resale pricing, too. It's better to get overbids on a newly listed house and sell it quickly than be forced to lower your asking price and pray for a buyer many months later. Never get caught holding a house that doesn't break even or better on rental income, either. You may have to hold a fall purchase until spring for the buying season to begin, so those six months should not provide negative cash flow. Typically, move-up or high-end houses do not break even. That's because prices have become disconnected from the rental market, especially in the overheated bicoastal markets. That's just one more reason to stay away from ex-pensive, move-up homes.

In my 20-plus years in the real estate business,
I've never lost money on a deal.

—Alexis McGee

Determining the Resale Value

You'll need a market value range for the property to help determine its resale value once it's fixed up. That amount should be based on comps—prices of com-parable property sales in the same neighborhood in the past six months. Keep in mind, though, the comps are strictly a starting point to help you weed your leads. The real value of a property will depend on market conditions at the time of sale and more.

When you are about to write an offer for a property, you need to know as closely as possible how much you can sell the property for *after* it's fixed up. Estimated market values aren't enough. Instead, you need an appraisal of the future value of the fixed-up property. But you won't have the time (or money) to hire an appraiser so you must learn to do your own appraisals.

Appraising for the Future

To do that, put on your rose-colored glasses and look ahead to visualize your prospective property with all the repairs completed—new paint, flooring, updated kitchen and bathrooms, clean landscaping, and more. (We detail which repairs provide the most bang for your buck in Chapter 13.) What is that fixed-up house worth? That's your starting point.

To help you find the details on accurate, comparable properties in an area, you'll need access to a credible source of data. A Zillow.com Zestimate, though free, isn't accurate enough. If you are using a premium foreclosure listing service, for a small additional fee you should be able to get a full report of recent comparable sales for a property on that web site. If your listing service doesn't have that information, you can subscribe to fee-based databases like SiteXdata (www.sitexdata.com) from Fidelity National Data Services (FNDS), First American Real Estate Solutions (www.firstamres.com), DataQuick Information Systems (www.dataquick.com), local Realtor Multiple Listing Services, or local title companies.

Your comparable sales report should list all houses that have sold within a quarter-mile radius of the home you're interested in (you can go out as far as one mile if needed) within the past six months. These sold houses must be similar in size, age, and style to the house you are appraising. Do not use fixer-upper comparables with low market values. You are looking for the *most* you can get for your house when it's in top condition after it's repaired and rehabbed. Then check your local MLS using Realtor.com, Metrolist.com, and others for all active properties on the market and for pending sales—both on the market and in escrow—with the same criteria to see what your current competition is doing.

Next, take your best comparables from among this data (solds, pending sales, and actives) and drive by them. Eliminate any comparables that you cannot replicate in your property. Your remaining comparables will give you your resale price range. Of course, until you've actually completed the rehab and rechecked your competition before you put a property on the market, you will not know for sure what your property is really worth. But you will be much closer to reality than you were when you started. The key is to minimize surprises and have your actual numbers come in as close to your price projections as possible.

Repair Costs

Once you have a resale price, calculate the costs of repairs needed on the property. Plenty of resources can help with that. Try the Sale Maximizer tool from Home-Gain™) (go to www.homegain.com, then click on "Resource Center," "Seller and Buyer Tools," and "Home Sale Maximizer"). It's a free Web-based tool that helps you choose the right touch-ups and repairs to improve a home's appeal, which in turn can boost the selling price and even shorten its days-on-market. The Sale Maximizer includes online tutorials and shopping lists for do-it-yourselfers, too. There's also a free downloadable brochure, *The Home Sale Maximizer Guide: Maximize Your Home Sale with Minimal Investment*.

More Deductions

Now deduct the cost of repairs and upgrades from your appraised future value of the property. Don't forget to also subtract the various *soft costs* associated with buying, fixing, and selling a house for profit. In a typical deal, soft costs alone can equal 8 to 20 percent of the resale value. They go way beyond simple closing costs and sales commission expenses. Some of those soft costs include:

- Buying costs (title and escrow closing fees).
- Operating costs (utilities, insurance, property taxes, maintenance).
- Money costs (monthly interest and hard-money points, when applicable).
- Selling costs (advertising, marketing, commissions, concessions, title, and escrow closing fees).

Finally, don't forget to deduct your profit. It should be at least 15 percent of the resale value or $30,000, whichever is higher, on every deal. That 15 percent is important because things can and *will* go wrong. As you've learned from some of the stories we've told you, costs can and do exceed budget, and all of it comes out of your profit margin. You take a risk, and you must be rewarded for it. In all my years of investing, I have never lost money on a house. I did make only $7,000 once. Luckily though, I had figured on a $30,000 profit so I had a cushion. Thank goodness for that 15 percent built in!

Your Goal

A deal is not a win-win situation if you help a homeowner but run yourself into the ground financially. That's not good business practice, either, and, after all, this is your business. It just happens to involve helping other people, too. Don't short-change yourself. Figure a reasonable profit, and build that into the deal.

It's as simple, or as difficult, as that. The key is to find motivated sellers who want your cash and services more than they want to keep their property. "It's an art, and it's a technique, and anyone can learn it—even an old dog like me," says ForeclosureS.com senior consultant Andy Anderson.

Miscalculations Add Up

Remember Ed from Chapter 5 who, on his first deal, used his own money instead of subject-to financing and then incorrectly figured his costs? Ed ended up biting the bullet on that first deal because, among other things, he was way off on his math. He didn't pay attention to the details of the property's needed repairs, so his repair estimate came up far short. He also failed to assess existing market conditions accurately, so he ended up having to hold—and pay related expenses on—the property much longer than he expected. As a result, Ed paid too much for the

Steps to Figuring Your Offering Price

Let's review how to figure the numbers for an offering price on a property:

1. Determine what a property's resale value will be *after* all the repairs and upgrades are made.

2. From that resale value, deduct the soft costs (what it costs to buy, sell, and hold a property—average 15 percent of the resale value).

3. Deduct your profit—15 percent of the resale value.

4. Deduct actual repair costs—not a percentage estimate.

5. The amount left is your offering price for the property.

6. From that price, deduct the cost of bringing all loans and liens current to stop the foreclosure.

7. The amount left is the cash you pay the seller at closing for his equity in the property.

property, overpaid the seller for his equity, and almost ended up with the property back in foreclosure. That's not the way to be successful in this business.

Luckily, Ed recognized his errors, regrouped, and went on to find great success in the business. The lesson, of course, is to be painstakingly accurate in your numbers when making offers to sellers. If you're not sure of the dollar amount for a repair, find out. Have your contractor look at the property to determine as closely as possible what a repair will cost. Don't be overly optimistic about the property's selling time, either. If the average selling time for a similar property in the area is five to seven weeks, figure on seven to eight weeks for your resale. It's far better to err on the side of caution than to end up facing unexpected, potentially crippling costs to yourself just because you tried to help someone out of a financial jam.

The Cost of Cash

In the end, though, recognize that you can't always anticipate every cost. You may end up having to borrow fast cash short-term to complete a deal. That's one reason you need to identify and thoroughly check out potential money partners ahead of time. As we mentioned, you should keep a Rolodex or equivalent list, as well as have a backup plan in place for fast cash.

If you must get a hard-money loan, typically the rates are double the normal interest rate (currently around 13 percent simple interest only monthly) plus 3 to 7 points (one point equals 1 percent of the loan amount) at close of escrow in loan fees. Keep in mind, too, that because the rates are so high, this kind of money should be considered a short-term (6 to 12 months maximum) bridge loan.

The Biggest Sales Mistakes

We all make mistakes. That's a given. But no foreclosure buyer can survive in this business if he repeats the same mistakes again and again. Instead, as Ed did, we must turn our mistakes into lessons. Mistakes help us anticipate what future pitfalls lurk and what steps are necessary to avoid them. Here's a list of some of the most common—and most damaging—mistakes and how to avoid them.

Lack of Preparation

Don't be caught flat-footed when your seller asks you a pointed question. You must develop a working outline ahead of time that highlights each of the benefits of your offer. Then do your homework. Find out how much the seller originally paid for the house, how much he borrowed against the purchase, how long he has owned the house, how much equity he has already taken out in the form of refinancing or second loans, what he does for a living, whether he owns any other property (and how it is doing), and his current financial condition. It's all public record.

The easiest way to access this is, again, through your premium foreclosure listing service. That service should be able to provide you on-site a report showing a property's deed and mortgage history. You also can get the information through the much more time-consuming and cumbersome search of records in the local county recorder's office. Of course, when it comes to a property owner's occupation and current financial condition, the way to get that is to talk to his or her neighbors, friends, and family.

Not Listening

Don't fall into the trap of thinking that your job is to talk and the seller's role is to sit silently and listen to the rationales behind your offer. Let the seller tell you what his situation is and why he needs the money, and then find ways to meet those needs in your offer.

Not Asking for the Deal

As simple as this sounds, many would-be buyers forget to ask for the deal. Nothing is wrong with asking the seller to accept your offer. Once the benefits of your offer exceed the pain of your requested discounted price, you've got the deal.

Moving Too Quickly

Instant rapport is difficult to achieve. Instead of trying to turn the seller into a buddy right away, focus on maintaining a professional attitude. Let any relationship develop naturally.

Not Customizing Your Presentation

A generic presentation isn't as convincing as one personally tailored to your seller's individual needs. Don't use scripts or forms when talking with your seller, either over the phone or in person. Each person is a unique individual and your dealings with them should come across that way. Take the time and you'll earn their respect as well as the deal.

Poor Follow-up

Many buyers cannot overcome a seller's initial objections and leave without the deal. If that happens to you, don't fret. As long as the house hasn't sold at the trustee sale auction, you have a second chance. (In some states, you can work a deal with a former homeowner even after the trustee sale.)

Make notes on your contact list/database, and then return in a week or so to see how things are going with your seller. Maybe that potential loan never came through. You'll be surprised at the deals you'll get simply for remembering to follow up.

A Final Note

Once a seller understands the benefits of your offer, he will sign on the bottom line. But how do you help a seller understand the advantages of your offer? The best way to guarantee that you buy a home pre-foreclosure is to stick with the process and evaluate yourself constantly. I've found that picking up a good sales/motivational book or audio download for my iPod gives me a chance to fine-tune my skills and close more deals.

Tips on Negotiating (With Sellers and Beyond)

The object of negotiating is to win, right? But what about the other guy? If you win, does that mean he loses? Not necessarily. That's where the term *win-win* originated. Ideally, the other guy feels he got a fair deal, too.

Negotiation is discussion with compromise between two or more parties that leads to an agreement, sale, resolution, or impasse. Sometimes negotiations fail, but that's never (supposedly) the fault of the person who's explaining what went wrong.

That sounds great, but in the heat of negotiation, definitions are of little value. What count are strategies and tactics. Before we delve into those concepts, consider and plan for possible moves from your opponent, or this *other guy*, across the negotiating table. In typical negotiations, informal or otherwise, he will likely:

- Withhold important facts until the end of the negotiation (or never reveal them at all).
- Lie.
- Change the deal to suit himself.
- Want it all his way.
- Pull out a deal breaker just when you think the deal is done.
- Hammer your price and terms.
- Refuse to tell you if he can't (or won't) do the deal.

Potential roadblocks like these make it a challenge to win. But it's not impossible to win the day and the deal, and still make the other guy feel like a winner, too. Consider a few lessons and strategies:

- Negotiate with yourself first. Run through all the possible outcomes and scenarios, and develop strategies for as many as you can. Make notes and bring them with you to negotiations.
- Don't burn bridges. Don't think, "I'll never do business with him again, so I'll just stick it to him." Be honorable and consider the long term in all your dealings.
- Uncover the true (as opposed to a good) objection or obstacle. By listening, questioning, and qualifying, you can ferret out the real stumbling block to a deal.
- Get to the real objection quickly. By discovering the true objections early, you stand a better chance of getting to the deal. The real objection is often masked by a stall ("Let me think it over," "I'm waiting for a loan," and similar lines).
- Take the blame—win the point. Who is at fault in a situation is less important than winning.
- Take notes. It helps you remember points and avoid interrupting.
- Know your trump card and when to play it. Save your surest tactic, most valuable information, best price, or greatest benefit to the seller until you need it. Use it as a closing tool or in an "If I did this . . . , would you . . . ?" situation.
- Ask a closing question. Let it precede (or preclude) the actual negotiation. Some examples: "What would you like to do?" or "Is that what you really want?"

- Ask the other guy to be you for a moment. Ask him, "What would you do if you were me?" To break an impasse, ask the other person to walk in your shoes.

- In negotiations, preparation can beat size and strength. Learn the rules of David and Goliath as seen from David's side:

  - Get to know the opposition.

  - Know your objective.

  - Keep your cool even if the opponent is bigger and stronger.

  - Know how and when to use your weapon(s).

  - Practice to be accurate.

  - Know when to shoot. Timing and delivery are paramount in achieving your objective.

- Everything is negotiable. All prices and terms have latitude (or room to move) if you take the right approach or make the right offer/concession.

- Give a concession, get a concession. Is price the last consideration? Double-check that the price is the *only* issue left. If you must give price, get terms.

- Think of yourself as a winner no matter what the outcome.

Limitations on Fast Turnovers

Some lenders now restrict the funding of loans for residential properties offered for sale within a certain number of days of acquisition because of fraud that's occurred. That can complicate matters for you if, for example, you plan to purchase a home in pre-foreclosure using subject-to financing, fix it up quickly, and resell it. As we've mentioned, in real estate jargon, such a purchase and quick resale is commonly known as *flipping* a property for profit. Unfortunately, with the new loan restrictions, your potential buyer might not be able to get a conventional loan.

The Federal Housing Administration (FHA), for example, won't provide mortgage insurance for resales that occur within 90 days of a purchase. The agency also restricts mortgage insurance to transactions where only the owner of record would qualify as a bona fide seller; it won't provide insurance in transactions in which the property had been assigned to others since the original purchase agreement. For resale transactions between 90 days and one year from the date of investor acquisition, FHA requires *documentation of repairs or upgrades* that add value to the property or an explanation of why the property was purchased at a below-market price.

Are You a Master Negotiator?

Take our quiz to test your negotiating skills. In the following statements, underline how the master negotiator skills apply to you:

1. I'm prepared when I begin negotiation.

   Never   Occasionally   Frequently   Usually   Always

2. I know my bottom line.

   Never   Occasionally   Frequently   Usually   Always

3. I have information about my opponent, the "other guy."

   Never   Occasionally   Frequently   Usually   Always

4. I am able to identify weakness in others.

   Never   Occasionally   Frequently   Usually   Always

5. I am solution-oriented.

   Never   Occasionally   Frequently   Usually   Always

6. I am open-minded.

   Never   Occasionally   Frequently   Usually   Always

7. I listen well and take notes.

   Never   Occasionally   Frequently   Usually   Always

8. I speak and communicate so others can understand me.

   Never   Occasionally   Frequently   Usually   Always

9. I don't interrupt.

   Never   Occasionally   Frequently   Usually   Always

10. I'm not afraid to talk hard dollars.

    Never   Occasionally   Frequently   Usually   Always

Are You a Master Negotiator? *(Continued)*

11. I use humor when I'm negotiating.

Never   Occasionally   Frequently   Usually   Always

12. I save my trump card and know when to play it.

Never   Occasionally   Frequently   Usually   Always

13. I try to get friendly with my opponent.

Never   Occasionally   Frequently   Usually   Always

14. I am cool under pressure.

Never   Occasionally   Frequently   Usually   Always

15. I am not easily intimidated.

Never   Occasionally   Frequently   Usually   Always

16. I know when to close the deal.

Never   Occasionally   Frequently   Usually   Always

17. I'm willing to walk away from a bad deal.

Never   Occasionally   Frequently   Usually   Always

18. I don't give in easily, but I'm not stubborn.

Never   Occasionally   Frequently   Usually   Always

19. I don't argue with or insult my opponent.

Never   Occasionally   Frequently   Usually   Always

20. I think of myself as a winner.

Never   Occasionally   Frequently   Usually   Always

All this means that you must thoroughly document the financial troubles of the homeowner that led to his selling the home to you at a discount. You also must record the money and sweat you poured into getting the property into shape to sell at fair market value. What are the specific repairs, the upgrades, the expenses, and the time and effort you invested into this property so you could sell it at fair market value? Document, document, document!

Make sure too, that the language in any purchase agreement with a seller in pre-foreclosure includes the following:

- Seller is aware that Buyer's purchase price is below market value.
- Seller is aware that Buyer is purchasing property for immediate resale.
- Buyer agrees Seller is selling the house "as is."

If you try to resell a property in fewer than 90 days from your purchase date, a lender may refuse a loan to your buyer unless you have this documentation, which helps to allay the lender's concerns. (*Note:* It's unlikely a property will be ready for resale in fewer than 90 days if improvements are needed. More likely it will take 120 days to accomplish all that's needed—including complete rehab, marketing, selling, funding, and closing.)

Your Cheat Sheet—Getting to the Deal

A step-by-step explanation of what to do once you target a potential property for purchase. Before the deal:

- Do the math to determine the top dollar you can offer the seller. Remember, the amount you should start with is 70 percent of a property's fixed-up market value. From that price, deduct your costs and the cost of all repairs, cleanup, and whatever else is needed to bring the property up to neighborhood standards.

- Find out from the seller (preferably by phone before you meet) all the loan and lien information on the property so you can determine how much equity he has to sell you.

- Verify that you have the right contracts to comply with your state's foreclosure laws. (See Chapter 4 for more specifics.) Then work with the seller so he will accept and sign your written offer.

TAKEaway

Essential points to keep in mind:

- When it comes to doing the deal, never lose sight of the Golden Rule: Do unto others as you would have them do unto you.
- Ask your probing questions, and then stop talking. Let the homeowner answer them and talk to you. That's the only way to learn the real truth behind a situation so you can offer the best solution.
- Don't make assumptions about a situation. Find out the truth.
- Be accurate in determining the value of a property once it's fixed up. That means learning how to find out comparable prices for similar homes in the neighborhood.
- Learn how to accurately appraise properties and figure out what it will cost you to fix up, hold, and resell a property.
- Know the current market for similar properties in the area. Be conservative in your estimates. If the average time on market for similar properties is five to seven weeks, figure six to eight weeks so you're not left unexpectedly holding a property, thus eating away at your profit margin.
- Negotiations involve compromise. Anticipate ahead of time a seller's possible objections, tactics, and more, and then know how to counter them. Give a concession to get a concession.
- Document your time, costs, and efforts involved in purchase, rehab, and resale of a property to avoid lender issues when flipping a property.

CHAPTER 11

The Other Options:
Short Sales, Foreclosure Auctions,
REOs, and REO Auctions

Foreclosure auctions are "senior class" stuff and not recommended for beginning foreclosure investors.

—Daryl White, ForeclosureS.com coach
and successful foreclosure investor

A cquiring a property through short sale, auction, REO—either bank-owned real estate, or banked-owned REO auctions—isn't the quick and easy road to riches that many people claim it is. But it can make sound financial sense in certain situations if the approach you take to acquire the property doesn't involve strong-arm tactics against property owners and if all parties really know and understand what's involved.

In the coming months, more properties likely will end up in foreclosure auctions or bank-owned and available for purchase because of the snowball effect from problems in the nation's subprime loan industry. As foreclosure numbers have mounted, lenders have been forced to tighten subprime loan qualifications; a number of subprime lenders have run into financial and legal difficulties; and some have even pulled out of the subprime market entirely. All of this combines to further limit bailout options available to homeowners in default and will lead to more REOs and properties auctioned.

An Explanation of the Options

Without a compromise by the lender, a property is likely to be foreclosed when its owner is in default and has negative equity with little prospect of recovery in the near term. Generally the property can't be sold to a third party or refinanced because the owner doesn't have enough equity even to cover the liens. At that point, available options generally include:

- Foreclosure through judicial or nonjudicial means so that the property ends up being sold at foreclosure auction and becomes a bank-owned property unless an outside bidder buys it.

- Granting a deed in lieu of foreclosure to the lender, who can then hold the property or sell it.

- A workout agreement between the existing lender and the property owner that allows time for the property to increase in value before being resold.

- A short sale or short payoff—negotiated either directly by the owner or through a third party—that allows the owner to sell or refinance the property.

- Scams to milk money from the property that include rent-skimming by the trustor or some other third party.

Before we more thoroughly examine short sales, auctions, and REOs, let's briefly define each.

- *Short sale*. In a short sale or short payoff, the lender agrees to write off the portion of a mortgage balance that's higher than the value of the home. A buyer must be on hand and ready, willing, and able to purchase the property at the fair market value.

- *Auction/trustee sale*. When a property is foreclosed on, it will be offered at auction on the courthouse steps. The maximum opening bid cannot exceed the amount owed the foreclosing lender, but it can be less. With the numbers of foreclosures increasing, lenders could instruct trustees to open bids at less than the full amount of the debt. Generally secondary or junior liens—except property taxes and IRS liens—are wiped out by the senior lenders' foreclosure sale.

- *REO or real estate owned*. If a property owner does nothing to cure the default on a mortgage, the property will go through foreclosure auction, and the bank or mortgage holder will end up owning the property unless an outside bidder buys it at the foreclosure auction. The property then becomes bank-owned REO. Sometimes if a bank ends up with a glut of REO properties, the bank will contract with an auction house to sell them.

Why Short Sales Usually Don't Work

The ads trumpet: "Buy properties at huge discounts!" "Learn how to steal properties from the banks!" "Create giant profits for yourself!"

Sorry to burst the bubble, but banks don't give money away. They are in the business of making money just like you and I are. Taking huge losses on their REO properties simply because they own them is not part of their business plan. Yes, there are cases when I have bought houses at big discounts from banks, but there was a reason. The economy was different and so was the banking system.

When I first started in the foreclosure business in the late 1980s, most banks didn't have a short-sales or REO department. Investors would contact banks directly on their REO or offer to do a short sale with quick cash *as is* (in existing condition) deals on the problem properties the bank didn't want.

Today it's a different story. Banks have gotten smarter and more sophisticated in how they manage their real estate. You can ask for deals, but with the amount of liquidity in the market—so much cash waiting to buy properties—the banks really don't need you. You have to be realistic about the amount of discount, if any, you will get from a bank. Any reputable bank has a team of professional agents, property managers, and asset managers ready to get the most money possible for its properties. Banks, after all, are your competition. They are experts at facilitating deals in their best interests.

A bank will, however, sometimes accept short sales because a short sale:

- Removes the loan from a potential nonperforming loan status, which may affect some lenders' reserve requirements.

- Eliminates the need (and cost) to foreclose and deal with managing REO properties.

- In a market moving downward, enables the amount of the loss to be immediately quantified rather than wait for a lower price after the REO sale.

- Allows any recovered funds to be reinvested far sooner than would be true if a short sale or payoff were not accepted.

What many short-sale promoters fail to mention, however, is the significant effort needed to close a short sale. Says ForeclosureS.com coach Daryl White, "I recommend even the seasoned investor stay away from them. They are complicated and hardly ever benefit the owner in default."

Let's look at some of the requirements for a short sale:

Tons of paperwork. Rather than having to prove their creditworthiness and financial stability to qualify for a loan, property owners in a short sale must demonstrate—and document—that they are broke in order to qualify. *Broke* means having no cash flow or assets, including savings, investments, trusts, liquid retirement funds, or other finances that could be tapped as potential sources of cash. The list of documents a homeowner must provide to qualify for a short sale will boggle your mind. Just because homeowners are *upside-down* on their loan—owing more than the home's value—doesn't mean the lender will simply forgive the debt. They signed a promissory note for a certain amount, and the lender wants to abide by that agreement.

Possibility of deficiency judgment. In most cases, the financial inquiries are legitimate and necessary for the lender to determine whether to accept a short sale. In some instances, however, lenders use the information to determine whether the homeowner may receive a deficiency judgment—remember, that's the difference between the amount of the outstanding loan and the fair market value of the house as determined by a court as part of the judicial foreclosure.

If the investigation reveals that the borrower may have liquid assets to cover the loss, some lenders will decline the short sale and require the owner to bear the loss and pay up. Even when a deficiency judgment is possible, however, lenders will compromise on a short sale, recognizing that deficiency judgments are difficult to obtain and collect, and can be had only through judicial foreclosures. Too, the potential amount of the lender's additional recovery through a judicial foreclosure (as opposed to a less costly, faster nonjudicial one) doesn't always justify the cost of obtaining a deficiency.

Fraud from the past. Ironically, a side effect of a homeowner proving insolvency is the possible revelation that the original loan application may have been flawed or even fraudulent. A homeowner only adds to his problems if it's demonstrated that he failed to fully disclose facts to the lender from the beginning.

Multiple liens/mortgages. The encumbrance of a second mortgage can kill a short-sale deal because you must persuade all junior lenders to remove or reduce their liens. A private mortgage-insurance holder also will want to protect its interests. Unlike foreclosure auctions, short sales do *not* automatically wipe out junior liens.

No wholesale deals. Before a homeowner in default can approach a lender about a short sale, he must have a firm market-value offer for the property from a *qualified* (read "financially rock-solid") buyer and a broker to negotiate the deal. A discounted or wholesale price offer is not acceptable. Banks are in business

---

TALES FROM FORECLOSURE INVESTORS

New foreclosure investors Earl and Louise were weeding default listings in their target area when they discovered that their neighbor Hank was about to lose his home. Hank, they knew, had also recently lost his job and divorced his wife. The couple approached Hank about his financial difficulties and offered to help him by purchasing his home through a short sale.

After Earl and Louise spent considerable time and energy working with Hank's lender, the company finally agreed to the sale because Hank had brought to the bargaining table a qualified, close-to-market-value purchaser—namely, Earl and Louise. The lender avoided the cost of foreclosure; Hank got out from under crippling mortgage payments; and Earl and Louise picked up a property that they then cleaned up and rented out with the intention of recouping their money through future appreciation.

---

and need to make money, so giving an investor a 30 percent discount isn't going to happen.

Serious credit consequences. One of the more serious concerns many borrowers have is that their credit will be ruined by whatever action they take. Unfortunately, many lenders are not responsive to requests for a short sale from such borrowers, insisting that they will discuss a short sale only if and when the loan is in default. For borrowers with good credit, a short sale may be the best way to proceed, particularly if there is little or no tax consequence. Companies that acquire property with negative equity sometimes have processes designed to mitigate credit problems of sellers.

Potential tax nightmare. If a homeowner does qualify for a short sale, the hassles are by no means over. Any remaining difference between a home's value and the balance on the mortgage is considered a "forgiveness of debt" and, in virtually all cases, means that an IRS Form 1099 will arrive in the mail. Yes, you read that correctly. The homeowner must pay taxes on the loss, as if it were earned income that year. One big problem is that most homeowners don't learn about these consequences until long after an investor has bought their property. That investor hadn't bothered to tell them because it might have torpedoed the deal.

> *If a homeowner sells his property through a short sale,*
> *the former owner may still owe taxes on*
> *capital gains associated with the property!*

This is true even though the owner receives no cash from the sale. If the property had a mortgage in excess of basis—more than the total of what you paid for the property plus the cost of all your improvements—the now-former owner still owes taxes on the capital gain just as if a third-party sale had occurred. The rationale is simple: A borrower cannot be allowed to pull out his equity (i.e., capital gain) through a loan and then dispose of the property by deed in lieu of foreclosure or by foreclosure, without paying taxes on the capital gain already realized from the property. Thus, rather than taxing the borrower when equity is cashed out through a loan, the IRS defers the taxable event until the property is sold or conveyed. Similarly, in short sales, the homeowner will often incur tax liability to the extent there exists mortgage debt in excess of that basis or the total cash you have put into the property.

To learn more about the tax consequences of short sales, check with a qualified real estate attorney. To find one, check out DSNews' Black Book (www.dsnewsblackbook.com), Lawyers.com (www.lawyers.com) from the well-respected LexisNexis Martindale-Hubbell, the American Bar Association (www.abanet.org, click on "Lawyer Locator"), or your local bar association.

Auctions: Buying on the Courthouse Steps

Many foreclosure gurus swear by auctions and trustee sales as the road to riches in the foreclosure investing business. That may be the only way to buy a property with junior liens that eat away the equity you need to make the purchase work for you. But keep in mind that a property bought this way is entangled with uncertainties. It's a crapshoot loaded with pitfalls and is not for neophyte foreclosure investors. Collusion between bidders and other forms of chicanery are not uncommon.

Different states have different timelines and processes for trustee sales and foreclosure auctions, which further complicate this method of buying property (see Chapter 4). In some states, the time between notification of default, notice of sale, and the actual auction date is short, while for other states, the process takes much longer. Before even considering auctions as an option, be aware of your state's rules. Some other considerations:

- A lien holder or owner in default may request on mutual agreement a postponement of sale. In fact, it's only rarely that a house goes to auction at the time and date originally posted. That means you must call and track the trustee sales personally to find out exactly what properties are being auctioned on any given day.

- At the sale, the note holder is entitled to *credit bid* the full amount of his debt plus penalties and charges. In other words, the note holder does not need to have physical cash (or a cashier's check) at the sale up to the amount owed him plus penalty fees and charges. But unless there are competing bidders, it's seldom wise to make a full credit bid.

- Acceptance of the highest bid completes the sale, and the bidder must deposit payment on demand. In some states, such as California, bidders must have 100 percent of the amount in advance of bidding in the form of cashier's checks. In other states, a portion of the bid is due at the time of sale and the balance later. Again, you must read your state's foreclosure laws to know the specific procedure required. Failure to deposit the payment subjects the bidder to liability for damages sustained by the trustee and, if the failure is willful, potential criminal penalties.

- The successful bidder takes the property free of all junior liens (except property taxes and federal income tax liens) to the foreclosed lien, but subject to any senior encumbrances.

- The successful bidder takes the property as is, with no warranties of title.

It sounds simple enough, but buying a property at a foreclosure auction is a very risky proposition because you don't see the property's interior before you buy, you don't know the home's actual condition, you must evict the former owner, and you must know how to do your title search—there are no title insurance policies here—or else liens on the property could prevent your getting clear title when you try to sell.

You also may end up bidding against a secondary lien holder who already has a vested interest in the property, says ForeclosureLink's Townsend. "These second mortgage holders look to us to actually attend sales and bid on their behalf so they protect themselves from getting wiped out (by actually buying the property at auction). That's a tough one (for you) to win."

When It Makes Sense

An auction purchase can work if you do your homework completely so that you fully understand a property's title documents. A property purchased at foreclosure auction or sale does not come with title insurance, so you must be aware of what the state of title is before the sale and what that means for you the investor, as well as what liabilities get wiped out at auction and why or why not. You may pay for an uninsured title search report online (a couple of fee-based sites you can try are http://www.titlesearch.com/ or http://www.americantitleinc.com) or pay for a preliminary title report from your local title company (average cost around $400). The problem with using a third party is that the research is costly, especially if you end up a losing bidder. It's preferable to research the title yourself with the county recorder (either online or in person).

Why should you worry about the title on a property? Let's say you're planning to bid on a $200,000 house at a foreclosure auction. The opening bid of $50,000 sounds awesome . . . or does it? That winning bid could be for the second mortgage (not the primary or first one) so that the winning bidder ends up paying $50,000 cash for the property and then automatically assumes the debt of the senior loan. That means if the first mortgage on the property was $200,000, you've just paid $250,000 for a house worth $200,000. Ouch!

Don't necessarily believe what other investors or people attending an auction have to say about a property or situation, either, says Townsend. "The regulars who attend these sales are not always up and up."

Title Tips

- Review your title research to see exactly the position and timeline of the loan in default that's going to the trustee sale.

- Keep in mind that junior liens and encumbrances—other than IRS and property tax liens—are wiped out by the deed of trust going to sale.

- Most states are "race notice" states—first to record is first in line—so typically the date that the original deed of trust, lien, or encumbrance was recorded will direct you to the position of that encumbrance.

- If your deed of trust at the auction is a second, then the first loan recorded will remain on the property (and you will get the property subject to that existing lien). However, most liens, loans, and encumbrances recorded after your second deed of trust was recorded will be wiped out. Of course, there are exceptions to this.

- Get legal advice on the state of title. It's easy for an amateur to miss a deed of trust, lien, or encumbrance that is senior to the position you're bidding on. If you want to invest in foreclosures at auction, get a good real estate attorney to help you with the title and keep you from losing your shirt.

You must also do your homework on money matters. It's much the same process as when you make a purchase offer directly to a homeowner. You must accurately determine a property's fully repaired and rehabbed resale value, estimate the costs of repairs and expenses, determine your purchase and holding costs, and then set your maximum offer price. That's your maximum bid at auction, too.

More Details

Call the auction trustee the day before the auction date to get the final minimum dollar amount you'll need for a particular property. Have the trustee sale number when you do that, says Townsend.

Then, the morning of the scheduled auction, call the trustee or attorney handling the auction to verify the sale date and time. As we mentioned earlier, sales can be postponed. If that happens, mark your calendar to phone the trustee again on that rescheduled date because the auction date will *not* be republished anywhere. If an auction is canceled because a homeowner cured his default, a notice of such will be recorded at the county as a "Canceled Notice of Default."

If the sale is to proceed as planned, get a cashier's check for the minimum bid amount in full, plus incremental checks for any overbidding you may plan to make, ahead of time. Find out from the trustee in advance to whom the check should be made out. Some states allow payment of a portion of the sale cost at the auction and the balance later. Make sure you know your state's requirements. It would be a shame if you had a winning bid for the perfect property only to lose out because you didn't comply with the process requirements.

Recheck a property's title to see if anything new has been recorded that could pose a problem. If you're not sure about something, get legal advice. Spending a little money on legal help now can save you big headaches and losses later.

At the Foreclosure Auction

Register to bid with the trustee or attorney's representative. They will ask to see your certified funds to make sure you are a real bidder. The bidding typically takes place on the steps of the courthouse in the county where the property is located. Bids are made orally, and you may or may not have competition at your sale.

After the Auction

The trustee will take your money and record a Trustee's Deed, noting you, the investor, as the new owner. Now that you own the property, don't forget to buy fire insurance to protect your asset. Now also is the time for the former owners (or tenants) to move out of your property—if they haven't already—so you can begin your remodel plan. We talk more about that in Chapter 12.

The REO Approach

An REO, or bank/lender-owned real estate, is a property that went to sale at a foreclosure auction but no one bid on it, and it *reverted to the beneficiary* and became REO. In most cases, the minimum bid at auction probably exceeded what a savvy investor would pay, so the lender ended up owning the property. On the positive side, the junior liens have been wiped out and the lender no longer needs to collect on a bad loan. On the negative side, the lender now owns a nonperforming asset that it must try to sell.

In a hot real estate market, the REO lender will simply fix up the property, list it with a Realtor, and sell it to a homebuyer for full market value. As markets cool and banks/lenders end up holding more and more real estate, those lenders likely will start selling their properties *as is* at a discount from market value. Keep in mind, though, that REO lenders are *not* highly motivated sellers, willing to sell at big discounts, until they have a backlog of bad loans and sizable REO inventory. Even when foreclosures are way up, if banks are making money or have plenty of cash, they don't need your cash and will hold some of their properties to sell at a higher price later.

Doing It Right

To succeed at REOs, you must take a tack different from that advocated by many investors. Avoid all HUD, VA, or highly promoted repossessed properties, especially those marketed by a Realtor. There is nothing wrong in working with Realtors, but they are hired to get the most money possible for a bank. Their allegiance is with their big REO lender who will give them repeat business if they get higher prices for properties.

Instead, locate REO properties from your public records foreclosure property lists. Watch for recently recorded trustee deed filings. A trustee deed is the document that transfers ownership from the owner in default to the lender from the foreclosure auction. See if those properties are on your local Realtors' MLS. If they are, chances are the lender wants a homebuyer willing to pay top dollar, not an investor looking to buy at discount—in other words, to take away the lender's profit.

A few points to remember when weeding REO leads:

- Deeds to REO properties are public documents also known as *trustee deeds*.
- You don't need to search for the amount of equity in an REO property when the senior lender already owns it because there are no loans remaining.
- If a junior loan has foreclosed, that lender may then take title subject to the existing senior loan. These properties are *not* then free and clear.

Whatever the case, if you tentatively identify a property as REO, contact the lender directly by phone. Ask for the head of the REO department or request the name of the specific REO asset manager handling that property. Ask if the bank is selling the property "as is" and if it is willing to discount the price for an "all-cash offer." Your timing is critical here. If you wait too long, the bank/lender will fix up the property, list it with a Realtor, and sell it for a profit itself.

Some banks/lenders will work with you; some will ask you to go through their Realtor; some will tell you they're already fixing up the property; and if you're lucky, you'll find one that is interested in discounting for a cash, as-is offer.

As with pre-foreclosure deals, make sure that what you pay for an REO property does not exceed 70 percent of the market value (purchase price plus the cost of all repairs) and that you will have no problem finding money partners.

REO Auctions

When a property ends up REO and a bank winds up owning lots of properties, sometimes that institution will opt to auction off some of its bulging portfolio. With the ongoing glut of foreclosures and REOs in some parts of the country, you'll be seeing more of these auctions taking place. That means plenty of good deals for you, right? Wrong!

Since the actual foreclosure auctions on the courthouse steps have already passed for these properties and they weren't purchased, they're now bank REO foreclosures. That means the bank sets the prices and terms. Of course, the goal is to sell the properties, so they're priced as close to market value as possible to maximize the price and minimize the hold time. Think of REO banks as your competition (only with deeper pockets).

Consider what happened at one recent auction in Detroit, Michigan, an area hard-hit by layoffs and cutbacks by the nation's financially troubled automakers. A group of lenders recently contracted with Texas-based auction experts

Hudson and Marshall to auction 450 REO properties. The terms for the auction included:

- Deposit in the form of a $3,000 cashier's check per property in order to bid.
- $1 opening bid; minimum reserve price set, but undisclosed to bidders.
- Thirty days to find financing and close on property.
- If property doesn't close, your only loss is $3,000 deposit.
- Open houses to inspect the properties prior to auction.
- Full title insurance and properties free of all liens and encumbrances.
- Commissions paid to buyer's agents who attended auction with their buyer.

> *If you're looking for a great deal at an REO auction,*
> *it's not going to come on a nice house on a nice street.*
>
> —Alexis McGee

The well-publicized auction drew lots of bidders, which, in accordance with the laws of supply and demand, led to a bidding war on the nice properties in good areas. As a result, many of these properties sold at or above their current price as listed in the local MLS. Other less desirable properties, though, drew few if any bidders, and sold for much less than market value or not at all.

Still, if you do your homework—and there's plenty of it—you can walk away with a gem. Some of those Detroit-area homes went for as little as $30,000 or less.

If you're interested in trying your hand at REO auctions, get ready to work hard to prepare. That preparation for the auction includes these steps:

- Preview *all* the properties being auctioned.
- Estimate repairs on every house—that means repair bid sheets or bringing the contractor with you (and paying him for his time).
- Estimate market values on every house. That means your own appraisals of all the houses—450 of them in the Detroit auction.
- Create a maximum bid sheet for every property whether you like that property or not. If it's a really bad house, then perhaps pencil in a bigger profit. (Make sure you include at least 15 percent profit or $30,000 no matter what.)
- Walk away from bidding on any property if it goes over your top price!

Another Source

As you make friends with Realtors along the way—perhaps through referrals from an REO lender—they may be able to help you find motivated sellers whose properties are *not* listed on the MLS. Let them know you can buy properties all-cash and as-is, and close quickly.

Your goal is to become that agent's *pocket buyer*, the one he calls when he wants to do a quick deal but doesn't have a listing agreement. You want to be that agent's best buyer, too, so he calls you first. You earn that privilege by sending him lots of listing referrals. Take care of your friends in the business, and they will take care of you.

Final Thoughts

As you can see, a plethora of opportunities exists in the foreclosure investing business if you take the right approach, do your homework, and pay attention to the details. Some avenues, as this chapter has shown, require more experience and knowledge than others. As you become more adept at the business, you'll be able to recognize the right deal for the right price in the right situation and know when, where, and how to make your move.

Personally, I prefer the lucrative approach of helping owners in default who need our expertise early in the pre-foreclosure process. That way we can offer them multiple solutions to their problems. Sometimes that means helping them keep their homes; other times it means buying their home from them so they can get a fresh start. Either way, we're there to help. You can be there, too, and make more money than you ever thought possible—while helping people in trouble and feeling great about yourself at the same time.

TAKEaway

Key points to remember:

- In a short sale, the lender agrees to write off the portion of the loan balance that exceeds the value of the property.
- A lender will agree to a short sale only *if* a qualified buyer is available and ready to purchase the property.
- Beware of all the paperwork involved with short sales.

- If a property owner does nothing to cure the default on a mortgage, the property will go through foreclosure, and the bank or mortgage holder will end up owning the property unless it's sold. It is then known as REO.

- Banks are in the business of making money, not discounting properties for your gain. In general, don't expect big discounts in short sales or with REOs.

- Homes that go to foreclosure end up for sale at auction or trustee sales generally held on the courthouse steps.

- If you decide to bid on a property at auction, make sure you do your homework on its title and are aware of the liens associated with the property.

- There are no guarantees when you purchase a property at auction.

- Consider limiting the variables in foreclosure investing by working with property owners in pre-foreclosure.

CHAPTER 12

After the Deal Is Sealed

Pay attention to the little things. It's the details that can determine your success or lack thereof.

—Alexis McGee

The property owner, with your help and counsel, has decided that selling his property and walking away with cash in his pocket is the best option for him and his family. He has also decided that he wants you to buy the house because he knows you are honest, fair, and above reproach—unlike the other prospecting buyers who promised him the moon and delivered nothing.

Although you've won the deal, your work isn't finished yet. There's the closing and helping the owner move on and move out. He will look to you for guidance and support. After all, in the overwhelming depths of his financial despair, you came forward to rescue him. Sounds like a soap opera? It's not. This is reality and where you really make a difference in others' lives.

A Note about Escrow

Once your seller agrees to your purchase offer, the first step is to open escrow. That usually takes only a phone call because you already should have identified the organization or individual to handle the process.

Escrow is an arrangement in which a disinterested third party—the escrow holder or attorney—holds legal documents and funds on behalf of a buyer and seller and distributes them according to the buyer's and seller's instructions. (Some

Your Cheat Sheet—After the Deal

Here's a step-by-step explanation of what to do once a homeowner agrees to sell you his/her property.

After the Owner Agrees to the Sale

- Open escrow with a simple telephone call to an independent and reputable third party; order a preliminary title report on the property; fax the escrow officer a copy of the signed purchase agreement.

- Review your preliminary title report to make sure there are no discrepancies between what the report shows to be owed on the property and what the seller says is owed. (If there is a discrepancy, notify the title company so it can check it out.)

- If you are to take title to the property "subject to existing liens and encumbrances," make sure you get from the sellers all loan payment books and/or loan statements so you can continue payments on the existing loans after closing.

- If you have not seen a recent termite report on the property, order one right away (cost: about $150, although it varies dramatically depending on locale) and ask the inspector to include a bid for all termite damage repairs in his report. That's essential, especially in warmer climates in the Southeast, Southwest, and West.

- Review the written termite report with your contractor; walk the house with the contractor, and review the property's potential remodel work. Ask the contractor for a written estimate of the cost to complete all repairs, including clearing all items as pointed out in your termite report.

- Call your property insurer and make sure the property will be covered by fire insurance at close of escrow.

- Ask the escrow company to call all lien holders to get the current balance on every lien and loan, as well as the amount of funds needed to reinstate those loans that are delinquent. This process usually takes three to five days of telephone work. Once you have those final numbers, the escrow officer can draft his settlement reports that show the final accounting of all proceeds for both the buyer and seller.

- When you're ready to close, the escrow officer will ask both you and the seller(s) to come to the escrow holder's office and sign final documents. Each seller must bring a valid driver's license or passport (or other approved form of picture ID) to the closing in order for documents to be notarized. There are no

Your Cheat Sheet—After the Deal *(Continued)*

exceptions. (I've learned this the hard way!) Make sure you remind the seller(s) that everyone named on the title must be present at signing and show a valid ID. If you're not sure whether a certain type of ID is allowed, check ahead of time.

- As buyer, you must bring certified funds for the cash needed to close your purchase. The amount typically includes the total cash needed to reinstate the delinquent loans plus whatever cash you've negotiated to give the seller(s) for the equity in the house.

- Do one last walk-through on the property before you sign final documents to make sure the property is in the same condition as when you signed the purchase contract and that the sellers have moved out.

After the Sale

- Call a locksmith to change the locks the minute you are "on record." (Recording is typically done the morning after you have signed closing papers.)

- Start work on your remodel and/or repairs. (Typically, it takes a contractor two to four weeks to complete needed work.)

- Offer the property for sale on both the MLS and with "for sale by owner" (FSBO) advertising.

- Make sure the prospective homebuyer has an adequate down payment (10 percent to 20 percent) and is prequalified for a new purchase money loan to cash you out entirely. Don't waste your time with homebuyers who are not qualified!

- Close your sale and take your money to the bank.

states require an escrow holder to be licensed.) When buying and selling real estate, escrow protects both the buyer and seller, and offers added convenience. The buyer can instruct the escrow holder to disburse the purchase price only upon the satisfaction of certain prerequisites and conditions. The seller can instruct the escrow holder to retain possession of the deed until the seller's requirements, including receipt of the purchase price, are met. Both buyer and seller rely on the escrow holder to carry out faithfully their mutually consistent instructions relating to the transaction and to advise them if any of their instructions are not mutually consistent or cannot be carried out.

Escrow involves an independent third party and is designed to protect the interests of both buyer and seller in a real estate transaction.

—Alexis McGee

Escrow also allows the buyer and seller to move forward separately but simultaneously in providing inspections, reports, loan commitments and funds, deeds, and many other items, using the escrow holder as the central depositing point. If the instructions from all parties to an escrow are clearly drafted, fully detailed, and mutually consistent, the escrow holder can take many actions on the parties' behalf without further consultation. This saves much time and facilitates the closing of the transaction.

Remember Mary Kay's frantic first deal, described in Chapter 10? Because she had a reputable and responsible escrow agent she could count on, the deal was done. Without such an agent, she likely couldn't have completed the deal.

Look for Experience

When choosing an escrow officer, it's generally best to use an established, independent escrow firm, an attorney, or an escrow officer with a title insurance company. Real estate transactions require a tremendous amount of technical experience and knowledge to proceed smoothly, and the escrow holder generally is responsible for safeguarding and properly distributing the purchase price. Escrow officers with established firms are usually experienced and trained in real estate procedures, title insurance, taxes, deeds, and insurance. They are also trained in how to act with complete impartiality.

Escrow Instructions

Both parties need to be clear in their instructions to the escrow agent. The instructions should be in writing and signed by both buyer and seller, directing the escrow officer in the specific steps to be completed so the escrow can be closed. Typical instructions include:

- Method by which the escrow holder is to receive and hold the purchase price to be paid by the buyer.

- Conditions under which a lapse of time or breach of a provision of the purchase contract will terminate the escrow without a closing.

- Instructions and authorization to the escrow holder to disburse funds for recording fees, title insurance policy, real estate commissions, and any other closing costs incurred through escrow. (In pre-foreclosure sales, such costs are paid by you, the buyer.)

- Instructions on prorating the cost of property taxes and utilities if prepaid.

- Instructions on payment by the escrow holder of prior liens and charges against the property and distribution of the net sale proceeds.

Because the escrow holder can follow only the instructions as stated and may not exceed them, it is extremely important that the instructions be stated clearly and be complete in all details.

Why Escrow?

The escrow process helps facilitate the sale or purchase of your home. The escrow holder accomplishes this by:

- Acting as the impartial stakeholder or depository of documents and funds.

- Processing and coordinating the flow of documents and funds.

- Keeping all parties informed of progress on the escrow.

- Securing a title insurance policy.

- Obtaining approvals of reports and documents from the parties as required.

- Obtaining final balances and reinstatement amounts on all loans and liens.

- Prorating and adjusting insurance, taxes, rents, and so on.

- Recording the deed and loan documents.

- Maintaining security and accountability of monies owed and owing.

Various Roles

During escrow, the *seller* deposits the executed grant deed to the buyer with the escrow holder, deposits evidence of pest inspection and any required repair work, and deposits other required documents such as tax receipts, addresses of mortgage holders, insurance policies, equipment or home warranty contracts, and more.

The *buyer* is responsible for depositing with the escrow holder the funds required, in addition to any borrowed funds, to pay the purchase price, funds sufficient for home and title insurance, and any deed of trust or mortgages necessary to secure loans. He also arranges for any borrowed funds to be delivered to the escrow holder, approves any inspection reports and title insurance commitments called for by the purchase and sale agreements, and fulfills any other conditions specified in the escrow instructions.

If a new loan is involved, the *lender* deposits proceeds of the loan to the purchaser and directs the escrow holder on the conditions under which the loan funds may be used.

The job of the *escrow holder* is to open the order for title insurance; obtain approvals from the buyer on the title insurance report and pest and other inspections; receive funds from the buyer and/or any lender; obtain final balances and reinstatement amounts on all loans and liens; prorate insurance, taxes, rents, and more; disburse funds for title insurance, recording fees, real estate commissions, lien clearance, and more; prepare final statements for each party indicating amounts to be disbursed for services and any further amounts necessary to close escrow; record deed and loan documents, and, finally, deliver the grant deed to the buyer, the loan documents to the lender, and the funds to the seller, thereby closing the escrow.

Closing Escrow

Once all the instructions of both parties have been fulfilled and all closing conditions satisfied, the escrow is closed and the safe and accurate transfer of property and money has been accomplished.

Closing also is when certain adjustments can be made. For instance, suppose the seller prepaid property taxes. In that case, the closing agent would compensate the seller for the prepayment at closing by having you, the buyer, pay the seller additional money.

It could also work in reverse. If the seller is behind on property taxes, as often happens when a loan is in default, the closing agent will reduce the money due the seller by the amount of the unpaid taxes.

What About Title Insurance?

Sure, you can and must do a preliminary title search on a potential purchase to make sure you know what you're dealing with as far as liens and ownership of a property are concerned. We've already discussed how to identify primary and secondary mortgages or liens. Other types of liens include property tax liens, federal and state tax liens, judgments, mechanic's liens, notice of pending action liens, and more, so do your homework up front.

Doing your homework early in the process, however, shouldn't preclude purchasing formal title insurance after a seller agrees to a deal with you. You're not afforded the luxury of title insurance when buying homes at a foreclosure auction or sheriff's sale, so take advantage of the protection and spring for it with pre-foreclosure purchases. Although you're not required by law to purchase title insurance, it's definitely worth the expense—usually around $1/2$ to 1 percent of the purchase price, but it can be less. Costs typically are regulated by state law, and often include title insurance and escrow fees.

Let's look a little more closely at what title insurance buys and ways you can cut your costs when purchasing it.

The Basics

Whenever a property's title passes to someone else, the seller—in a normal home purchase—usually provides a deed containing certain guarantees or warranties (hence the name *grant deed* or *warranty deed*). The seller warrants that title is good and that no one will challenge its integrity. Any irregularities in what's called the *chain of title* can place a *cloud* on the integrity of the title.

In a pre-foreclosure deal, it's up to you to pay a title company or real estate attorney to do a title search—that is, to warranty the title is good. You'll need to provide the title insurance anyway when you resell the rehabbed property.

The title searcher generally follows the chain of title—or the ownership—back until he finds a "full value" transfer (that's the zero point in the title search), tracing ownership through deeds recorded at the county recorder's office. The searcher also checks to make certain that previously recorded mortgages and other liens have been released. Based on documents found in public records, the title company or attorney will prepare a *title insurance commitment*. A commitment is a statement that, based on certain documents found by a search of public records, the company will issue a title insurance policy for a certain fee.

The Title Insurance Policy

Unlike typical insurance policies, a title insurance policy covers past events. For example, the daughter of a previous owner could suddenly claim that her father conveyed a deed while not mentally competent. Such a claim could jeopardize the current ownership. In that case, the title insurance company would defend against the claim and pay for any damages (usually the value of the property).

The policy does not cover claims based on events that occur after the policy is issued. Furthermore, the policy usually contains numerous exceptions, such as claims based on information undisclosed to the title company. For example, if you're aware of any potential problems that might lead to a claim, your failure to disclose that information to the title company could lead to a denial of a claim based on those events.

Cash Savings

Title insurance coverage starts from the last full-value transfer and ends with the date the title is transferred. Since most transfers are insured by a title company, the longer you own the property, the more expensive the policy. Keep in mind that when you purchase a property in pre-foreclosure, buy title insurance on that deal, rehab the property, and then turn around and sell it in six months, most likely nothing has gone wrong with that title. For that reason, title companies offer reissue rates, usually discounted about 40 percent, if title insurance was issued on the same property within the past few years.

The rate is lower because any claims that arise from events before the previous owner are covered by the previous policy. Thus the new policy really deals with the risk of claims from events that occurred while you owned it.

Try a Hold-Open Policy

If you plan to resell a property within a year, ask the title insurance company for a hold-open policy (or a *binder*). For a small fee (usually an additional 10 percent on the policy), the title company will hold a title commitment open for a year or more. Rather than issue a policy based on the first transfer (from the seller to you), the company will issue a policy on the second transfer (from you to the next buyer). Because the seller usually pays for title insurance, you can pay the additional 10 percent when you buy, saving 90 percent on title insurance when you sell.

About Liens

As we've discussed, it's important to pay attention to and quadruple-check the mortgages and liens on any property before you purchase it. A lien, you remember, is a claim that attaches to a person and is secured by property owned by that person for the payment of a debt. That means the lien holder could foreclose on a property if the debt is not paid off. People often fail to pay attention to the fact that once a lien is recorded it attaches to all property owned by the individual. When a lien is satisfied (paid off), it should be recorded as a release of lien or *reconveyance*.

There are several types of liens, all of which can cloud the title and prevent the seller from conveying marketable title to the buyer. A mechanic's lien, or a construction lien, is a claim made by contractors or subcontractors who have performed work on the house and have not been paid. A supplier of materials delivered to the job may also file a mechanic's lien.

In some states, contractors and subcontractors must notify the homeowner when they intend to file a lien, but in other states they can file it without prior notification of the owner. An owner could face a mechanic's lien if his contractor fails to pay a subcontractor or a materials supplier. (After the remodel of an investment home, be sure to obtain a release of lien form signed by all subcontractors and material suppliers before making the final payment to the contractor. That avoids any potential lien hassles on your resale.)

Also paid and removed before any sale are recorded liens for unpaid debts, such as credit card judgments or unpaid child support.

If you discover any of these liens on a potential investment property, contact the lien holder and negotiate to pay off the debt so that you get a release of lien. Again, be sure to have the lien holder sign a release of lien form and deliver it to your escrow office, or have him file it at the county recorder's office to clear the title in the official records.

Remember, if you're buying a property pre-foreclosure with subject-to financing, you agree to take over any other liens against the property that are recorded at the county, too.

The Actual Closing

Be prepared for the unexpected up until the time of the actual closing. Remember Mary Kay's deal with Anita? At the last minute Mary Kay had to hop a plane to get a necessary signature because of a problem with the property's deed. She did her homework, recognized the issue ahead of the closing—just barely—and dealt with it, and the deal squeaked through.

Avoid Last-Minute Fiascos

You must do your homework, too, to avoid last-minute deal-breaking fiascos, whether they're physical, financial, or emotional.

Double-check your title search with what the owner says, and get that title insurance to protect your investment and your seller's future. Walk a property with your seller and your contractor to make sure you're aware of all the necessary repairs and the cost of those repairs ahead of time, and that the property is in the same condition as when the seller agreed to the deal.

If your seller hasn't moved out already, make sure you and he have a signed agreement with a firm date for his departure (no longer than two weeks after you close escrow on the purchase). It's important the sellers know you are not going to let them live in the house and are only helping them move in a more organized manner. When Mary Kay bought Anita's house, she gave her several weeks to move out but also offered extra cash if she left sooner. Anita took the cash incentive and was out in three days.

Check with your home insurance provider, too, to make sure that the house is covered for fire insurance once the deal closes. That usually can be taken care of with a simple phone call as long as you know the property's exact address and legal parcel information.

If you're using someone else's cash and getting a finder's fee, have a backup funding source ready and willing if your designated cash cow doesn't show up at closing. Your involvement in the deal aside, this is someone else's home and future on the line. Think about the what-ifs and plan for them.

If you are getting deed to the property via subject-to financing, make sure you have all the necessary loan booklets, pay stubs, and any other related material so you can keep making those loan payments until you sell the house.

As part of their escrow procedure, your escrow officer will use the designated funds to make the back payments to bring the loan current (reinstatement), thus canceling the default.

Be prepared in case your seller gets cold feet, too. This, after all, is his home, and it's quite possible that, at the last minute, he'll be afraid to leave. Always have a few extra benefits in mind that you can use as soft persuasion to help a homeowner let go. As always, though, don't be cruel and hurtful, but gentle and kind. For example, if Sol is hesitant, remind him that with his equity check and the chance to start anew, his son will be able to play in a safer neighborhood. Or perhaps, as happened with Anita in Mary Kay's deal, the equity check will provide the cash to return to school and fulfill a dream to get a degree.

You are a solution provider. Remember the problems, and remind the sellers of the benefits of the solution they have chosen. That goes for whether the solution is a sale, refinance, workout, or whatever. This kind of gentle persuasion goes a long way toward making it easier for a seller to transition out of his or her home and into a new home and a new life.

Preparing for Closing

In advance of closing, review the purchase agreement and make sure all the conditions of the purchase contract have been met. Has the closing agent followed all the instructions? Before signing your name to any closing documents, check and double-check that everything is correct, especially interest rate, fees charged, and condition of the property.

The Process

For the actual closing, you and the sellers will go to the escrow holder's office, usually at different times, to sign the final documents. Each of the sellers and you (or your buyer if you're the deal finder only) must present a valid driver's license at closing so the documents can be notarized. If a seller doesn't have a valid driver's license, a passport or state-issued identification will suffice. There are no exceptions. If a seller doesn't have a valid driver's license and you're not sure that the type of ID he has will work, find out from the escrow agent ahead of time so there are no last-minute snags.

As the buyer, you must have certified funds for the cash needed to close the deal. A personal check won't do. Typically that includes the cash needed to reinstate the delinquent loans as well as the cash you've agreed to pay the seller. You should receive a settlement statement that itemizes the costs before signing so you can wire the money or bring a certified cashier's check with you.

Make sure you get the keys and the garage-door opener, if applicable, from the seller. Even though you'll have the locks changed immediately after the deal closes, you'll need the keys to get in initially.

Once all the papers are signed and notarized, the deal is sealed and the property is yours. Go out and celebrate, and then get going with your remodel!

Closing Checklist

If You're the Buyer

- Have you made a final walk-through inspection of the property?

- Is the condition of the house or property as it should be?

- If the seller has vacated, have any personal property items been left behind?

- Is everything in working order?

- Are you satisfied that the seller provided all required disclosure documents of any known defects on the property?

- Have you carefully reviewed the mortgage closing documents? If applicable, are the lender's closing costs as expected? Are there any junk fees you don't agree with? Are the names correct on the mortgage or deed of trust documents?

- If applicable, are the loan amount, interest rate, term of the loan, and prepayment penalty correctly stated? When is the first payment due? Where will the payment be made?

- Do you agree with the fees to the title company, attorney, or escrow agency? Are they the same as previously quoted to you?

- Do you understand any prorated costs such as taxes or other items? Are they correct?

- It is clear on which day you will take possession of the property? When will the seller hand over the keys?

- Is the purchase price correct on the closing documents?

- Have you been credited for all deposits put into escrow either by you or on your behalf?

- Is your name correct on the grant deed? Is it spelled correctly, and does it include your correct middle initial?

- Is the manner in which you will take title stated correctly?

- Is the legal description of the property correct? Does this description conform to the one in the title report? Are all the easements and rights-of-way properly listed?

- Were any questionable items on the title report removed or explained to your satisfaction?

Closing Checklist (*Continued*)

- If any personal property is to be included, are you being given a bill of sale, and do you agree with the items included?

- Are you paying for fire insurance yourself outside of escrow or through the closing agent? Is the premium correct and is the policy for a full year?

- Are the property taxes being paid in full? Ask when the next property tax bill will be due.

- Check that the return address on the deed is where you will want the recorded deed sent.

If You're the Seller

- Are all personal property items removed?

- Have you left the property in the condition you promised you would?

- Are the sale price and payoff information correct on your closing documents?

- Were you given credit for any items agreed upon to be credited to your account?

- If applicable, is a satisfaction of mortgage or payoff document being prepared for your old loan?

- If you will be signing a bill of sale for personal property items, is it correct?

- Are any prorated fees or costs correct? Check the dates on these debit and credit items.

- When must the property be vacated?

- Have you agreed to perform any repairs or other work before or after closing?

- Are the title and closing costs as you understood them to be?

- Are the attorney's, closing agent, transfer tax, or title insurance fees correct?

- Did you correctly make any disclosures as required by your state or federal law to the new buyer? Or did you sell the property in as-is condition?

- If a Realtor was involved in the sale, is his fee correct?

- Is any money being held back in escrow on your behalf? If so, how and when will it be released?

Footing the Bill

Dividing charges for the services performed through escrow or as a result of escrow varies from place to place. The fees and service charges to be divided might include, for example, the title insurance policy premium, escrow fee, any transfer taxes, recording fees, and costs in connection with any loan being obtained. Sometimes, however, the buyer and seller have a special agreement as to how these charges are to be paid—often in a pre-foreclosure sale you, the investor, foot the bill to make things easier on the seller.

After the Deal

If you truly practice the white-knight approach to foreclosure investing and are mindful of the Golden Rule in your dealings with others, you won't be surprised at all the new friends you make and at how many property owners feel indebted to you even though you bought their home at a discount. In almost all of those instances, you become an integral part of their lives, even if only temporarily.

Foreclosure investors constantly tell me stories of people who have kept in contact with them over the years. For some, it might be as simple as a card exchanged at holidays. With others, the communication may be more frequent. There is no right or wrong approach. It's an individual choice in every situation. This is truly a win-win business for all involved, and in the end you will have made many new friends. It is my goal for you to be able to throw a party and invite everyone you ever bought a house from—all those you helped to keep their homes, too—and they would all happily show up! That is the true meaning of success. (Of course, it also helps that you have the financial wherewithal to foot the bill for the party!)

It's Your Business

An important point to remember is that your business is helping others find solutions to their financial problems related to their homes. You can do only so much. You can't make all their decisions for them. You're not a lawyer or an accountant. You offer a rational look at the benefits and drawbacks of the options available in their unique situation. But the final choice is theirs to make.

If you help someone choose refinancing and they end up in default six months later, that's the path they've chosen. If you buy a property and the seller ends up in financial trouble or even default again on their next house, that's their choice. You must accept that and remember that you did your best to help.

Very often you'll deal with people who do wind up in financial trouble again. Sometimes you can help them yet again, and sometimes you can't. You'll also run into many people like Anita, who take their new start and make the most of it.

Tim Rhode, a 20-year-plus real estate broker, successful foreclosure investor, and ForeclosureS.com coach, recounts the story of one elderly homeowner in poor health—we'll call him Joe. Victimized by his son who had used the home's equity to fund his gambling habit, Joe was about to lose his home. Tim stepped in at the last minute and was able to purchase Joe's home, structuring the deal in such a way that the son could not access the cash settlement.

"At one point, the social worker in the case called the police on me because she thought I was taking Joe's house away and giving the son the money," says Tim. "But when the social worker realized that I actually had put together a deal to protect Joe and get his money away from his abusive son, she was thrilled. The son ended up in prison for elder abuse, and Joe was finally able to get the medical care he needed."

Not all stories have such a happy ending. Tim recounts another tale of a divorce case in which he had put together a deal that would have given both former spouses $20,000 each to start new lives. At the last minute, the husband decided to back out, which left the ex-wife and their two young children with nothing.

"Sometimes it's not about money," says Tim. "It was a case of revenge. I felt so bad for the now-single mom and her kids. They were left with nothing, and I couldn't do anything about it."

TAKEaway

Key points to remember:

- Once a seller agrees to your purchase offer, the first step is to open escrow.

- Escrow involves bringing in an independent third party, the escrow holder or agent, to hold legal documents and funds on behalf of a buyer and seller and distribute them according to their instructions. It's designed to protect the interests of both buyer and seller.

- Make sure the escrow holder is an independent, reputable, and experienced third party. A neighbor or friend generally won't do. You want someone who knows the real estate and title business.

- Title insurance is a must to make sure you purchase a property with a clear or unencumbered title.

- If you're purchasing a property subject-to, the title company is also responsible for disbursing the funds to bring a loan current and clear the credit of the homeowner in default.

- Don't forget that *all* individuals named on a title must be present (or other arrangements made) at closing and present a valid driver's license or other form of acceptable ID. Check with your title company to determine whether a specific ID will suffice.

- Plan for contingencies. Do your homework ahead of time to make sure you've checked and double-checked all aspects of the deal, the property, and the closing.

CHAPTER 13

What's Next: The Right Way to Flip a Property

Maximize your price; minimize your hassles.

—Alexis McGee's mantra for successful
foreclosure investors

To be successful in the foreclosure investing business, you must know how to buy *and* sell properties for profit. As we've discussed, that means buying property at a discount—at least 30 percent off the top resale value and minus the cost of repairs—knowing how to spruce up the property, and then pricing it right, marketing it, and reselling it. If you do that, your property will sell no matter what market conditions prevail.

If you think you've done all that yet you're not inundated with top-dollar offers on a property, don't blame a slow market. The culprit instead is that you have failed in one of these areas:

- You did not complete the proper repairs to maximize your value.
- The price you are asking isn't consistent with the quality of your product.
- You have not properly marketed your product.

Learn from your mistakes, go back to the drawing board, and try again. You will succeed in this business if you're persistent, consistent, compassionate, and savvy.

Let's look more closely.

Right Pricing

Selling your foreclosure investment is part science, part marketing, and part negotiation. All transactions are different, and there are no foregone conclusions. If it all works out as planned—and you did your figuring based on what you paid for the property in pre-foreclosure—you should make a 15 percent net profit on the resale of your foreclosure investment.

Ideally, as investors we all want to get the best possible price and terms when selling a property. What we eventually get for a property, however, depends on several factors, including current market conditions. If your property is in a community with an expanding job base, a growing population, and a limited housing supply, it's likely that prices are rising. Alternatively, if that same community is losing jobs and people are moving out, prices likely will be declining.

When considering your property's value for resale, you must first have a list of current, sold properties. Remember, you should be able to get accurate comparable sales reports for a fee from your foreclosure listing service and it will be much more accurate than those online freebies. The value of your property is relative to the value of recently sold properties in the immediate neighborhood. That means the same home located elsewhere would likely have a different value.

A seller's needs can affect the selling price, too. If a neighbor must sell quickly, he will have less leverage in the marketplace. Buyers may think that the seller will take a lower price—and they may be right. (Hopefully, you will buy his house!) Conversely, when there is no incentive to sell quickly, you have an advantage in negotiations. (Remember, you *want* to sell, but you don't *need* to sell.)

Finding Data on Comps

The following are good sources for finding prices on current sold properties to use in figuring a property's resale value include.

- ForeclosureS.com (*www.foreclosures.com*).
- SiteXdata (*www.sitexdata.com*).
- Realquest (*www.realquest.com*).
- First American Real Estate Solutions (*www.firstamres.com*).
- DataQuick Information Systems (*www.dataquick.com*).
- Local Realtor Multiple Listing Services.
- Local title companies.

Sale prices are not based on what sellers need. If you say, "I must sell for $400,000 because I need $100,000 in cash now," a buyer will quickly ask if $400,000 is the right price for your property. If similar homes in the same community sell for $350,000, your offers will come in at $350,000 or not come in at all.

How much, though, is too much to ask for your property? That depends. Markets are flexible. How flexible depends again on local conditions. For example, if recent sales of comparable properties have ranged from $400,000 to $450,000, in a strong market perhaps you can ask $450,000 and get offers for a little more. If the market has slowed, though, $399,000 may be the right price to attract the most buyers.

Imagine a different scenario. Suppose you live in a community of arts and crafts bungalows built in the 1920s. All the homes are different in terms of size, condition, modernization, style, and features. In such a neighborhood, an average sale price has little practical meaning. On a single block one home may sell for $400,000 while another is priced at more than $1 million. The asking price may be outrageously high for one home and staggeringly low for another.

In those situations, you will need to drive by each comparable property and talk to the sellers about the condition of their property when they closed the sale. You'll learn a lot through these interviews. Most of all, you will have a clearer picture as to what repairs your property needs in order to fetch a specific resale price.

Next, compare your house with others currently on the market in the same area in the same price range. How do you think yours stacks up? Does your home seem inviting? Well-maintained? Do you see more value in your home than in the others? Would you want to buy this home at this price?

Your answer to these questions should be a big "yes." If not, consider why not, and then make sure you've done all the necessary rehab and polish on your property (more on what counts in the next section). Make it your goal to become knowledgeable in all aspects of the real estate market, as well as to understand what repairs will bring full market price. Make it your priority to maintain your ethical standards, too, as well as your personal honor and sense of empathy, while fine-tuning your truthful negotiation skills and successfully selling your property.

The Rehab/Remodel

If you want to get top dollar for a property you've purchased, it must be in top condition, period. That means the property should be as nice as the top comparable homes used in your original appraised valuation. Remember, that involves like homes in the area.

If a property is priced right, it will sell. Your job, then, is to make sure it *is* priced right so you can flip it for a solid profit. That entails making sure your original valuations, cost estimates, outlays, repairs, and more are on target up front. Too often, investors do not get their house in great condition for resale because they can't afford to. They can't afford to because they paid too much for the property in the first place and now must cut corners. The original big mistake quickly leads to new-investor demise.

To avoid that, you must know what the rehabbed and repaired home is worth (we talked about figuring that with comparables), and then you must decide what repairs will give you the most return on your money and how much those repairs will cost. Of course, you should already have a pretty good estimate from when you determined your offering price to the seller. Typically, repairs/upgrades will cost $15 to $25 or more per living-area square foot unless you are a contractor and can do the work yourself.

The repairs that offer the most bang for your buck vary depending on the age and condition of the home and how well it competes with other homes on the market at selling time. Figure 13.1 lists some repairs and popular upgrades, along with their average cost and return on investment (ROI).

Must-Haves

A typical home should have the following fixes:

- *Termites and dry rot.* Clearance on Section 1 of a termite report. That means repairing any damage already done to a property, such as damaged wood due to dry rot or bugs. Any action on Section 2 of the report (issues that could lead to potential problems) depends on the extent of damage and how the property compares with others in the area. A water leak, for example, might in the future lead to dry rot.

- *Roof.* Needs to be repaired with a three-year, water-tight guarantee, or another layer of composition added (check your local rules on how many layers of roofing your building codes allow), or replaced with a new 30-year composition roof.

- *Landscape.* Clean up, spruce up, and fix up any broken sprinklers or fencing; plant trees, shrubs, and flowers to increase curb appeal.

- *Paint.* Apply new paint inside and out.

- *Flooring.* New carpet, padding, and vinyl/linoleum even if you have hardwood.

- *Kitchen.* New appliances, new faucet, new or reglazed counters, cabinets cleaned up.

- *Bathrooms*. Reglaze tub/shower, new or reglazed sink/vanity, new toilet or at least toilet seat.
- *Heating and cooling system*. Clean vents; repair or replace condenser unit.

Full Appraised Value or Not?

If you want to get full-appraised value for a property, it must be in cherry condition. That means, as we said earlier, in as good condition as top comps in the neighborhood. It's not enough simply to replace the heating and cooling system or

---

HomeGain™ (www.homegain.com), an online resource that connects real estate professionals with homeowners and homebuyers, in its Prepare-to-Sell study* asked real estate agents nationally what home repairs result in the greatest return. Here's a summary of the 10 top areas for home improvement:

Product	Typical Cost	Sale Price Increase	ROI
Lighten/brighten home	$86–110	$768–935	769%
Clean/declutter home	$305–339	$2,093–2,378	594%
Landscape and trim front and back yards	$432–506	$1,594–1,839	266%
Stage a home for sale	$812–1,089	$2,275–2,841	169%
Repair damaged electrical/plumbing	$338–381	$922–1,208	196%
Repair damaged flooring	$1,531–1,714	$2,267–2,589	50%
Update kitchen/baths	$1,546–2,120	$3,823–4,885	138%
Replace or shampoo carpeting	$2,602–2,765	$3,585–3,900	39%
Paint exterior walls	$2,188–2,381	$2,907–3,233	57%
Paint interior walls	$1,453–1,588	$2,342–2,600	63%

*HomeGain™ surveyed approximately 2,000 real estate agents in 46 states nationwide. Agents might not necessarily agree on the same pre-sale strategy.

FIGURE 13.1   Return on Your Rehab/Repair Investments

reglaze the counters. Pay attention to the type of air-conditioning and heating systems, kitchens, and baths in the home and make sure they're comparable with current sold, pending, or competing sales on the market in the area. For example, if the property has wall air-conditioning, a floor furnace, and the original kitchen and bath from 1955 while your top comparables have central air and heat, a remodeled kitchen with new appliances, and a remodeled bath, you had better plan to upgrade your house to that extent, too.

If your walls are inconsistent in texture, have holes that need patching, or have many layers of wallpaper to remove, you had better plan to retexture the entire house for a consistent, fresh look. In some cases you'll need to entirely replace the drywall (when there is significant damage from roof leaks). Pay attention to baseboards; you'll want to make sure they match in all rooms as well.

If the front yard is dried out, brown, and weedy, you'll have to install automatic sprinklers, rototill the soil, and reseed the lawn. If the backyard fence is in poor repair or nonexistent, you'll need to repair or replace it, too. Use wood fencing, because chain-link fences are less attractive and don't hide the neighbor's ugly yard very well.

Think curb appeal, first impressions, and what makes a home show well.

More Ways to Spruce Up a Property

It's easy to fix up a property if you have unlimited cash and plan to live in the home. However, when it comes to repairing and rehabbing a property for sale or even rental, keep repairs to a minimum to attract buyers and still keep your deal profitable. Following are a few inexpensive ways to polish your property without lots of extra cash.

> *New electrical switch plates and plug.* This is a minor yet overlooked improvement. A switch plate and plug can cost less than a buck but few people bother to replace them. To give your property a cleaner look, replace them all. For the foyer, living room, and other obvious areas, spring for nice brass plates. They run about $5 each, which isn't much for that added touch of class.

> *New or improved interior doors.* Another overlooked yet cheap replacement item is doors. If you have ugly brown doors, replace them with nice white ones (you can paint them, but unless you have a spray gun it will take three coats by hand). A basic hollow-core door costs about $150 or a little more and comes preprimed and prehung. For about $20 more, you can buy stylish

six-panel doors. If you are doing a rehab, the extra cash per door is well worth the cost.

New door handles. Consider changing the handles on doors, too. An old door handle, especially if it's crusted with old paint, looks drab. For about $10, you can replace it with a new brass-finished handle. Replace the guest bathroom and bedroom door handles with fancy "S" handles (about $20 each).

Paint/replace trim. If the entire interior doesn't need a paint job, consider at least painting the trim. New, modern, custom homes typically come with beige or off-white walls and bright-white trim. Use a semigloss bright white on all the trim in your houses. If the floor trim is worn, cracked, or just plain ugly, replace it! Do-it-yourself home stores such as Home Depot carry inexpensive prepainted foam trim in several finishes.

New front door. You get one chance to make a first impression. A cheap front door makes a house look cheap. An old front door makes a house look old. If a property already has a nice heavy door, paint it a bold color using high-gloss paint. If your front door is old, consider replacing it with a new, stylish door.

Tile the foyer. After the front door, the next first impression is the foyer area. Consider upgrading it with tile or at least upscale, low-maintenance vinyl flooring.

Remove shower doors and curtains. This is a no-brainer. Old shower curtains and doors look awful. It amazes me that so many sellers show properties with a dirty shower curtain or ugly old shower door in the bathroom. Remove it all so the bathroom looks clean, bright, and much bigger.

Paint kitchen cabinets. If you don't want to spring for the cost of replacing kitchen cabinets, consider painting them instead. It's inexpensive and makes a big difference in how a house shows. If you have old 1970s-style wooden cabinets in a dark brown, paint them with a semigloss white and finish them with a cool knob.

Add a fancy kitchen faucet. For an added extra, put in a fancy, modern, kitchen faucet. Americans spend 99 percent of their time in the kitchen (when they are not watching TV) so why not make the experience more pleasing to the eye? Faucets can be expensive, but look for sales at a big-box retailer. You can pick up a discontinued style for half the normal cost.

Add a nice mailbox. Everyone on the block has the same black or brown mailbox. Make your property stand out. For about $100, you can buy a nice colorful mailbox and wooden post for it. People notice these things, and they like them!

Four Steps to Marketing Success

Market conditions constantly change, but if you rehab the property and market it correctly, you'll always find a buyer whether it's a seller's market (few properties, many buyers) or a buyer's market (many properties, fewer buyers). Let's look at the essentials for successful marketing of your pre-foreclosure purchase.

Step One: Mailer to Neighbors

As a professional investor, you need to make sure you have access to the tax assessor's data (aka sales comparables) for current ownership and property information. An easy way to generate a mailing campaign to neighbors is simply to search all properties within a one-mile radius of your subject property and print labels for a postcard mailer.

Your postcard basically should say, "Hi, I just bought your neighbor's house at (property's address). I am fixing it up and will be selling it shortly. Here's your chance to choose your neighbor! Have your friend or family member call me at (your contact number) ASAP. If they call quickly, they can even pick their colors! P.S. If you are thinking about selling, call me at (your contact number)! I am very interested in investing in your community. Thank you!"

Step 2: MLS Listing and FSBO Services

You have a choice to list your home with a Realtor or sell it yourself. I prefer to work on my own. But I still want the world to know about my house so I pay a flat-

Realtor versus FSBO

When listing a property for sale, you can opt to sell it yourself—FSBO—or through a Realtor. The choice is yours and depends on how much time and effort you want to invest in selling the property.

Whatever the choice, though, keep in mind that chances are you can't sell a property unless people know it's for sale. That means it needs to be listed in the local MLS or other online services.

rate broker to list my house on the MLS, and then offer the buyer's agent 3 to 4 percent commission if he brings me a bona fide buyer. I use flat-rate broker sites such as Homeseller's Assistance (www.whypay6.com) or FlatFeeMLSListing.com (www.flatfeemlslisting.com). For as low as $399 to $799, depending on your area and services provided, you'll be able to list a property on the local MLS as well as on FSBO sites, and obtain yard signs, disclosure and purchase agreements, online photos, lockbox, help with pricing, and more.

It's up to you to show the house, qualify the buyer, write the contract, and close the deal. But if you want help, the web site will handle those responsibilities for only 3 percent commission. If you want them to negotiate the deal for you, add another 1 percent commission. You can't beat that.

Step 3: Advertising

Now it's time to advertise your property in the classified section of your local major Sunday newspaper (print and online) as well as on Craigslist (www .craigslist.com) and other free advertising web sites. Advertise a brand-new listing FSBO, and announce the open house with address and hours. The ad should be brief. Generally an ad runs only a couple of weekends while you hold your open houses.

Step 4: Hold an Open House

Open houses are common in some communities but rarely used in others. They're an especially good tool to get the neighbors to come in to see the new finished product. They are also a great way to bring in people who are just checking out the area. Even if the house isn't right for them at this time, they could be potential buyers of your next property. Start making a list of their names and contact numbers for the future. A guest register is a great way to gather those names.

During the open house, make sure your property is inviting. Because it won't have furniture in it, bring a few barstools into the kitchen. Arrive early and bake some cookies (what a great smell) for your visitors. Have a plate of warm cookies and glasses of milk available. Beside your cookie plate, have a list of "what's on the market." Ask your buyers if they have seen those houses. How does your house look compared with the others? Do they see more value in your home than in the others? Listen carefully and note all feedback. This will help you find out quickly if you have priced your property right.

Negotiating the Sale

Selling your investment property is an important event. Big profits are involved and complex issues negotiated, so it's critical that you do it properly.

If you've done it all right thus far, your efforts should bring in multiple potential buyers with multiple offers. Don't jump at the first one. You want to make sure your buyer qualifies for a loan on your property.

Choosing the Best Offer

In a buyers' market, you'll likely get fewer offers than in one primed for sellers. But that doesn't mean you can't and won't get good solid offers. Evaluate each offer with the following in mind:

- Is the offer near, at, or above your asking price?
- How much down payment and deposit will the buyer put down?
- Is the potential buyer preapproved or prequalified, and is the approval in writing?
- In speaking with the mortgage broker, how far along is the potential buyer in the application process?
- If a contract were signed today, how soon could their lender fund their loan and close?

What Next?

Before you immediately jump at an offer, keep in mind that most offers, no matter how good the price and terms look, will have certain clauses or contingencies that are simply unacceptable. Contract clauses, for example, can have very important consequences that could include:

- Personal warranties for a home you never lived in.
- Hidden seller costs that could seriously affect your net profit.
- Inspections that could lead to further price negotiations.
- Extensions of time to close escrow, which would increase your holding costs.

Evaluate all the offers and then make a counteroffer to the most solid buyer. That's the buyer who can close the quickest with the fewest contingencies. Include your own terms and conditions in your counteroffer, and then let the other buyers know they are second or third in line. That way if the first-choice buyer can't or won't accept your counteroffer, you move to the next in line.

More Negotiating Tips

Successful negotiations involve compromises by both sides and end with a win-win deal. Everyone should be happy not only when the deal closes but many years later.

If you were to have a big party and invite every buyer and seller with whom you ever did a deal, they'd better all want to show up! If they don't, you did something terribly wrong along the way.

—Alexis McGee

Here are some points to keep in mind from the outset of negotiations to sell your property:

- Begin all negotiations with an understanding of your deal's strengths and weaknesses.
- Never underestimate the attractiveness of competing houses on the market.
- Make sure you have the best product at the best price.
- Make sure you have a product everyone wants and needs.
- Make sure you are not competing against too many other houses in the same category and market. You must begin with the leverage that having the best house in your market gives you.

The Next Step

Once you and a potential buyer reach agreement on a deal, you'll go through the closing process. The same rules apply in this closing as when you closed on your purchase of the property. Don't forget that all selling parties in the deal *must* bring a valid driver's license (or acceptable equivalent) to closing so documents can be notarized. Contact the title insurance company and take advantage of that hold-open discount you negotiated when you initially purchased the property.

You can expect your paycheck at the end of escrow. Hand over the keys, and smile all the way to the bank. After that first deal, the sky indeed is the limit. Before you're ready to jump on the next deal, though, look back at what you did and did not do throughout the process. Ask yourself the following questions:

- What worked?

- What didn't work, and why?

- What could you have done differently to make the process and the deals smoother?

I also keep spreadsheets of all buying, holding, and selling expenses for each deal, both projected and actual. Then I keep track of the average costs and apply them to the next deal. This can be a big help down the road on other properties when you need to make a quick offer and don't have time to research every item. Nor do you always have time to get a contractor's estimate until after you've bought a property. If you are new to the business, this can be somewhat problematic because you don't have a history of costs to work with.

Once you've done the follow-up paperwork and analysis, it's time to revel in your personal and financial success as well as in the satisfaction that you helped someone out of their financial troubles. Consider your future, too. Success will happen again and again if you truly accept the approach, processes, and procedures we've detailed in the past pages.

Dream big, and then plan the next steps to achieve your dream. You've earned it!

TAKEaway

Key points to remember:

- If your rehabbed and updated home doesn't sell right away, you've done something wrong. Have you priced it right? Did you complete the necessary upgrades and repairs? Did you misdiagnose markets?

- When it comes to rehabbing a property, think first impressions and curb appeal. Pay attention to what your house looks like and how it shows. Cosmetics count.

- Pay attention to top homes in the neighborhood, too. How does your property stack up? It had better be comparable or it won't sell for top dollar without a lot of headaches and hassles.

- Price your property right. Pay attention to those comps you used in your initial appraisal and the current state of the local real estate market. Price your home to sell it.

- Market your property properly, too. That means tell the neighbors about it, advertise it, place it in the local MLS, and hold an open house. Make sure everyone knows about the open house.

- Polish up your negotiating techniques. Don't jump at the first offer. Make sure any potential buyer is well qualified and can close with the fewest hassles.

*We all want financial success, but there is much more to
life than just money. What really matters is what the
money brings you and what you do with it!*

—Alexis McGee

Completing a deal requires a great deal of preparation. As a professional investor, you must be aware of the many factors we've discussed throughout this book, including:

- Where to buy your houses.
- What type of property to buy.
- Where and how to find motivated sellers.
- How to talk to those sellers.
- How to find solutions to their problems in a selfless way.
- What you should say and *not* say to owners in foreclosure.
- How to practice the Golden Rule with strength and high moral standards.
- How to develop a good team of Realtors, investors, mortgage brokers, title officers, escrow agents, and contractors.
- What price to offer so you will make a reasonable profit.
- How to get the seller to say yes to your offer.
- How to find the money you'll need (when you don't have or don't want to use your own) to close on time.
- What repairs are needed to get top dollar when you resell.
- How not to overimprove your property so you don't lose money.
- How to minimize your holding time and carrying costs.
- How to set the right price and market your house to get a stampede of buyers.
- How to choose the most qualified buyer.
- How to get your buyer to sign your contract.

Some of these issues may seem simple, others extremely difficult. But, as with any new venture, you will succeed if you learn what you need to know and make the right decisions.

You may decide to learn on your own for a while. I call this getting an education from the "school of hard knocks," which generally ends up costing you much more in lost profits than if you invest in learning the business first. Remember, education always precedes wealth.

You don't know what you don't know. Are you ready to eat a $50,000 mistake? What is it worth to you to *not* have that happen? What about the cost of not closing any deals for a year? That happened to me when I first started 15 years ago. How much money have you left on the table?

After 20 years of investing and 15 years of training investors, I know what it takes to be successful. I hope in these pages I've been able to impart some of that knowledge to you.

Where you go from here truly is up to you. Whatever you choose, though, try not to lose sight of treating homeowners in default with dignity and respect, and as you would like to be treated if in the same situation. Your gains will be magnified financially and personally, and you will sleep well at night!

I hope to hear about your successes next. Good luck, and happy deal-making!

The leader in foreclosure-investing education, ForeclosureS.com boasts teachers who are nationally recognized experts and who have been involved in buying investment property since 1983.

ForeclosureS.com offers cutting-edge, investor-oriented learning programs for both new and seasoned professional investors. Students have access to exclusive learning programs as well as the experts in foreclosure investing. Personal foreclosure-investing coaches work closely with our students, sharing up-to-date techniques and life experiences to guide each student through the investing process and—ultimately—to success.

Intensive Help Through Our Exclusive Learning Programs

Alexis McGee has developed a proven four-step system to help investors maximize their foreclosure lists and, subsequently, their foreclosure-investing success. Step 1 introduces you to what works now in the foreclosure business. Steps 2 to 4 teach you exactly what to do (and what not to do) so you can begin generating pre-foreclosure profits in your own backyard and without your own money!

- **Step 1: Sign up for Alexis' Webinar and Teleconference Call,** *Jump-Start Your Foreclosure Profits*: Chat with Alexis and her guest panelists in a 90-minute webinar teleconference call with live chat.

- **Step 2: Order the Home-Study Course,** *Seven Steps to Mastering Foreclosures*: Step-by-step, complete systems for buying great deals and selling them in any market (includes home-study CD course with digital forms and bonus DVD).

- **Step 3: Enroll in Mastering Systems Lab:** Three days of hands-on tutoring from Alexis and her coaches in their new, state-of-the-art training facility.

- **Step 4: Join the Personal Foreclosure-Investor Coaching Program:** Get one-on-one training with your personal ForeclosureS.com coach (for lab graduates only).

Start Learning Now!

We invite you to check us out. You'll see why so many people agree that **ForeclosureS.com** is more than a database. It's *your* knowledge base for success in foreclosure and pre-foreclosure investing.

I look forward to helping you succeed and serve others for many years to come. Happy investing.

Alexis McGee and the ForeclosureS.com Team
800-310-7730, ext. 2

abandonment Situation in which homeowner leaves house with no intention to return.

abstract of judgment Summary of a judgment in a lawsuit; includes who won, who lost, amount owed, the court making the decisions, date of judgment, and winning attorney. Once recorded (filed with county clerk or recorder), it creates a general lien on judgment debtor's property that's usually discovered by title company in conjunction with property sale. Most title companies require lien be paid as a condition of insuring resale.

acceleration clause Part of trust deed or mortgage that gives lender right to call/demand all money owed as due and payable immediately in the event a specific event (such as a sale) occurs.

acceptance When seller's or agent's principal agrees to terms of the agreement of sale, approves negotiation on the part of agent, and acknowledges receipt of deposit.

accrued items of expense Incurred expenses not yet payable; seller's accrued expenses credited to purchaser in closing statement.

adjustable rate mortgage (ARM) Loan with an interest rate that can vary up or down at certain intervals (periods) and within certain limits (caps); loan is secured by house on which lender will foreclose if loan is not paid.

alienation Transferring property from one person to another.

alienation/acceleration/due on sale clause States that on sale or transfer of certain property, a loan is immediately due and payable.

all-inclusive deed or trust Also known as a wraparound contract, a mortgage document that includes amount actually financed as part of a property purchase as well as amounts of any prior deeds of trust.

amortization Repayment of a debt in installments.

amortization mortgage A debt in which periodic repayments reduce the outstanding principal and pay off current interest charges.

apportionment Adjustment of income, expenses, or carrying charges on real estate, usually computed to the date of closing of title so seller pays all expenses to that date and buyer assumes all expenses after that.

appraisal Estimate of property's value as made by a trained, licensed professional.

appraisal by comparison Estimate of property value made by comparing sale prices of similar properties in the same area.

appurtenance Something outside of a property but belonging to the land and adding to its greater enjoyment, such as a right-of-way, barn, or dwelling.

as is When a property is sold as is, its seller does not warrant or guarantee the property is free of defects; buyer accepts property in present condition without modification.

assessed valuation Value placed on property by public officer or board as basis for taxation.

assessment Charge against real estate made by a unit of government to cover a proportionate cost of an improvement such as a street or sewer.

assessor Official who has responsibility for determining assessed valuation.

assessor's parcel number Numeral assigned by county tax assessor to identify parcel of real property.

assignment Method or manner by which a right or contract is transferred from one person (the assignor) to another (the assignee).

assignment of rents Procedure in which borrower gives lender the right to receive rents collected from a tenant in a house owned by borrower.

assumes and agrees to pay Clause in deed or related document in which a buyer who takes over payments on a seller's old loan also agrees to pay the old loan; buyer normally receives title and makes payments. Clause is often found in section of document that transfers title from the seller to the buyer; seller may or may not be released from liability.

assumption of mortgage Occurs when person takes title to property and assumes liability for payment of existing note or bond secured by mortgage against the property.

auction Process of selling property at public sale to highest bidder.

automatic stay Court order when bankruptcy is filed that prevents any creditor from attempting to collect any debt from the person who declared bankruptcy; creditors may not undertake foreclosure, repossession, eviction, or seizure, or even call or write the debtor demanding payment, and instead must join all other creditors and go through bankruptcy court to seek any money owed them.

balance owed on loan The part of the original loan that remains unpaid by the borrower at a given point in time.

balloon payment Final installment on a loan that pays off debt; larger than previous installments.

bankruptcy Action filed in federal bankruptcy court that allows creditor to reorganize or discharge credit obligations due to insolvency; property owner may restrain foreclosure action by filing bankruptcy.

bearer Lender in whose hands the promissory note remains until it is paid in full.

beneficiary (1) One entitled to the benefit of a trust; (2) one who receives profit from an estate, the title of which is vested in a trustee; (3) lender on a security of a note and deed of trust.

beneficiary's statement Also known as a "benny statement," a written statement of conditions and remaining balance on loan secured by a deed of trust.

bill of complaint Initial paperwork filed in many states to begin foreclosure; part of the process of filing a lawsuit.

bill of sale Document that passes title to personal property from seller to buyer.

bond Set sum of money or assets available if needed to pay to court or other named person upon a certain event.

broker price opinion Real estate broker's estimate of property's reasonable selling price; often less than professional appraisal but often more useful because it's a realistic marketing price.

buydown Arrangement in which seller pays some or all of buyer's loan costs, usually measured by increments (points) of 1 percent of loan; seller pays enough points so that lender can offer loan at reduced interest rate (and lower monthly payment); cost to seller is small, but the reduction in payments to buyer can be substantial; often structured to reduce interest rates (and payments) in early years of loan. In a 3-2-1 buydown, the seller pays enough points to reduce the buyer's interest rate 3 percent the first year, 2 percent the second year and 1 percent the third year; in the fourth year, the loan interest rate and the monthly payments would return to the normal market rate of interest as set initially.

capital improvement Permanent structure change that extends useful life and value of a property, such as a new roof.

certificate of sale Document indicating a property has been sold to a buyer at foreclosure sale subject to right of redemption for a set period after the sale; redemption periods vary, but with IRS, it's 180 days; foreclosures often take place without a certificate of sale indicating sale is final or near final, and buyer gets deed instead.

chain of title History of conveyances and encumbrances affecting a title from the time the original patent or right to the land was granted, or as far back as records are available.

Chapter 7 Chapter in the federal Bankruptcy Code that calls for liquidation; a debtor's nonexempt assets are gathered together and given up or sold for benefit of creditors in order of their priority; debts are not discharged; secured creditors receive continued payments or the asset as collateral for the loan; unsecured creditors usually get little or nothing.

Chapter 13 Chapter in the federal Bankruptcy Code that gives wage earner the right to reduce debt payments through a bankruptcy court order according to the terms of a plan that will allow the debtor to pay much or even all of the original amounts owed.

chattel Personal property such as household goods or fixtures.

chattel mortgage Mortgage on personal property.

clear title Ownership rights to piece of real estate that are not diminished by liens, leases, or other encumbrances.

client Principal who employs and compensates a broker.

closing date Date on which buyer takes over the property.

cloud on the title Outstanding claim or encumbrance that, if valid, affects or impairs owner's title.

collateral Additional security pledged for payment of debt.

collections Activity in which lenders or their agents employ various techniques to pressure borrowers to pay what's owed.

color of title Apparent invalid title.

condemnation Acquisition of private property for public use with what's considered fair compensation to the owner.

conditional sales contract Contract for sale of property that calls for seller to deliver property, but title remains vested in the seller until conditions of contract are fulfilled.

condominium Land ownership arrangement in which one owns an individual unit and a percentage of common area.

conforming loans Loans that meet Federal National Mortgage Association (Fannie Mae) standards.

conservatorship When the Federal Deposit Insurance Corporation takes over and runs a bank or S&L until it can be sold either complete or broken down into its major components. (During the S&L crisis of the 1980s, the Resolution Trust Corporation was also involved in conservatorship.)

consideration When parties in a contract exchange something of value such as goods, services, or promises.

constructive notice Information someone is assumed by law to have because it could be ascertained by proper diligence and inquiry in public records.

contingency fee Employment arrangement commonly used by attorneys in which payment is a percentage of whatever monetary damages are awarded in a lawsuit's final judgment.

contract for deed Sales arrangement in which seller holds title until buyer completes payment for property and then receives title/deed; terms of sale and payments are set in written contract signed by buyer and seller.

conventional lender Group or individual that makes conventional loans.

conventional loan Private loan not insured or guaranteed by any agency of the federal government.

conversion Exchange of personal real property of one character or use for another.

conveyance Process of transferring title or some interest in real estate to a new owner.

correlation Final state of the appraisal process in which appraiser reviews data and estimates property's value.

covenants Agreements written into deeds and other instruments promising performance or nonperformance of certain acts or stipulating certain uses or restrictions on a property.

coverage Amount of money insurance company will pay in response to a claim.

cram-down Chapter 13 bankruptcy arrangement in which plan to repay lenders and creditors developed by debtor's attorney is ordered into effect by the court; it's *crammed down* on sometimes unwilling creditors.

credit Willingness of borrower to repay loaned money; usually measured by borrower's past record of payments on loans and debts as maintained in a *credit report*.

cured default When borrower's failure to make payments or meet the terms of a loan is corrected to the lender's satisfaction.

current value Value of a property at time of appraisal.

damages Monetary compensation set by court for loss suffered by party to a lawsuit.

debt service Annual amount to be paid by debtor for money borrowed.

decree Final order of a court in many states.

deed Legal document commonly used to transfer ownership of real estate from one owner to the next.

deed in lieu of foreclosure Borrower deeds property, usually to lender, instead of waiting for lender to force sale of house in foreclosure.

deed of reconveyance Instrument that releases and discharges deed of trust.

deed of restriction Limits use of land; might include clauses preventing sale of liquor on property or defining size, type, value, or placement of improvements.

deed of trust (trust deed) Type of mortgage given by property owner to secure performance of an act (such as making payments on a loan).

default Failure to fulfill duty or promise, or to discharge an obligation; omission or failure to perform an act. In property foreclosure, usually the failure to pay loan installment repayments when they become due.

defeasance clause Part of a mortgage that permits borrower to redeem his or her property on payment of mortgage obligations.

defeased To lose ownership; in medieval times ownership rights constituted a fee and to be defeased meant to lose the fee.

defendant's original answer First responsive pleading of a defendant in a lawsuit.

deficiency Money that a borrower who has lost real estate in foreclosure still owes to the lender because the foreclosure sale failed to generate enough money to pay off the loan. Frequently lenders acquire title to real estate at foreclosures and often only credit fair market value of property against balance due on the loan; any unpaid balance on loan after all just credits are applied generally is amount of deficiency. Many states limit or restrict deficiencies.

deficiency judgment A court judgment that the defaulting borrower owes a deficiency.

delinquency The state of affairs when payments on a note or other loan obligation are past due.

demand note A note payable on demand of the holder.

Department of Veterans Affairs Federal government department that guarantees loans and performs other services for veterans; formerly known as Veterans Administration (VA).

discharge of indebtedness or debt Lender informs borrower a loan does not have to be repaid.

discovery Phase of lawsuit when parties may ask each other formal written and oral questions, obtain copies of documents, and in general find out facts related to the lawsuit.

documentary transfer tax Applicable to transfers of real property, notice of payment entered on face of the deed or on a separate paper filed with the deed.

double whammy When lenders refuse to permit loan assumptions while, at the same time, insisting on hefty prepayment penalty when a nonassumable loan is paid off early.

down payment Initial cash a borrower pays to seller to purchase a property; does not include closing costs.

due on encumbrance Clause in mortgage preventing a borrower from encumbering title to the property with liens, leases, or other encumbrances without the lender's consent.

due on sale Mortgage clause demanding that borrower pay off the loan in full if the house is ever sold; lender can't prevent sale but can demand payment in full on the loan balance. Without a due on sale clause, loan is assumable without lender's consent; older FHA and DVA loans are assumable without lender's consent.

earnest money Down payment made by purchaser of real estate as evidence of good faith.

earnest money contract Agreement in which seller agrees to sell and the buyer agrees to buy.

easement Right that may be exercised by the public or individuals on, over, or through the property of others.

encroachment Building, part of building, or obstruction that intrudes on the property of another.

entry and possession Method of foreclosure in some states in which lender, who already owns property, reenters it and takes possession away from borrower, either peacefully or by court order.

equity Excess of fair market value over the outstanding loan balance.

equity cushion Amount of equity required before lender will make a loan.

equity loan Junior (subordinate) loan based on a percentage of the equity.

equity right of redemption Right of property owner to avert foreclosure by paying the debt, interest, and costs.

equity skimmer Scam artist who assumes loan, collects money up front, and possibly rents, then refuses to pay the payments on assumed loan while keeping cash paid up front.

escrow Deposit held ready for some use, such as to pay taxes and insurance on a mortgaged property.

estate Degree, quantity, nature, and extent of interest (ownership) that a person has in real property.

estoppel certificate Instrument executed by the mortgagor setting forth status of and balance due on mortgage as of date of certificate execution.

eviction Legal procedure to forcibly remove a tenant from dwelling.

exclusive right to sell Agreement to give, for a specified period, only one broker the right to sell a property; if sale during term of agreement is made by owner or any other broker, the broker holding exclusive right is entitled to compensation.

execution sale Sale of property by a sheriff pursuant to a court order.

extending loan term Giving borrower more time to repay a loan.

extension agreement Accord that extends life of a mortgage.

Fair Credit Reporting Act Federal law regulating credit bureaus and credit reports that grants individuals certain rights regarding both.

fair market value Amount a willing and knowledgeable buyer would pay and seller would accept in a property transaction.

Fannie Mae See *Federal National Mortgage Association*.

FCL Abbreviation for *foreclosure*, used on borrower's credit record.

Federal Deposit Insurance Corporation (FDIC) Agency set up by the federal government to insure deposits at banks and S&Ls.

Federal Home Loan Mortgage Corporation (Freddie Mac) A government-chartered, privately owned entity that buys mortgages from S&Ls.

Federal Housing Administration (FHA) Federal agency that regulates many aspects of the real estate industry and insures repayment of certain home loans.

Federal National Mortgage Association (Fannie Mae) Government-chartered, privately owned corporation that buys mortgages from mortgage companies.

Federal Savings and Loan Insurance Corporation (FSLIC) Corporation formerly run by the federal government that insured deposits in S&Ls; FDIC took over its function; leftover FSLIC deposit insurance funds were transferred to Savings Association Insurance Fund (SAIF).

FHA guidelines Rules specifying income and credit requirements for borrower and condition and value of property to allow an insured loan of a specific amount.

FHA mortgage Loan insured by Federal Housing Administration.

FHLMC See *Federal Home Loan Mortgage Corporation*.

first lien Debt recorded first against a property.

first mortgage Loan with priority as a lien over all other mortgages; in cases of foreclosure, the first mortgage must be satisfied before other mortgages are paid off.

FNMA See *Federal National Mortgage Association.*

for sale by owner (FSBO) A property marketed by its owner without help of a real estate broker.

forbearance Lender voluntarily accepts lower payments than originally agreed to in loan documents for a specific time period to allow borrower to recover financially; borrower eventually must repay missing or reduced payments and all other remaining payments on loan.

foreclosure Forced sale of real estate to repay debt.

fraud Intentional false statements believed and relied on by an individual who suffered a loss as a result.

Freddie Mac See *Federal Home Loan Mortgage Corporation.*

freeze order Automatic stay; bankruptcy court order that prevents creditors from attempting to collect debt from individual who declared bankruptcy. Creditors may not undertake foreclosure, repossession, eviction or seizure, or even call or write the debtor demanding payment, and instead must join all other creditors and go through bankruptcy court to seek any money owed them.

FSA Designation for Federal Savings Association.

full assumption Arrangement in which buyer takes title to property and takes over payments on seller's old loan with the full permission of lender; new buyer also must prove to lender (qualify) adequate income and creditworthiness.

Ginnie Mae See *Government National Mortgage Association (GNMA).*

good repair Borrower's obligation to maintain condition of mortgaged property.

Government National Mortgage Association Also known as Ginnie Mae (GNMA), arm of federal government that purchases loans.

grace period Additional time allowed to perform an act or make payment before a default occurs.

grant Term used in deeds of conveyance of land to indicate a transfer.

grant deed Conveyance document that implies grantor (seller) is granting an actual interest and has not previously granted such interest to anyone else.

grantee Party to whom the title to real property is conveyed.

grantor Person who conveys real estate by deed; the seller.

guarantee Federal insurance, such as from the Department of Veterans Affairs, that agrees to cover loss up to a certain dollar figure on a loan made by a private lender if it goes into default and foreclosure.

hearing A proceeding in court.

homestead Special legal protection that many states give to an individual's principal residence.

Housing and Urban Development (HUD) Department of federal government that administers housing programs.

hypothecate To use something as security without giving up possession of it.

impound account Account held by lender, used to advance payments of certain expenses or charges incidental to property ownership and that may protect lender's security.

incumbrance Any right to or interest in property interfering with its use or transfer, or subjecting it to an obligation; with foreclosures, incumbrance likely includes mortgages and unpaid tax claims.

installment Parts of the same debt, payable at successive periods as agreed; payments made to reduce a mortgage.

instrument Written legal document.

Internal Revenue Service (IRS) Arm of the U.S. government that collects taxes.

involuntary lien Lien imposed against property without consent of owner-such as taxes, special assessments.

jeopardy To have property or liberty subjected to a possibly adverse decree of a court or agency.

joint tenancy Ownership of property by two or more individuals, each with an undivided interest and right of survivorship.

judgment Final decision of court.

judicial foreclosure Foreclosure action executed by the court.

junior lien holder Holder of a right to force sale of property that is subordinate to another lien holder's right to do the same. A junior lien holder who forces the sale of real estate must either pay off senior lien or make arrangements to make payments on it to prevent it from being foreclosed. Foreclosure of first lien eliminates right of junior lien holder to foreclose, but foreclosure of a junior lien does not affect right of senior lien to foreclose.

junior mortgage Mortgage second or subsequent in lien to a previous mortgage.

land sale contract Document transferring ownership rights but not title that may be used to sell property.

late payments Set amount that may be paid past its due date in accordance with loan documents.

lease with option to buy Arrangement in which property owner rents to a tenant who has the right to purchase the property on agreed terms.

lender approval Lender's agreement to allow assumption after review of borrower's creditworthiness and income; can also apply to initial loan.

lender liability Holds lenders legally responsible to pay damages for legal misdeeds committed against borrowers in course of making loans.

liability Obligation to pay a debt.

lien Right to force sale of property to pay a debt.

lien holder Person or institution that controls a lien.

life estate Conveyance of title to property for duration of the life of grantee.

life tenant Holder of a life estate.

liquidating plan Arrangement in which borrower repays missed payments to lender over time.

liquidation appraisal Estimate of property's value in a forced sale (when it's sold quickly); usually less than fair market value.

lis pendens Recorded notice indicating a lawsuit is in progress that could affect title to a piece of land.

listing agreement Accord in which seller hires a real estate broker to sell a property, usually for a commission.

loan balance Amount a borrower owes on a loan.

loan modification Procedure in which a loan's terms, such as interest rate, monthly payment, or duration, are altered.

loan officer Person who is paid commissions to find and sign up borrowers for loans.

loan pool Group of mortgages in which investors own shares.

loan processor Person who gathers and prepares paperwork used by lender to determine whether to make loan.

lot book report Document from title company that identifies encumbrances recorded against a particular property; does not identify liens recorded in the name of the owner that may affect property.

marketable title Property title considered free from defect by court that will enforce its acceptance by purchaser.

maven (Also mavin or mayvin) Regarded by cohorts as a trusted expert in a particular field, and who seeks to pass his or her knowledge on to others.

mechanic's lien Claim that secures the price of labor done on and materials furnished for uncompensated improvements.

metes and bounds Land description that sets forth all boundary lines together with their uncompensated improvement.

misrepresentation Making false statements in the course of a business transaction.

mortgage Instrument in writing, duly executed and delivered, that creates a lien on real estate as security for payment of specified debt, usually in the form of a bond.

mortgage commitment Formal indication made by lender that grants a mortgage loan on property for a specified amount and terms.

mortgage company Group that makes home loans to borrowers; most then resell the loans on secondary market to loan buyers but continue to service the loans under contracts, collecting payments from borrowers and handling trouble (such as default and foreclosure) with the loan.

Mortgage Guaranty Insurance Corporation (MGIC) Major private insurer of mortgage loans in the United States.

mortgage instrument Legal paperwork to create mortgage.

mortgage lien Right of lender to force sale of mortgaged property if borrower fails to repay the loan as agreed.

mortgage reduction certificate Instrument executed by mortgagee that gives status of and balances due on loan as of the date document is executed.

mortgagee Lender.

mortgagee's title policy Title insurance policy that will pay off lender's loss if title to the mortgaged property fails.

mortgagor Borrower.

motion to lift stay Formal request to bankruptcy court to dissolve an automatic stay that prevents a lender from foreclosing; once granted, lender may proceed to foreclose unless borrower can keep up payments.

negative equity Position in which outstanding loans on property exceed its worth.

nonjudicial foreclosure Foreclosure on a mortgage without filing lawsuit or obtaining court order; generally occurs because borrower has signed document such as deed of trust that gives trustee right to sell property to pay off debt.

notary public Person legally authorized to take sworn affidavits and certify certain classes of documents, such as deeds, contracts, mortgages.

note Legal document specifying terms of a loan (including rate, duration, provisions dealing with failure to pay in timely manner).

notice of default Letter sent to party as reminder loan has not been paid; may include a grace period and penalties for failing to cure the default.

notice of rescission Document that cancels notice of default.

one-action rule Rule of law, used heavily in California, forcing lender to bring only one court action or proceeding against a borrower in foreclosure; hampers lender's ability to obtain deficiency judgment.

open mortgage A mortgage that has matured or is overdue and, therefore, may be foreclosed at any time.

origination Creation of a loan.

owner-occupied Home used by borrower as his/her primary residence.

partial payments Those that are less than the full amount borrower owes on a loan.

performance bond Used to guarantee completion of an endeavor in accordance with a contract.

plat book Public record containing maps of land showing division into streets, blocks, and lots and indicating the measurements of individual parcels.

PMI-assisted presale Private mortgage insurance (PMI) company pays part of loss when house with negative equity (loans exceed property value) is sold by regular means prior to foreclosure.

points Discount charges by lenders that raise loan yields.

positive equity When a property's value exceeds amount due on mortgage.

posting Placing legal notice of foreclosure sale on public display as legally specified.

power of attorney Document signed and executed by owner of property that authorizes agent to act on his/her behalf.

power-of-sale clause Portion of deed of trust or mortgage in which borrower preauthorizes sale of property to pay off loan balance in case of default.

prepaids Costs of purchasing home that buyer pays at closing to a third party.

prepayment clause Statement in mortgage granting mortgagor right to pay off debt early.

primary lender Lender that deals directly with borrower.

private mortgage insurance (PMI) Insurance that protects a lender in the event borrower defaults on loan.

property condition Property's physical state.

prorations Allocation of closing costs and credits to buyers and sellers.

purchase money mortgage Mortgage given by grantee in part payment of purchase price of real estate.

qualifying Process lender undertakes prior to agreeing to make a loan that evaluates a buyer's income and credit, the property's physical condition, and compares figures with the lender's guidelines.

quiet title suit Lawsuit to ascertain legal rights of an owner to a certain parcel of real property.

quitclaim deed Conveys grantor's rights or interest in real estate; generally considered inadequate except when interests are being passed from one spouse to the other.

real estate owned (REO) Property acquired by lender through foreclosure and held in inventory.

recasting Restructuring loan with new interest rate and term; can be same loan from same lender.

receivership What happens when FDIC takes over bank to liquidate its assets; REO is taken over by FDIC's liquidation division; existing contracts with institution can be voided at the option of the FDIC.

recording Act of writing or entering in public record instruments affecting the title to real property.

recourse Right to claim against prior owner of property or note.

redemption Right of mortgagor to property by paying debt before sale at foreclosure; right of owner to reclaim property after its foreclosure sale to settle claims for unpaid taxes.

refinance Process of replacing old loan with new one, usually at lower interest rate.

release clause Statement in mortgage that gives property owner right to pay off part of debt, thus freeing part of property from mortgage.

release of liability Document relieving individual's obligation to pay loan; may be obtained when buyer takes over payments on seller's old loan if buyer meets lender's standards for income and creditworthiness.

relief Various types of special payment plans or other assistance offered to borrowers who have missed payments; enables borrower to bring loan current.

removal Process of transferring a case from state to federal court.

repayment plan Plan for repaying missed payments over time.

request for notice of default Document that under statutory provisions allows certain interested parties to request and be entitled to notification of default.

right of rescission Authorization to back out of contract.

right of survivorship Opportunity for surviving joint owner to take over interests of deceased joint owner; a distinguishing feature of joint tenancy or tenancy by the entirety.

sales contract Legal document in which buyer and seller agree to terms of sale.

satisfaction piece Receipt for paid-off mortgage.

scire facias Court order to borrower to attend hearing and show cause why fore-closure should not be authorized.

second deed of trust Subordinate position to another deed of trust securing same parcel.

second mortgage Mortgage made by home buyer in addition to existing first mortgage.

secondary market The market in which investors buy loans from primary lenders, who deal directly with borrowers to originate loans.

servicing Process of administering mortgage loan including collecting payments, maintaining insurance, and undertaking special measures such as workouts and foreclosures as necessary.

short sale/also short payoff Workout procedure in which lender accepts less than full balance due on loan as part of deal in which borrower cooperates with lender to obtain quick sale.

simple assumption Arrangement in which seller conveys property's title to buyer and moves out while buyer moves in and makes payments on old loan; lender does not qualify buyer's credit and income, so this may be a *no-approval loan*; seller re-mains liable on old loan under such circumstances. (Only loans without strong *due on sale* clauses are assumable without approval, including DVA loans made before March 1, 1988; FHA loans made before December 15, 1989; and conventional loans made before 1973.)

special assessment Assessment made against a property to pay for a public im-provement.

strict foreclosure Legal premise in some states that gives lender ownership to property, allows borrower to be evicted for nonpayment, and then gives lender full and complete title by waiting a set time period until borrower's right to redeem ends (lender also gets any property value in excess of what's owed on loan).

subdivision　Tract of land divided into lots or plots.

subject-to clause　Statement in a deed that transfers title from seller to buyer in an assumption transaction, or in other paperwork for the assumption transaction, in which buyer refuses to accept legal liability to make payments, although buyer expects to make them; lender's remedy for nonpayment is limited to foreclosure, and lender can't sue defaulting buyer for missed payments on the loan balance.

subordinate clause　Statement in a mortgage that gives priority to mortgage taken out at later date.

subrogation for mortgage insurers　Right of mortgage insurance company to file suit to recover losses due to borrower's default from the money borrower already paid to lender.

summary judgment　Legal procedure in which one side wins lawsuit without trial by showing the case involves no material fact issues but only legal issues that can be decided by the judge; if judge agrees, then one side wins by *summary judgment*.

survey　Process by which parcel of land is measured and its area ascertained; also the blueprint showing measurements, boundaries, and area.

tax sale　When property is sold after a period of nonpayment of taxes.

temporary injunction　Court order freezing the status quo for extended time period, typically until full court trial can determine merits of case; can require posting bond, though many states' laws waive that in cases involving home foreclosure.

temporary restraining order　Court command that freezes status quo for short time until other legal relief is awarded or settlement between litigants can be reached.

tenancy at will　A license to use or occupy lands and tenements at the will of the owner.

tenancy by the entirety　An estate that exists only between husband and wife with equal right of possession and enjoyment during their joint lives and with right of survivorship.

Tenancy in common　Ownership of real estate by two or more people, each of whom has an undivided interest without right of survivorship.

title　Evidence of ownership of land.

title defect　Unresolved claim against ownership of property that prevents presentation of marketable title; such claims may arise from failure of owner's spouse or former part-owner to sign deed, as well as from current liens against property or interruption in title's records of property.

title insurance Insurance policy that protects holder from any loss caused by defects in title.

title report Document indicating current state of title, including easements, covenants, liens, and any other defects; does not describe the chain of title.

title search Examination of public records to determine ownership and encumbrances affecting real property.

trust deed A type of mortgage that gives lender the power to foreclose and take title away from borrower.

trustee Person named in deed of trust or other mortgage to conduct any foreclosure proceedings and sell property to pay off mortgage loan balance.

trustee's deed Type of deed issued to buyer at foreclosure by trustee.

trustee's sale Nonjudicial action in which trustee may auction and sell property secured by a deed of trust subsequent to default in terms and conditions of loan.

trustee's sale guarantee Title insurance policy for benefit of trustee handling foreclosure action.

Truth in Lending Act Federal law that requires lenders to make certain disclosures (such as interest, annual percentage rate, total cost of loan, total of all payments, and use of disclosure forms at the loan application and closing) to borrowers concerning loan.

turnover order Court command to debtor to give title to certain assets to creditor.

underwriter Person who makes final decision at most mortgage companies on whether loan should be granted or not.

undivided interest Ownership of real estate by joint tenants or tenants in common under the same title.

upside-down home A house worth less than what is owed on mortgage it secures.

vendee's lien A lien against property under contract of sale to secure a deposit paid by purchaser.

verification of deposit Form sent to bank by lender to verify that borrower has certain sum on deposit.

verification of employment Form sent to employer by lender to verify borrower is employed at certain salary.

Veterans Administration See *Department of Veterans Affairs*.

wage earner's plan Nickname for Chapter 13 bankruptcy.

warranty deed Conveyance of land in which grantor guarantees title to grantee.

without recourse Words used in endorsing note or bill to denote that future holder is not to look to endorser in case of nonpayment.

workout Process in which borrower comes to mutually acceptable financial arrangement with lender to avoid impending foreclosure.

wraparound Type of mortgage in which obligation to pay second or later lien includes obligation to pay earlier lien mortgage; later mortgage wraps around the earlier mortgage; default on earlier-lien mortgage is automatically a default on later-lien mortgage.

wraparound loan New loan encompassing any existing loans.

writ of execution Court order authorizing holder to seize and sell debtor's property to pay off judgment.

writ of garnishment Court order commanding someone who holds assets for another (for example, a banker who holds funds on deposit, employer who holds a paycheck, or a stock broker who holds account for investor) to give those assets up to creditor.

writ of possession Court document authorizing constable or other law officer to break down tenant's door, drag tenant from premises, and throw tenant's belongings out of house or apartment.

wrongful foreclosure Foreclosure that was legally improper and caused borrower to suffer damages.

Books

Carnegie, Dale. *How to Win Friends and Influence People*. New York: Pocket paperback, 1998.

Covey, Stephen R. *The Eighth Habit: From Effectiveness to Greatness*. New York: Free Press, 2004.

Covey, Stephen R. *The Seven Habits of Highly Effective People*. New York: Free Press, 1989.

Hill, Napoleon. *Think and Grow Rich*. New York: Ballantine, 1987.

Mandino, Og. *The Greatest Salesman in the World*. New York: Bantam, 1983.

Rohn, Jim. *The Treasury of Quotes*. Southlake, TX: Jim Rohn International, 2001.

Tracy, Brian. *The Psychology of Selling*. Niles, IL: Nightingale-Conant, 1999.

Vass, Jerry. *Soft Selling in a Hard World: Plain Talk on the Art of Persuasion*. Philadelphia, PA: Running Press Book Publishers, 1998 (second edition, revised and updated).

Willingham, Ron. *Integrity Selling for the 21st Century: How to Sell the Way People Want to Buy*. New York: Currency, 2003.

Ziglar, Zig. *Zig Ziglar's Secrets of Closing the Sale*. New York: Berkley Trade, 1985 (reissue edition).

DVD

The Secret (www.thesecret.tv)

Web Sites

Bob Bruss's Real Estate Center (www.bobbruss.com). From nationally syndicated columnist Bob Bruss, this site offers real estate commentary, advice, and information.

Census Bureau (www.census.gov). From the federal government, check out its consolidated location for construction statistics, many tracked monthly, including new residential construction, new residential sales, construction price indexes, construction spending, manufactured housing, residential improvements, and more.

Council for Community and Economic Research (www.C2er.org). Formerly ACCRA; click on "Cost of Living Index" for quick, easy, and current online cost-of-living comparisons.

DataQuick Information Systems (www.dataquick.com). A solid source of up-to-date property information ranging from appraisals and financials to insurance, mortgage lending, and more.

DSNews.com (www.dsnews.com). The online counterpart to *DS News* (formerly *REO Magazine*), this site provides helpful information and news on the default mortgage-servicing industry. Check out its Black Book (http://dsnewsblackbook.com) to locate default-servicing attorneys and firms, and its REO Red Book (http://reoredbook.com) to find specialized brokers/agents.

Fannie Mae (www.fanniemae.com). A congressionally chartered private company with information and details on mortgages, home buying, and more.

Federal Deposit Insurance Corporation (www.fdic.gov). Access financial information on specific banks as well as analyses on the banking industry and economic trends.

Federal Housing Finance Board (www.fhfb.gov). Government entity that surveys rates and terms on conventional mortgage loans in its monthly interest rate survey (MIRS).

Fidelity National Data Services (www.fidelityinfoservices.com). (See Sitexdata).

First American Real Estate Solutions (www.firstamres.com). (See RealQuest).

FlatFeeMLSListing.com (www.FlatFeeMLSListing.com). The largest network of flat fee MLS listing brokers in the United States.

ForeclosureLink.com (www.foreclosurelink.com). National foreclosure-processing company that services all aspects of real estate default including nonjudicial foreclosures as trustee/agent in Arizona, California, Idaho, Nevada, Oregon, Utah, and Washington; judicial foreclosures in all 50 states; land/private real estate contract forfeitures; homeowners associations pre-lien, lien filing, and foreclosure services; and more.

ForeclosureS.com (www.foreclosures.com). Premium national foreclosure listing and property information service that includes easy to use investor friendly Web-based interface for more than 1,500 counties and growing across the United States as well as extensive foreclosure investing training and information resources; both free and fee-based.

Home Loan Learning Center (www.homeloanlearningcenter.com). The consumer web site from the Mortgage Bankers' Association (www.mbaa.org), this is a comprehensive, unbiased source that provides information to prospective homebuyers and sellers.

HomesellersAssistance.com (www.whypay6.com). Flat-rate licensed real estate broker throughout California.

HOPE for Homeowners (www.995hope.org). A nonprofit agency formed in 2004 through a $20 million contribution from a General Motors Acceptance Corp. subsidiary. It includes toll-free hotline for homeowners facing foreclosure (888-995-HOPE) and is associated with the nonprofit Homeownership Preservation Foundation (www.hpfonline.org).

Housing Predictor (www.housingpredictor.com). Source for general information on specific state and metropolitan markets across the country; check out its predicted top 25 markets (www.housingpredictor.com/top25.html).

HSH Associates (www.hsh.com). Major publisher of independent mortgage and consumer loan information and statistics, much of it free.

InfoSpace (www.infospace.com). Find businesses, people, neighbors, family, and more.

Inman News (www.inman.com). Solid resource for real estate news, information, advice, direction, blogs, and more; check out the InmanWiki for the latest in terminology, guides, blogs, and more (www.inmanwiki.com).

International Real Estate Digest (www.ired.com). Source of international real estate data.

InvestorWords.com (www.investorwords.com). From the Annandale, Virginia–based financial Internet company WebFinance Inc., this site includes definitions of more than 6,000 terms, with more added regularly.

Jim Rohn (www.jimrohn.com). Get motivation, advice, and information from business philosopher, author, and motivator Jim Rohn.

Joint Center for Housing Studies at Harvard University (www.jchs.harvard.edu). Solid source of information on housing trends, economics, and more.

Lane Guide (www.laneguide.com). A complete reference on banks, savings banks, finance companies, mortgage lenders, loan servicers, credit unions, and other major creditors.

Marketwatch.com (www.marketwatch.com/personalfinance/realestate). This free site from Dow Jones Incorporated includes news, rate information, real estate and personal finance resources, and more.

Mortgage Bankers Association of America (www.mbaa.org). Industry organization that tracks real estate money trends including mortgages, delinquencies, refinancings, and more.

National Association of Homebuilders (www.nahb.org). From the industry organization, click on "Resources" for information on home maintenance and care, remodeling, and mortgages; also provides look at current markets and amenities.

National County Recorders Directory (www.zanatec.com/home.html). Listing of contact information for county recorders nationwide by state.

NETRonline.com (http://netronline.com). Public records and real estate information portal; find access to deeds, vital records, tax data from state and county governments nationwide.

Office of Federal Housing Enterprise Oversight (www.ofheo.gov). From the federal government and also known as OFHEO, its quarterly House Price Index reflects pricing trends nationwide; the site also has free home-pricing calculators.

PACER (http://pacer.psc.uscourts.gov). Administrative office of the U.S. Courts, PACER Service Center, the federal judiciary's centralized registration, billing, and technical support center for electronic access to U.S. district, bankruptcy, and appellate court records.

The Paper Source (www.papersourceonline.com). Free e-newsletter, discussion forum, and resources for trust deed investors and brokers; solid source for information on cash-flow industry.

RealEstateABC.com (www.realestateabc.com). Information source for everything from researching and comparing Realtors® to housing trends, buying and selling real estate, pricing, calculators, articles, tips, and more.

Real Estate Consulting (www.realestateconsulting.com). John Burns, real estate consultant to builders and investors, helps executives make informed decisions. Sign up for his three free monthly e-mails on building marketing intelligence.

RealEstateJournal.com (www.realestatejournal.com). From the publishers of the *Wall Street Journal*, a source of solid information, property listings, resources, remodeling direction, and more.

RealQuest (www.realquest.com). Access 97 percent of all U.S. real estate transactions via RealQuest.com from First American Real Estate Solutions (FARES). Delivering unmatched coverage, accuracy, and 24/7 availability, RealQuest makes it simple to find and use the latest data for customer prospecting, risk management, or investment purposes. Gather information necessary for verification, compliance, analytics, research, list kits, and database enhancement from one easy-to-use source.

Realtor.com (www.realtor.com). The official Internet site of the National Association of Realtors; includes real estate economic information, calculators, and more, as well as home, neighborhood, and Realtor listings. Check out its Real Estate Insights (http://www.realtor.org/reinsights.nsf/pages/home?openDocument).

Robert Bruss (www.bobbruss.com). See *Bob Bruss's Real Estate Center*.

Sitexdata (www.sitexdata.com). From Fidelity National Data Services (FNDS), a user-friendly, affordable Internet program for the up-to-date, accurate, and comprehensive county real estate data. The information is compiled directly from the county recorder and assessor offices nationwide. Database is updated *daily* and available 24/7 online. A full report includes a profile on a property, its history, comparables, a map, and more.

Skipease (www.skipease.com). Free people search and public record directories online; includes military, inmate, Social Security number, deceased persons searches, and more.

Trulia Real Estate Search (www.trulia.com). Real estate search engine that includes blogs and information; helps locate homes for sale nationally and lets user visually compare prices and sales by state, county, city, or neighborhood with the help of its aerial maps.

U.S. Courts (www.uscourts.gov). From the federal government, a free source of information, links, and resources to U.S. courts.

WhitePages.com (www.whitepages.com). Free telephone white pages and people search; find neighbors and more by business, person, reverse address, and reverse phone numbers.

ZabaSearch (www.zabasearch.com). Free people search and public information search; premium search capabilities available for a fee.

Zillow (www.zillow.com). New online real estate service from the founders of Expedia.com; includes free blogs, listings, news, and information on real estate.

FREE TELECONFERENCE!

JUMP-START YOUR PRE-FORECLOSURE PROFITS

Listen to foreclosure expert *Alexis McGee* discuss her innovative approach to buying pre-foreclosures in a special *90-minute teleconference* for FREE!

What You Will Learn:

- What Alexis' successful students are doing NOW to make it BIG in the pre-foreclosure business.
- How you can make plenty of money ethically and honestly in this business and sleep well at night, too.
- What's ahead for real estate and foreclosures and how that affects you.
- How you can find great deals in your changing real estate market.
- The best way to buy a foreclosure-pre-foreclosure (default), short sales, auctions, bank owned (REO), or REO auctions.
- How you can set yourself apart from the pack and gain the seller's trust and confidence.
- How to JUMP-START your own pre-foreclosure business now and be successful without using any of your own money or credit.

As an Added Bonus:

- **Guest Panelists:** *Successful graduates of Alexis' learning program* share their inspiring pre-foreclosure experiences.

This FREE "Jump-Start Your Foreclosure Profits" Program Includes:

- **FREE audio replay** of Alexis' special teleconference call for holders of this book. (*$50 value*)
- **FREE digital outline** of the entire presentation, including all of Alexis' web page links. (*$40 Value*)

Here's How to Get Your FREE OFFER NOW:

- **Go to www.ForeclosureS.com/book.**
- **Submit your full contact information.**
- **Include your FREE OFFER CODE: Maven.**
- **We will e-mail you the link to download the audio file (MP3) and full outline (HTML).**
- **If you need assistance, please contact 800-310-7730 x3.**

Then sit back, read, listen, and enjoy the teleconference. Make sure to e-mail your feedback to alexis@foreclosures.com. She would love to hear from you!